WOMEN IN ROMAN BRITAIN

Wall-painting of a woman at Sparsholt (© Winchester Museums Service)

WOMEN IN
ROMAN BRITAIN

Lindsay Allason-Jones

Council for British Archaeology
2005

New edition 2005 © Lindsay Allason-Jones
Published by the The Council for British Archaeology
St Mary's House, 66 Bootham, York YO30 7BZ

First edition 1989, published by the British Museum Press
(The British Museum Company Ltd)

British Library Cataloguing in Publication Data
A catalogue card for this book is available from the British Library

ISBN 1-902771-43-5

Typeset by Heritage Marketing & Publications Ltd
Printed in England by Pennine Printing Services Ltd

Front cover illustration and frontispiece Wall-painting of a woman at Sparsholt (© Winchester Museums Service)

Contents

List of Figures

Acknowledgements

A book of this type relies heavily on the work of other people and I would like to express my thanks to all the archaeologists whose detailed excavation and research provided the facts which support my comments and generalisations. In particular I am indebted to the following, with whom I have discussed their work: Mr P T Bidwell, Professor A Birley, Dr M C Bishop, Dr R Brickstock, Dr B C Burnham, Mr J Casey, Dr Hilary Cool, Dr Hazel Dodge, Dr S Greep, Dr Karen Griffiths, Mrs Kay Hartley, Dr M Henig, Dr Gill Hey, Mrs Margery Hutchinson, Dr Catherine Johns, Dr G Lawson, Dr D Mackreth, Prof M Millett, Dr Theya Molleson, Dr Jenny Price, Miss Pat Southern, Dr R S O Tomlin, Dr Carol van Driel-Murray, Dr D A Welsby, Dr J P Wild, and Mr Tony Wilmott. Specifically, I must thank my sister, Dr Erica Allason-Jones, Dr Ian Cameron, Prof W Dunlop, and the late Dr F Miller for checking my medical facts, and Margaret Cox and Eleanor Scott for allowing me to read their unpublished theses and discussing their ideas. Mr and Mrs P Smith were more than kind in allowing me access to the female burial on their property in York, as were my colleagues at the University of Newcastle upon Tyne Dr Dr K T Greene, Dr J D C Harte, Dr J Richards, Dr D J Smith, Dr Tony Spawforth, and Miss Catherine Johns, Mr R Jackson and the late Dr T W Potter, at the British Museum, who read various drafts. Their helpful comments, assistance and encouragement have been much appreciated.

Both before and after the publication of the first edition I was heartened and helped by the questions and interest of many members of Womens' Institutes, Townswomens' Guilds, Retired Gentlemen's Associations and local history societies, as well as students of the Open University, University of the Third Age and the University of Newcastle upon Tyne; through their curiosity and enthusiasm to learn more about the women who lived in Britain in the Roman period I was encouraged to explore aspects of Romano-British history which are often ignored but which provide the details which fascinate modern readers.

Finally my gratitude must be expressed to Mrs Wendy Young who struggled with my handwriting to produce a readable text for the first edition, the staff of British Museum Publications who patiently guided me through the birth pangs of the book and the staff of the Council for British Archaeology who encouraged and assisted in its rebirth.

Preface

To begin by saying that this was an impossible book to write may be seen as a defeatist attitude, but to chronicle the lives, habits and thoughts of half the population of a country over four centuries could never be easy. In the case of Roman Britain the attempt has been made more difficult by the fact that only in the first few years of the occupation can we be said to be dealing with a native population which was entirely British born or a homogeneous invading force. Even some of the earliest governors of the province came from Gaul or Africa, and most of the legionaries who first invaded the country came from Spain, Gaul, and the two Germanies; as these soldiers and their auxiliary colleagues retired and intermarried with the native population, and merchants and slaves entered the country, so the population became more and more mixed. To talk about Romano-British women, even in the first century AD, as if they all had the same background, traditions and tastes is to oversimplify a complex situation. Any foreigner living in Britain could be described as 'British' by right of residence, while every inhabitant automatically became a 'Roman' when Britain became a province of the Roman Empire, and all were awarded citizenship by decree in AD 212. In Scotland the situation was particularly confused as the various incursions by the Roman army over the centuries meant that Scotland was occasionally part of the province but more often not.

In some areas of Britain the ways of the native population, for which we have only limited direct evidence, will have flavoured and dominated life, while the minorities may have kept together and continued their familiar practices with little effect on the majority. Even so, trends and fashions will have been brought in by new immigrants, and the wealthier natives with political or social ambitions will have looked to Rome for indications as to acceptable behaviour and the latest ideas. This cosmopolitan nature of Romano-British society may tempt us to use our knowledge of the life led by women in Rome, as described by classical authors, to fill in the gaps in the evidence from Britain itself. Indeed, the use of literary motifs in mosaics and wall-paintings makes it clear that works by such writers as Ovid and Pliny must have been widely read in the province, so that ideas which were familiar to women in Rome would have been available to their contemporaries in Britain.

However, although I have used quotations from classical sources to give some indication of both the Roman and Celtic attitudes towards women, it is dangerous to rely too heavily on literary evidence unless its relevance is supported by the archaeology: there are very few specific references to Britain in these sources. The difficulty of discussing women's rights, for example, illustrates our problem. Recent research has shown that each province in the

Roman Empire had its own legal code based on an amalgam of Roman and native laws. Assumptions about life in a province based on classical Roman law have often proved to be inaccurate and as we have little knowledge of the pre-Roman legal code in Britain, nor any idea of the extent to which the Roman code was adapted to fit native mores, even the most general discussion is fraught with difficulties. We are also quite unable to make any kind of estimate of the numbers of women in different classes of society – freedwomen, slaves, wives of military men, foreigners, and so on. In fact, as we have no census returns for the period we cannot even say confidently how many people there were in total in the province at any one time.

We do have a certain amount of information about some native women. Boudica and Cartimandua were both mentioned in classical authors' discussions on the political and military affairs of the Empire, but their status cannot be thought of as typical for women in the province, and even in these cases the evidence is severely limited and on occasion contradictory. The bulk of the evidence concerning most individuals comes from inscriptions – tombstones, altars, writing tablets and curse tablets – but this is still slight. Of all the inscriptions surviving from Britain only about ten per cent refer to women, and dating them can be problematical. Many relating to women have previously been dated on doubtful premises, and none of the few surviving fourth-century inscriptions mention women at all.

The quantity and quality of the information in the inscriptions varies considerably from potted biographies to mere names. They are also strongly biased towards the upper- and middle-class Romanised population, particularly those with links to the military, for these were the people who could afford to erect imposing tombstones or dedicate altars and were living in a milieu which favoured written records. Of the women referred to in the inscriptions only some fifteen per cent were of low status. Every female slave and freedwoman known by name and status in Roman Britain is mentioned in this book, but the thousands who must have lived in the province have disappeared without trace. Lead curse tablets found at Bath and other sites may do something to redress the balance for the less wealthy native population, but they hardly constitute overwhelming evidence: of 110 curse tablets from Bath with any decipherable text, just sixteen mention women by name; of these six simply give a name, and only three could be said to give useful information about their status and position. Curse tablets found at Uley, Gloucestershire, promise to add to our information, but it may be some time before they are all ready for scholarly publication.

The bias of the inscriptions is also reflected in the archaeological record: the lower the class the sparser its material remains. However, these remain the most comprehensive body of evidence we have. It may be felt that the emphasis on material culture (dress, jewellery, cooking utensils, furniture and so on) gives a somewhat distorted view of the preoccupations of Romano-British women. However, an enormous number of hairpins and jewellery have been found in excavations and women are often portrayed on their tombstones wearing their jewellery or holding mirrors. Although there can be problems in attributing some of this excavated material to the gender of its erstwhile owners, its sheer quantity strongly indicates that the women of the province were interested in their personal appearance.

It cannot be claimed that the Romans were a politically correct civilization; indeed, the attitude towards women which developed in the western world through the eighteenth, nineteenth and twentieth centuries, against which the Feminist Movement was a reaction, was largely the result of the political and religious leaders of those times having received a sound classical education and thus becoming imbued with the ideas of such writers as Cicero and Tertullian – both men whose forthright views on the status and position of women make most modern readers very uncomfortable. Many generations of archaeologists were also brought up in a similar educational tradition and this coloured their interpretation of the evidence they were uncovering.

Despite the problems of the evidence, I have attempted to present a fair view of the lives and concerns of the women of Roman Britain, even if these are not always to modern taste. My aim has been to stimulate discussion in what has been a neglected area in the hope that new information from excavations in the future may be interpreted with the female population in mind, and not just the male inhabitants, as has been the case in the past.

In order to keep references to a minimum, women cited in the text are listed at the end of the book with their source. Inscriptions discovered before 1956 are published in *Roman Inscriptions in Britain*, by R G Collingwood and R P Wright. Those found since have been published annually in either *Journal of Roman Studies* or in *Britannia*. The list does not include every woman known to have lived in Roman Britain, but none have been excluded who could in any way add to our knowledge of the period. The bulk of the exclusions are simply names scratched on pots.

The notes are restricted to classical texts and a few comments. Wherever possible quotes from the classical authors have been taken from the Loeb edition translations, as these are readily available in libraries and bookshops, and have the further benefit of carrying the original text and English translation side by side, allowing the reader to investigate the evidence at first hand. Works by modern authors which are referred to in the text can be found in the Bibliography, along with other publications which might be useful for further reading.

Introduction

The British Isles had been known to several generations of Romans before the first invasion by Julius Caesar in 55 BC. Among some sections of Republican society there was a belief that Britain was one of the 'Isles of the Blessed' to which one journeyed after death, and the stories brought back by shipwrecked sailors and traders reinforced the idea of a fabulous land inhabited by shadowy beings. Even Tacitus was able to relate that, of the survivors of Germanicus' fleet who fetched up on the shores of Britain, 'not a man returned from the distance without his tale of marvels – furious whirlwinds, unheard of birds, enigmatic shapes half human and half bestial: things seen or things believed in a moment of terror'.[1] Although early visitors had not ventured far inland, the Roman authorities were aware of the many natural resources of the island, such as the grain, cattle, gold, silver, iron, hides, slaves, and hunting dogs listed by Strabo.[2] This potential bounty may have provided some incentive to Julius Caesar, and later the Emperor Claudius, to invade the country. Caesar also considered it essential for the security of the European mainland to stop the tribes of Britain sending reinforcements to the Gallic and Germanic tribes in their struggles against the Roman army. The close connection between the people of Britain, Gaul and Germany can be traced back to the fifth century BC, and successive waves of immigrants and invaders across the English Channel meant that by the first century BC there were strong tribal links. Caesar noted that Diviciacus, whom he described as 'the greatest man in Gaul', had also been 'powerful in Britain',[3] while a number of Britons had served in the Gallic armies and rebellious Gallic nobles had found sanctuary in Britain after their unsuccessful resistance to Roman policy in 57 BC.

The two campaigns by Julius Caesar had little long-term political impact on Britain but they did help to develop the trade links with Roman merchants, which in turn strengthened the cultural links between Rome and the British tribes via a Gaul which was rapidly becoming Romanised. Between the Julian campaigns and the Claudian invasion Roman ideas and culture were absorbed by the peoples of the south-eastern tribes, and information about the Britons, plus a steady supply of various commodities, were received by Rome in return. Britain was no longer seen to be a land beyond the edge of the world, and the way was paved for a determined attempt to include the island in the Roman Empire.

For various reasons it was not until the reign of Claudius that Britain was successfully invaded and became a province of the Roman Empire. The invaders of AD 43 found a country divided between powerful tribes who either lived in peaceful coexistence or were sworn enemies (Fig 1). These tribes all appear to have spoken variations on the same language, which today is called Celtic.

1. Distribution of the native British Tribes (© D A Welsby)

The meaning of the terms 'Celt' and 'Celtic' have altered over the centuries and they have often been used in the absence of any better term to describe the native population of Britain before and during the Roman occupation but it is important to remember that the British population at the time may not have thought of themselves as Celtic at all. According to Julius Caesar, the tribes along the coast of south-east Britain were all Belgae who had emigrated from France and Belgium, but this may be a simplification of the tribal histories, and as the Romans expanded their control further north and west they found fewer people with any claim to either tribal or trade links with the Continental Belgae.

Despite our increased knowledge of Iron Age Britain we know surprisingly little about the female population before the Roman invasion,[4] and the lack of evidence about the native law codes, social mores and tribal government makes it difficult to assess the impact of Roman domination. It would be rash to presume, because the tribes in Britain have been described by ancient and modern writers as Celts, that they behaved in the same way as the tribes of Germany and Gaul. Certainly they shared elements of an ethnic tradition, but how far this affected the details of daily life is not easy to determine. Nor is it wise to rely on the accuracy of early writers, such as Julius Caesar or Tacitus, as their works have a political bias and as a result tend to dwell on the barbarity of the Celtic people throughout Europe in order to emphasise the civilisation of the Romans. Neither writer showed much interest in the women of the newly conquered province, and it was not until AD 51 that any female is mentioned by name. Regrettably, we have no information about the female members of the families of Togodumnos or Cogidubnus, or any of the other eleven British kings who surrendered to Claudius.

The number of inhabitants of Roman Britain has been variously estimated at four to five million, which Martin Millet broke down into a figure of 3.6 million people living in rural areas, 250,000 in towns and 125,000 in forts, but this may be a conservative estimate.[5] Without census returns it is impossible to calculate the size of the population with any accuracy, nor can we estimate the ratios of the sexes. The proportion of men to women may have fluctuated over the centuries, and no doubt there were local variations as well. The invasion, for example, may have decimated the male population, particularly amongst the recalcitrant tribes, with the result that there may have been a considerable number of widows and unmarried girls in the first century AD. This balance may have been redressed during the Boudican revolt, when women joined in the fighting and thousands of women were slaughtered at Verulamium, Colchester and London. Later rebellions, and the transfer of troops abroad, will again have upset the balance between the sexes. Analysis of cemeteries gives a varied picture as to exact ratios: at Poundbury the ratios were equal, at Trentholme Drive, York, there were four men to every woman, while the Cirencester cemetery indicated a population of five men to two women. Lamyatt Beacon gave a contrary statistic of eleven women to every man. This varied pattern may

3

2. Boudica and her daughters in heroic vein at Cardiff, as visualised in 1913–15
by J Havard Thomas (Cardiff City Council. Photo © Rob Watkins)

be explained by the segregation of the sexes in cemeteries or by the bias in a military area which would result in a preponderance of men.

The cemetery evidence is more useful in giving a picture of the physical characteristics of the people. The average height of men was 5 feet 6.5 inches (1.69 m) with the women consistently smaller at 4 feet 11 inches to 5 feet 6 inches (1.50 to 1.68 m) with a mean average of 5 feet 2.6 inches (the average height of a British woman today is 5 feet 4 inches: 1.625m).[6] This represents a decrease of 3 cm in women's stature from the Iron Age, although the average man appears to have grown by 1 cm. As only a few women were taller than 5 foot 4 inches this contradicts the classical writers' impression of the women of Britain being as tall and as well-built as their husbands. In particular, the contemporary descriptions of Boudica[7] bring to mind a Wagnerian contralto: 'in stature she was very tall, in appearance most terrifying, in the glance of her eye most fierce, and her voice was harsh; a great mass of bright red hair fell to her hips'. (Fig 2)[8]

There is no way of telling whether this is an accurate picture or merely propaganda – it certainly bears a remarkable resemblance to the description of another female leader who defeated the Romans, the Candace of Meroe, which may suggest that it was a generic description of an idealised female enemy.[9] The preponderance of red hair among the southern tribes has been confirmed by traces of hair found in graves, but the physical attributes of the population will have varied from tribe to tribe. The Silures of the Welsh Marches, for example, are more likely to have been small and dark, while the tribes along the east coast may have shared the physical characteristics of their Gallic and Germanic relations. Within a few generations of the Roman invasion several women with African, Scandinavian, and Mediterranean characteristics would have joined the population and throughout the centuries the intermarriage of native Britons with those of the other races of the Empire will have resulted in a mixed population with every colour of hair and skin being commonplace.

As more and more of Britain was absorbed into the new Roman province of Britannia, so the population become Roman in name, if not necessarily with full citizenship. There has been a tendency among modern writers to presume that because Roman law was valid throughout the Empire all the people of that Empire were subject to exactly the same legal and social restraints. The evidence of papyri from Egypt has shown that there were, in fact, local interpretations and variations on the central theme. In the provinces the interpretation of written law, particularly those laws which affected women – marriage, status, and inheritance – would have been influenced by tradition, local custom, and social moral values and the Roman government had learned not to interfere with the law in relation to these issues unless absolutely necessary.

To add to the confusion, any discussion as to the status and legal rights of Roman women has tended to be biased by the literary evidence of the late Republic, and by our knowledge of the empresses and aristocratic ladies of Imperial Rome, which may bear scant similarity to the reality of life in a province. In Britain we have only the limited evidence of inscriptions, writing tablets, and curse tablets to give any clues as to how rigidly Roman laws were followed, so to evaluate the status of women in Romano-British society we can only look at conditions in the other parts of the Roman Empire and compare the limited evidence from Britain to judge the degree of similarity or disparity.

Throughout the Empire the population was divided between those who were free, freed, or slaves, with various social subdivisions within the classes. The free population included those who were full Roman citizens with all the privileges which this brought, those who had the more limited Latin rights, and peregrines, as non-citizens were known. These different grades of citizenship or non-citizenship, up to AD 212 when all those of free status were given citizenship, largely depended on where one lived, as we will see in Chapter 3, but initially the majority of Romano-Britons will have had peregrine status, with full Roman citizenship accorded to only a few influential tribal leaders and their families.

At first glance the constraints on women under Roman law might make the term 'free' appear misleading. A woman had no political status and no vote; nor could she hold political office or join the army, and in essence she remained a 'minor' all her life. No action taken by a woman had any legal validity unless it had the sanction of her father, husband or guardian. A Roman family had at its head the father who, as *pater familias*, had control over his wife, his children, his son's children, and his slaves. On the death of the *pater* his wife and children became *sui iuris*, that is, legally independent of a *pater's* control, and each adult son was promoted to *pater familias* in his own right. Under Roman law no woman could be head of a family or exercise *potestas* (control), and it was the lack of *potestas* which limited a woman's legal role, as without it she could not own property, adopt a child, or exercise legal control over her children. For girls, the initial control, known as *tutela impuberis*, ended when she was twelve and legally old enough to marry, but it was replaced by the *tutela mulieris*. Cicero voiced Roman opinion as to why this was necessary: 'our ancestors established the rule that all women, because of their weakness of intellect, should be under the power of guardians'.[10] Even an adult woman who became independent on the death of her father or husband was required at law to have a guardian appointed by her former guardian's will or by a magistrate's decision. These secondary guardians were usually brothers, paternal uncles or cousins, but could be appointed from outside the immediate family circle.

The duties of a minor's guardian included arranging, and consenting to, a suitable marriage, as well as administering property for his ward. An adult woman's guardian had less onerous duties, only being expected to give or withhold consent to her actions. Whether the role of guardian was a sinecure or not probably depended on the character of the people concerned, rather than on any demands made by the legal system, and a woman had the right to apply to the magistrates to have her guardian replaced if he proved unreasonable.

Was this male domination of women shared by the native British population? The careers of the first women known by name in the province, Cartimandua and Boudica, would appear to suggest not. The career of Cartimandua, ruler of the Brigantes, a large tribe or confederation of tribes who controlled the north of England, exhibited all the scandal and intrigue of a modern soap-opera. According to Tacitus she owed her position to 'the influence which belongs to high birth',[11] a position consolidated by her betrayal of Caratacus, leader of the Silurian tribe, after he had sought refuge with her following his defeat by Ostorius Scapula. Cartimandua was married at the time to Venutius, but the contemporary texts make it clear that it was she who held the reins of power and not her husband. She may have inherited her throne by native law, or have been installed as ruler by the Roman authorities. The former is the more likely explanation and may be supported by the behaviour of the wife and family of Caratacus when they were displayed as captives in Rome: according to Tacitus, when 'released from their chains, they offered to Agrippina, conspicuously seated on another dais nearby, the same homage and gratitude as they had given to the Emperor'.[12] Tacitus took this as an indication of the forwardness of the Empress Agrippina but the incident also says much about the British attitude to women: not only could a woman be a leader in her own right but the female consort of a ruler was of equal importance and entitled to respect.

Cartimandua did very well out of her act of treachery to Caratacus for 'from this came her wealth and the wanton spirit which success breeds'.[13] Domestic disharmony, however, also resulted, and she separated from her husband, taking Vellocatus, Venutius's armour-bearer, as her lover. Tacitus gives two versions of the subsequent events: in the *Histories* he suggests that 'her house was at once shaken by this scandalous act'[14] and as a consequence her husband was supported by the outraged populace in his attempt to remove her from office. In the *Annals* he commented that 'her enemies, infuriated and goaded by fears of humiliating feminine rule, invaded her kingdom with a powerful force of picked warriors'.[15] As she was already acknowledged as ruler this last comment might indicate that she had threatened to extend her influence to neighbouring tribes or other sections of the Brigantes. Even though a female leader was an alien concept to Roman thought, the authorities were still willing to support a female ruler if they felt it was in their best interests to do so, and troops were sent to Cartimandua's aid. Venutius and his rebels were driven back, only to succeed in ousting Cartimandua in AD 69.

Although the exact sequence of the events in Cartimandua's life are confusing and open to several interpretations, it does appear that among the Brigantes a woman could be a ruler, hold property, divorce her husband, lead armies and be accepted as a force to be reckoned with.

The career of Boudica is even more complex (Fig 3).[16] She was the wife of Prasutagus, the leader of the Iceni tribe who had been confirmed as a client king of Rome after AD 47. She herself was descended from a royal house, although which one is not recorded, and was probably in her thirties when her husband

3. The Snettisham gold torc. Cassius Dio described Boudica as wearing such a torc when leading her troops into battle as a symbol of her leadership (© British Museum)

died, leaving his kingdom jointly to his two daughters and the Emperor Nero. It should be noted that there was never any suggestion that Boudica had a right to her husband's throne in her own name, nor did she subsequently claim the throne for herself, but acted on behalf of her daughters, whose rights were recognised by the Iceni if not by the Romans. In making the emperor and his daughters co-heirs Prasutagus had vainly attempted to preserve his kingdom as an entity. The motives behind the Roman authorities' arrogant disregard for his last wishes are not far to seek or understand. While Cartimandua was a mature woman with an established claim to her throne, Prasutagus's daughters were young girls; their youth, and the fact that there were two of them, made each a potential focus of resistance and rebellion. An unstable client kingdom would not be to anyone's advantage, nor would it be conducive to peaceful provincial administration. An agreement between a client king and Rome was a personal arrangement rather than a treaty between two states, and on the death of a king the Roman authorities would feel no necessity to continue the arrangement into the second generation. Even so, it is hard to explain why Tacitus should report that 'as a beginning his widow, Boudica, was flogged, and their daughters raped. The Icenian chiefs were deprived of their hereditary estates as if the Romans had been given the whole country. The king's own relatives were treated like slaves.'[17] This excessive behaviour has been blamed on the procurator, Decianus Catus, the high-handed attitude of the local officials and the low morals of the army veterans, but none of these explanations fully covers the events. Flogging was not a punishment normally meted out to free women for any criminal offence, while rape, far from being condoned, was a capital offence. The Emperor Hadrian was later to take a lenient view of those who, taking the law into their own hands, killed a rapist. A woman could not prosecute for rape herself but her relatives were entitled to do so and if they did not fulfil their responsibilities it was open to outsiders to press charges without the constraint of a time limit. According to the legal writer Ruffus, the result of a successful prosecution meant that 'a soldier who takes a girl by force and rapes her shall have his nose cut off, and the girl be given a third part of his property'.[18] For anyone to flog the widow of a client king and rape his daughters was not only reprehensible according to contemporary mores, but also an act of political folly and it is hardly surprising that the Iceni revolted, supported by the Trinovantes.

Cassius Dio's explanation of the revolt was that it was caused by 'the confiscation of the sums of money that Claudius had given to the foremost Britons' by Decianus Catus[19] and the calling in of Seneca's loans to the local nobility. He claimed that 'the person who was chiefly instrumental in rousing the natives and persuading them to fight the Romans, the person who was thought worthy to be their leader, and who directed the conduct of the war, was Boudica, a British woman of the royal family and possessed of greater intelligence than often belongs to women'.[20] He gave no indication that Boudica had suffered any personal indignity, nor did he refer to her daughters' claim to the Icenian throne.

The speeches of Boudica and the Roman commander, Suetonius, to their respective troops before battle, as reported by Cassius Dio and Tacitus,[21] are likely to be as historically accurate as the speech by King Henry V before the Battle of Agincourt as related by Shakespeare.[22] However, they do give an impression of the different Roman and Iron Age British attitudes towards women, and it is this difference which appears to have struck the classical writers. There is an inference that the Roman army was prepared to behave with forbearance and gallantry towards women as long as the women stayed at home, knew their place and did not meddle in affairs of state. It was the British woman's lack of womanly virtues which was considered to lie at the bottom of the trouble; not only were the tribes willing to be led by a woman but the female population joined in the fighting. Suetonius tried to rally his men by saying that the majority of those massed against them were mere women. Boudica took the same line with her troops, describing the heavy armour and weaponry of the legionaries as the defence of feeble men who were as weak as their womenfolk. British women were not only equal to their men but 'possessed of the same valour'.

Both classical writers refer to the British tribes being used to female leadership. We know of few Iron Age generals by name, so cannot estimate how many were women nor whether some tribes were more likely to be led by a woman than others. Apart from Boudica and Cartimandua, Tacitus also hints at a third female general, unfortunately anonymous, who led the Brigantes against a Roman fort and colony some time between AD 71 and 83. This cannot have been Cartimandua but may have been one of her successors, if Tacitus has not confused several incidents.[23]

It is clear that native women attached great significance to their tribal identity and it was common for a woman to claim to be a member of a particular tribe. For example, at Ilkley, Ved..ic.. (Fig 4) was recorded on her tombstone as a tribeswoman of the Cornovii, while at Templebrough, Verecunda Rufilia's epitaph referred to her as a tribeswoman of the Dobunni. Both these women had married away from their native area and the references to their tribal origins on their tombstones shows the importance of an individual's tribal identity as well as making the point that this identity was not affected by marriage. To a Romanised woman it was more important to record one's status. At Lincoln Volusia Faustina was remembered as 'a citizen of Lindum', and it is clear that for her family it was more important to record her citizenship on her tombstone rather than her birth or residence in Lincoln (see Figure 23).

With a tradition of female leadership and participation in events it is unlikely that British women would overnight relinquish all their rights and submit to the control of a *pater familias*, although several tombstones hint that the *pater familias* system was followed to some extent by some families. The inscription at Old Penrith set up to Crotilo Germanus and Greca by their brother Vindicianus gives the impression that Vindicianus had assumed the role of *pater familias* after the death of their parents, while a soldier called Tadius Exuperatus, who was commemorated by his sister Tadia Exuperata on the same memorial at Caerleon as their mother Tadia Vallaunius, may also have seen his protection of the two women as the formal relationship of a *pater familias* to his wards. These references, however, may simply reflect the tradition of the extended family, with several generations living together. The tombstone of Aelia Matrona, erected by her husband, commemorated Aelia herself, as well as her son and her mother, and carries with it the implication that the whole family lived together. The tombstone of Mantinia Maerica also suggests that her mother lived in the marital home. Other households included sisters, cousins and nieces – Lifana, for example, appears to have been living with her uncle Lucius Senofilus at Carvoran. To have several generations living under one roof was clearly not uncommon and may not have had any legal implications.

A curse tablet from Bath gives a somewhat different picture, as Veloriga is listed as the head of a family, equal in status to Trinnus, Marcellinus, Morivassus and Riovassus – a situation contrary to traditional Roman law. Other women's names on curse tablets add to the evidence that even as late as the fourth century AD British women took part in transactions and owned property.

From an early period Roman women had the technical right to inherit and bequeath property, although at times this was subject to various restrictions. Wives had no right at Roman law to claim any of their husband's estate in cases of intestacy, although in practice most husbands seem to have tried to provide for their widows rather than rely on their nearest male relative to shoulder the responsibility for maintenance as well as guardianship. Julia Similina referred to herself as 'wife and heiress' of Titinius Felix, *beneficiarius* of the XXth Legion Valeria Victrix, but this is the only British example where a wife is specifically

4. Tombstone of Ved...ic.. at Ilkley: 'a tribeswoman of the Cornovii' (© West Yorkshire Archaeology Service (WYAS))

recorded as her husband's heiress. The number of wives who erected a memorial to their husbands, however, might indicate that they had inherited money, or at least had enough cash to pay for a tombstone and the right to carry out the transaction themselves.

Daughters are more often recorded as heiresses and they were fully entitled to claim on intestacy. A father might leave a married daughter a minimal share of his estate, taking the view that she had already had her share in the form of a dowry. Equally a daughter, married or single, might be left nothing in a will in order to ensure that the property was kept in the male line. Martiola, from Penrith, an unmarried woman in her twenties, however, may have inherited considerable wealth when her father, Flavius Martius, a councillor of quaestorian rank in the *civitas* of the Carvetii, died at the age of forty-five.

To be eligible to make a will one had to be a free citizen and capable of attesting. As a consequence slaves, prisoners, the insane, congenital deaf-mutes, and those who had been declared *infamia* as a punishment were excluded. One also had to be *sui iuris* and have reached puberty. Girls were considered to have reached adulthood at twelve (boys had to be fourteen), so the thirteen-year-old mourned by Vitellia Procula on a tombstone from York is likely to have been a daughter rather than a son: Vitellia describes herself as the 'heir in part' as well as the mother. Whether this child had inherited the estate from a father who left Vitellia Procula nothing or only a part of his estate is open to speculation. Another mother, also from York, who is recorded as inheriting from her offspring is Emilia Theodora, whose son Valerius Theodorianus died at the age of thirty-five years and six months. Under Roman law a mother could in theory only be left the usufruct of a property but it was not uncommon for a mother to be left the estate outright. There is a notable lack of inscriptions which refer to offspring inheriting from their mothers.

Other Romano-British heiresses are known by name, although we are left in doubt as to their relationship with their heirs or benefactors. It is likely that a girl at Chester called Tiberia inherited from her father, although all that survives of his name is '-berius' and he could have been her brother. Lucius Ulpius Sestius inherited from Rusonia Aventina, but she was probably not his wife as a wife's property automatically became her husband's on marriage. Aurelius Mercurialis referred to himself on the tombstone of Julia Velva (Fig 5) as her heir, whilst mentioning that he had erected a tomb at York 'in his lifetime for himself and his family'. It would be odd for a father to see his relationship with his daughter as purely that of heir, and the lack of a common name between Julia and her heir suggests that she was neither his daughter nor his sister, yet there is the implication that she was part of the family. It is possible that she was Mercurialis' mother-in-law but the phrase 'lived most dutifully' is used most often to refer to wives or much loved freedwomen. Epigraphic evidence from Rome shows that freedwomen were regarded as part of the *familia* and as such were entitled to a place in the family tomb. This is pure speculation however. The lavishness of Julia Velva's tombstone might indicate that her estate

5. Tombstone of Julia Velva at York. She reclines on a couch with her heir, L Aurelius Mercurialis, standing at its head(© York Museums Trust (Yorkshire Museum))

was worth having, as does the appearance of Mercurialis standing at her side with a firm grip on the will.

Claudia Crysis, who died at Lincoln, was remembered by more than one heir, although they remain anonymous and their relationships are unspecified. The property of another woman, Pervinca, went to a man called Delfinus along with the estates of a large group of other apparently unrelated people. Why Delfinus should benefit from so many deaths is not stated, although it is possible that they were all members of a burial club or a guild, but it is clear that Pervinca, who may have been a slave or a freedwoman, was as free to leave him her property as her male colleagues, and there is no suggestion that he was a husband, brother or father.

Literary references indicate that slavery was as much a fact of life in Roman Britain as it was throughout the rest of the Empire and it is clear that slavery had been prevalent in the country long before the Roman invasion. A writing tablet from London in which Rufus apparently recommends that his friend Epillicus turns 'that slave girl into cash' recorded an everyday occurence; both Rufus and Epillicus would have been astonished at any suggestion that their transaction was either immoral or unethical.[24] A writing tablet of late first or early second-century date, recently discovered in the City of London, adds to our knowledge of the purchase of a slave.[25] It describes the sale by Albicianus of a girl referred to as 'Fortunata, or by whatever name she is known' to 'Vegetus, assistant slave

13

of Montanus, the slave of the August Emperor and sometime assistant slave of Iucundus' for the sum of 600 *denarii*. The rest of the text is in the form of legal formulae ensuring that 'the girl in question is transferred in good health' and 'that she is warranted not to be liable to wander or run away'. This transaction is of interest for its evidence that a slave of an imperial slave could own a slave himself as well as being a man of some affluence – 600 *denarii* was a substantial sum, equal to two years' salary for a legionary at the time. The tablet also reveals how formulaic and thus how business-like such a transaction would be.

Some slaves may have accompanied their owners to Britain, but there was also an import and export trade by which slaves from different provinces changed hands – Fortunata was 'by nationality a Diablintian', that is, from the area between Britanny and Normandy. The fashion for giving slaves Greek names regardless of their origins makes this trade difficult to trace or evaluate, while the case of Regina (Fig 6) suggests that there was an additional domestic market. She was described on her tombstone as being of the Catuvellaunian tribe and the freedwoman and wife of Barates of Palmyra. For her to have been a freedwoman presupposes her to have been enslaved at some time, and in the late second century AD it is difficult to see how a member of a British tribe, and thus presumably freeborn, could have become a slave unless sold by her parents. This practice was banned by Roman law until AD 313 but evidence from Noricum (modern Hungary/Czech Republic) and other parts of the Empire suggests that it was widespread in the second and third centuries, if families found they could not afford to bring up all their children unassisted. It may also have been judged worth the risk that a girl would attract her master, who might as a consequence free her and marry her. Regina, unlike other freedwomen such as Calpurnia Trifosa, does not appear to have received Roman citizenship on gaining her freedom.

Roman law recognised the status of a slave and made due provision, particularly in the areas concerned with children and sexual relationships. Female slaves could be sold for breeding and it was considered sound commercial practice to breed one's own slaves for sale or use. Three children commemorated at Chester, Atilianus, Antiatilianus and Protus, may well have been *vernae*, that is children born to a slave woman on her master's estate.[26] A slave woman who produced a number of children might claim her freedom as a reward but she had no automatic right, for in this, as in all matters, she was dependent on the generosity of her owner. Any child born to a slave woman belonged to her owner and she had no claim to keep her children or have any say in their subsequent upbringing or education. Some Italian estate owners passed all *vernae* over to slave nannies to rear so that their mothers could return to work as soon as possible, whilst others split up families for financial gain.

Slaves could not contract legal marriages but in many households stable relationships were formed. The slaves themselves regarded these relationships as true marriages and British slaves are referred to with their wives on inscriptions and curse tablets: for example, Cunitius and his wife Senovara, the slaves of

6. Tombstone of Regina from South Shields: 'freedwoman and wife of Barates of Palmyra', 'a Catuvellaunian by tribe' (© Museum of Antiquities of the University and Society of Antiquaries of Newcastle upon Tyne)

Cunomolius and his wife Minervina at Bath. These 'marriages', however, could be terminated through one or both of the partners being sold or freed.

After AD 52, if a Roman free woman had sexual relations with a slave without the consent of the slave's master she ran the risk of becoming a slave herself. If consent was given, the woman's status was still reduced to that of freedwoman, whilst any children resulting from the union might become slaves 'by agreement'. In Britain this may have affected the marriage of the free Roman citizen Claudia Martina to the slave Anencletus. Anencletus was not, however, an ordinary slave, but a slave of the Council of the Province, which gave him the superior position of a civil servant. Claudia Martina's situation, therefore, may not have been as invidious as it appears.

In Britain the majority of female slaves may have been occupied in domestic work as maids, cooks, laundresses, spinners, weavers, wet-nurses, nannies, or bath attendants, and the quality of their lives will have depended on the number of other slaves employed with whom they shared the work, and on the personality of their owner. In Italy there is evidence for a hierarchy among slaves in a household and the case of Fortunata's new owner, Vegetus, indicates that this was also so in Britain. A large number of superior slaves will have accompanied the imperial family on their visits to the province or administered their property in the province, whilst others will have formed part of the household of the governors and other high officials. For these people the fact of their slavery may have made little impact on their daily lives, but this was not always the case. The Elder Cato is known to have established slave brothels on his estates in Italy for the entertainment of his male slaves and, while it is not known whether this precedent was ever followed in Britain, slaves who fell into the hands of brothel owners, tavern keepers or gladiatorial trainers were truly to be pitied, particularly as they were unlikely to live long enough or earn enough to be able to buy their freedom. A female slave was also at the mercy of her male owner should he wish to take her into his bed. Whereas it was regarded as adultery for a married woman to have sex with a male slave, for a married man to have sex with a female slave was considered unexceptional, unless he was not her owner, in which case he could be sued by her master on the grounds that personal property had been damaged. If a female slave was raped, the accused was not punishable by death, but again the slave's master could bring a charge for damages.

A female slave could obtain her freedom in several ways. Firstly, if she was over thirty she could be manumitted under the terms of her owner's will. During their lifetime owners could free slaves by verbal declaration before witnesses or by letter, or the slave herself could buy her freedom with money saved during her working life, or with a loan from a third party. The freeing of a slave by her master in order that he might marry her appears to have been common, although it was an opportunity denied to owners of senatorial rank. By an Augustan law a freedwoman married to her former master might not divorce him and marry a second time without his consent. It was also possible for a master to free his slave and live with her without going through a marriage ceremony: any children of the union would be illegitimate and take their mother's status, but this type of stable relationship, known as concubinage, was recognised, even encouraged, by Roman law. Concubinage allowed those unable to marry by law, such as soldiers, to have a long-term relationship, but might also be used when the girl's family was unable to raise a dowry. A married man was forbidden to keep a concubine and it was frowned upon for a bachelor to keep more than one.

Alternatively, a freedwoman, and on rare occasions a free woman, could live as a courtesan, whereby she was kept by a man but did not live under his roof. Courtesans were expected to register with the magistrates like common prostitutes, but were regarded as being of higher social standing. Most courtesans lived with their mothers or sisters and were considered to be cultured, well-read women. For obvious reasons it is impossible to estimate how many men in Roman Britain kept mistresses or even how many preferred to support a concubine rather than a wife. The reference to the 'carrying off' of a woman called Vilbia on one of the Bath curse tablets may suggest that there were potential difficulties in keeping a concubine.

Not all freedwomen were linked to their former masters by sex or marriage. By law a freed person was tied to their previous owner by a new relationship: that of patron and client. A patron was *tutor legitimus* to his freedwomen and could thus ensure that they died intestate, whereby he was entitled to first claim on their estates, over and above any children they might bear. If the patron allowed his freedwomen to make wills then he had little claim if they left him no part of their estates. Freedwomen, like freedmen, could become very wealthy, particularly if their patron set them up in business. Women could learn skills such as spinning, weaving, midwifery, metalworking and other crafts whilst a slave, and continue to practise their crafts after manumission. There was some argument as to whether a former slave could set up in business in direct competition with her owner, but the jurist Papinian was of the opinion that 'a freedwoman is not considered ungrateful because she practises her trade against the wishes of her patron'.[27] Exactly how many freedwomen set themselves up in business in Britain is unknown but there is a possibility that a number of crafts were carried out by either self-employed women or paid workers (see chapter 3). Collectives may also have been established, although there is no evidence that women in Britain, unlike those in Gaul, either formed guilds or joined them. In the other provinces there are a number of references to freedwomen joining the professions as doctors, accountants or librarians – opportunities not easily open to free women.[28]

A freedwoman need not necessarily leave her master's household on gaining her freedom, and the majority appear to have continued to fulfil their old duties without a break and without any noticeable alteration to their lifestyle. Some even transferred to the heir's household on the death of their patron of their own free will, and it would seem from the many dedications of freedmen and freedwomen to their former masters and mistresses, and of patrons to freed clients, that many servants had an affectionate relationship with the families for whom they worked.

Chapter 1

Birth, marriage and death

In Roman Britain, as for centuries before and after, the pattern of a woman's life was preordained. No matter what her social standing or ethnic origins might be, birth, puberty, marriage, children, the menopause, old age, and death were the seven stages of female life which she was expected to follow and could do little to avoid.

A baby girl took her father's status if she was legitimate and her mother's if she was not, this status being determined at the moment of conception in the case of a child conceived in wedlock, but at the time of birth in the case of an illegitimate child. If the mother was of slave status and belonged to her owner at the time of giving birth then the child was deemed to belong to the owner, who could either rear her, sell her, or otherwise dispose of her, as he wished. If the mother happened to be free at the time of the birth, then her offspring would be born free.

Various rites surrounded a birth, one of which, according to the medical writer Soranus,[1] was the laying of the new-born child on the earth and allowing it to cry for a while, before being washed and swaddled. The Germans, Scythians and some Greeks had a tougher attitude, condemned by Soranus, of plunging the baby into cold water in the belief that those who became livid or convulsed were not worth rearing.[2] Soranus also mentioned various superstitious beliefs surrounding the cutting of the umbilical cord, and it might be presumed from anthropological parallels that the native Britons had their own procedures and superstitions surrounding the birth of a girl.

A Roman family would name a girl on the eighth day and a boy on the ninth and the ceremony would be accompanied by rites of purification. During the Republic a Roman woman had only one name, the family name, and she was distinguished from her sisters by the use of terms such as 'the elder' or 'the younger' or by the use of numbers: *prima, secunda*. By the time of the invasion of Britain Roman women had acquired two names, the first being the family name, and the second taken from her father's name – for example, Fabia Honorata, daughter of Fabius Honoratus at Chesters, or Aurelia Victorina, daughter of Aurelius Victor at Halton Chesters. In Britain the family name (*nomen gentilicium*) was often derived from that of the emperor from whom the family had first received citizenship. This accounts for the large numbers of Julias, Claudias, Aurelias, Aelias and Flavias recorded in the province: they were not necessarily related.

On marriage a Roman woman might take her husband's name in the genitive, but this was not inevitable in Britain where we have records of Aelia

Ammillusima, wife of Marcus Trojanius Augustinus at Stanwix; Afutianus (son of Bassus) and his wife, Flavia Baetica at Birrens; and Aurelia Eglectiane, wife of Fabius Honoratus who, as we have seen, followed conservative Roman practice when naming her daughter. Even so, some women appear to have been identified simply as the wife of a man; an altar erected at High Rochester was dedicated by a woman who referred to herself merely as 'she who is married to Fabius'.

Most families from the Celtic provinces had assorted names: Lurio, a German living at Chesters, had a sister called Ursa, a wife called Julia, and a son called Canio, while Limisius at Old Penrith had a wife called Aicetuos and a daughter called Lattio. Other offspring took their names from their mother, for example: Tadius Exuperatus and his sister Tadia Exuperata took their family name from their mother, Tadia Vallaunius, and the other, presumably, from their father. A lead tablet from Bath gives the family tree of Uricalus: his wife Docilosa, his son Docilis, daughter Docilina, his brother Decentinus, and sister-in-law Alogiosa. Why the children took their name from their mother rather than their father in these cases is unclear as there is no suggestion that they were illegitimate.

British families appear to have had more choice of names available to them and were more imaginative when naming their offspring than orthodox Roman families. Celtic names can often be translated, for example, Boudica: 'victory', Cartimandua: 'white filly', or Grata: 'welcome', but many make it difficult for us to be certain as to the gender of the person concerned. This difficulty seems to have led to problems at the time: the female who is recorded on her tombstone at Old Carlisle as 'Tancorix, a woman' has the full sympathy of the present female author who is also blessed with an ambiguous Celtic first name.

Nicknames and pet-names were used by Romans and Britons alike, indeed many famous Roman names originated in a private nickname. In Britain a four-year-old at Corbridge is remembered as 'Ertola, properly called Vellibia', while another name on a Corbridge tombstone, Ahteha, may also have been a pet-name. Slaves and freedwomen were often given Greek names, although they were not all of Greek origin: for example, Calpurnia Trifosa, whose Greek name Trifosa means 'delicious', whilst her nomen, Calpurnia, is derived from the name of her husband and former owner, Gaius Calpurnius Receptus, the priest of Sulis at Bath.

A legitimate child was expected to be registered within thirty days of its birth, and by the second century AD it was possible to register an illegitimate child. A birth certificate was available on request and it was wise to acquire one or obtain some other legal recognition of one's offsprings' legitimacy, particularly if one was the mother of a soldier's child, in order for the children to be in a position to claim on their father's estate if he died intestate. In Egypt, a woman called Demetria attempted to rectify this lack of a birth certificate by preparing a document in which she claimed to have been 'previously married' to Gemellus, 'and from which marriage she bore sons, Justus aged fourteen and Gemmelus aged ten'.

The childhood years of a well-born daughter would be spent in play and education, but other children might be put to work at a very early age. In Italy slave children acted as companions for their richer playmates or had jobs on farms or in workshops from as young as five years. Even in freed or free families children would be expected to help in the family business or sent out to work.

At Poundbury, Thea Molleson has noted a high proportion of the burials were of girls aged around twelve years.[3] Her conclusions were that adolescent girls were not considered to be of much worth and were, as a consequence, not as well fed, but there is little corroborating evidence that girls were regarded as second class citizens in Roman Britain. Indeed, a society which could trace its roots back to such redoubtable female leaders as Cartimandua and Boudica is unlikely to have presumed that daughters were not worth having. It is also unlikely that, should such an attitude have prevailed in a specific tribe, the girls would survive to adolescence. It is more likely that the burials reflect a cause of death which doesn't show up in the archaeological record, such as rituals accompanying a girl's first period.

Soranus stated that menstruation started at the age of fourteen in most cases, and recommended that girls should be prepared for this from the age of thirteen by daily baths, regular gentle exercise and massage, as well as having 'the mind diverted in every possible way'.[4] Economic factors, particularly diet, will have affected the age of menarche, and Soranus listed several professions, such as those of singing and dancing, where the strenuous exercise hindered menarche altogether.[5]

Soranus also recognised the problems of pre-menstrual tension: 'one has to infer approaching menstruation from the fact that at the expected time of the period it becomes trying to move and there develops heaviness of the loins, sometimes pain as well, sometimes also a flush of the cheeks ... and in some cases approaching menstruation must be inferred from the fact that the stomach is prone to nausea and it lacks appetite'.[6] There was little understanding of the causes or mechanism of menstruation, due to the fact that the function of neither the ovaries nor the Fallopian tubes had been recognised, although Soranus dismissed his colleagues' opinion that menstruation was nature's way of purging the female body of noxious substances, recognising that 'conception does not take place without menstruation'.[7]

How women coped with their menstrual cycle is not a question which can be answered confidently. The medical writers gave copious advice as to what should be done if periods were irregular, too frequent, too painful, too heavy or non-existent, but gave no practical advice on hygiene. Possibly they regarded this matter as a mother's responsibility and not worthy of comment. There are references to tampons of lamb's wool in connection with contraception and medical treatment but not for monthly use. A suggestion has been made that pads secured by leather briefs (Fig 7) were used for feminine hygiene (see below, Chapter 5) but it is more likely that a form of washable linen 'nappy' was used, as in nineteenth-century Europe. It is interesting that the old wives' tale that

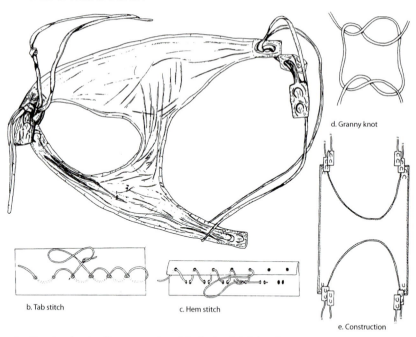

d. Granny knot

b. Tab stitch

c. Hem stitch

e. Construction

7.   Drawing showing the construction of the leather briefs found in excavations at Queen's Street, London (© Tony Wilmott)

menstruating women should not bathe may have started with Soranus, who otherwise gave sensible advice ahead of his time.[8]

From the time of Augustus the minimum age of marriage for females under Roman law was twelve, but some girls went through a form of wedding ceremony earlier. Tacitus mentioned that 'a girl who has married before twelve will be a legitimate wife when she becomes twelve'.[9] Hopkins' analysis of inscriptions in Italy indicates that eight per cent of pagan girls and three per cent of Christian girls in his sample were married before the age of twelve, and that Aurelia Philmatio, who married at the age of seven, was not unique.[10] In the provinces girls appear to have married later: Tacitus, in his discussion of the Germans, said 'the girls, too, are not hurried into marriage',[11] while Caesar commented that for a German 'to have intercourse with a woman below the age of twenty is considered perfectly scandalous'.[12] Romano-British tombstones have not proved to be as helpful as those in Italy in ascertaining the age at which girls produced their first child, but the majority indicate that girls usually postponed marriage until they were in their early to mid-twenties. Claudia Martina, at the age of nineteen, is the youngest wife so far known from a tombstone. Inscriptions, unfortunately, only give evidence for a particular level of society, but the study of skeletal remains appears to produce a similar picture throughout the social range. At Poundbury, Margaret Cox assumed from the age at which girls produced their first child that only seven and a half per cent of the female population had been married by the time they were seventeen, while 54 per cent had married by the time they reached twenty-one, and 62 per cent by the age of twenty-eight. This late age of first marriage and first child may have been due to economic conditions rather than moral traditions, with only the richer brides being able to marry in their teens, although an early marriage may have been seen to be 'the Roman thing to do'.

In wealthy families first marriages may have been arranged, as in Rome, although a woman would have had more choice if she married a second time. An Italian mother had a duty to find her daughter a husband but how much say a Romano-British mother had in the choice of her daughter's husband, or indeed how much say the bride had herself, is difficult to evaluate and may well have depended on the characters of the people involved. In artisan circles and among the freed, where dynastic considerations were of less moment, love and lust will have played their usual part along with practical considerations such as finance, and a proportion of the population may not have bothered with a formal wedding ceremony at all. Slaves could only marry with their owner's permission, although even then it was not regarded as a legal marriage: Senovara could only call herself the wife of Cunitius as a courtesy title.

It was expected that a girl would be a virgin when she first married but that her husband would not be. There was also a tendency for men to be much older than their brides, particularly military men who were expected to wait until retirement in their forties before they married (see below, Chapter 2). The marriage might be preceded by a formal betrothal ceremony at which both families made promises that the bride and groom would be married, and at which rings might be exchanged.

There was no legal minimal age for betrothal: children could be betrothed from the cradle and there were many stories of men in Rome avoiding pressure to marry and father children by deliberately betrothing themselves to babies.

No religious ceremony was required to make a marriage binding or legal. The fact that a couple was married legally rather than simply cohabiting depended on whether there were witnesses or a written agreement that they intended to live as man and wife for the purposes of producing children. From the first century AD signed and witnessed marriage contracts became the norm, setting down the amount of dowry and other financial settlements, which facilitated matters should the marriage fail. In Rome the wedding was a civil ceremony performed at the bride's house, in which promises were exchanged and sacrifices made to the gods. Weddings did not become specifically religious in character until the acceptance of Christianity but it is possible that provincial marriages had a religious content. Unfortunately, nothing is known of the native British ceremonies, although it is likely that these differed from tribe to tribe.

The Romans, and most of the tribes from the Celtic provinces, were monogamous although the wording of army retirement diplomas suggests that some cultures in the Empire recognised polygamy, and some foreigners in Britain may have had more than one wife. Both Diodorus Siculus and Strabo were convinced that British men had sexual relations with their mothers and

8. Jet pendant from Vindolanda portraying a betrothed couple (© The Vindolanda Trust)

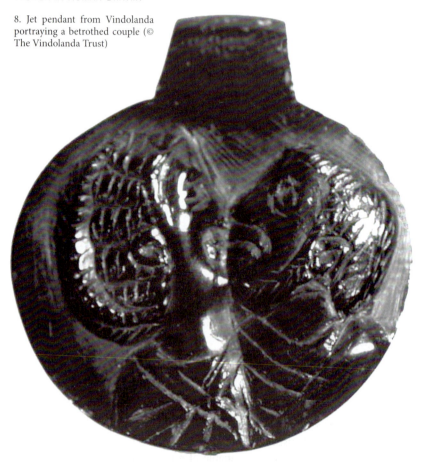

sisters while Julius Caesar noted that 'groups of ten or twelve men have wives together in common, and particularly brothers along with brothers, and fathers with sons, but the children born of the union are reckoned to belong to the particular house to which the maiden was first conducted'.[13] Caesar was not a trained anthropologist nor was he always reporting his own observations, but it is interesting that the idea that British women could have sex with male relatives other than their husbands was apparently still believed in Rome two centuries later, and that the Empress Julia Domna (see Fig 13), when visiting Britain with her husband Septimius Severus, could still ask the wife of the Caledonian chieftain Argentocoxus 'about the free intercourse of her sex with men in Britain'. It is possible that the writers had misunderstood the situation and that, whereas under the Roman system a widow became technically the daughter of her new *pater familias*, in the Caledonian tradition she became his wife, but in name only. Alternatively it has been suggested that the system followed was that of the Levirate, still practised in parts of modern Sudan, whereby widows capable of child-bearing are taken into the household of their husband's brother in order to keep the children within the tribal sub-group and to keep the family from dying out. This system has been practised throughout history by cultures where warfare resulted in many men dying young, leaving a high proportion of fertile widows. Whatever system was referred to one feels that Argentocoxus' wife got the best of the engagement in her reply to Julia Domna's impertinent question: 'we fulfil the demands of nature in a much better way than do you Roman women; for we consort openly with the best men, whereas you let yourselves be debauched in secret by the vilest' – a sly dig at the empress, whose private life was reputed to leave much to be desired.[14]

The subject of sex was openly discussed in Roman society before Christianity tightened its moral grip. Objects of domestic, religious or decorative purpose were often embellished with sexual imagery or scenes of sexual activity, reflecting the importance of fertility and its association with good fortune in Roman religious thought. The Roman sense of humour also contained much that was sexual or lavatorial. A number of writers provided information as to love-making positions, although invariably indicating that this advice was for the use of prostitutes and courtesans rather than respectable married women. The scenes of complex sexual positions decorating oil lamps and samian pottery, however, might indicate that married ladies were not ignorant of the possibilities.

Homosexuality between men was recognised to be common and was referred to many times in Roman law and literature, but female homosexuality was neither written about nor illustrated to any noticeable extent. Whether this reflects a lack of female homosexuality or simply indicates that lesbian activities were considered to be uninteresting by the classical writers or potters is not clear, but the latter is more likely to have been the case. The inclusion of three women in the list of suspects accused of 'carrying off Vilbia' at Bath may be relevant here but, as the text is capable of a range of interpretations, hardly conclusive.

Soranus considered that the reason for marrying was to produce children and he suggested that women 'who digest their food easily, and have not loose bowels continually, who are of steady mind and cheerful' were the most likely to conceive.[15] Unfortunately, the Roman medical profession was not able to tell with any degree of certainty when a pregnancy had begun, nor was there any agreement as to the length of gestation. Aulus Gellius voiced the opinion that a child could be born after seven, nine or ten months, but never during the eighth month.[16] The difficulty of diagnosing pregnancy must also have been exacerbated by the number of women who, for dietary or other reasons, either had no periods at all or were very irregular.

Soranus included the care of the pregnant woman in his treatise on gynae-cology, mentioning treatments for morning sickness and pica, that is the craving for 'things not customary, like earth, charcoal, tendrils of the vine, unripe and acid fruit'.[17] He listed the food which would benefit a pregnant woman and discouraged 'eating for two'. Gentle exercise was encouraged but he declared that 'sexual intercourse ... is always harmful to pregnant women'.[18] Miscarriages were commonplace – Thea Molleson has identified the bodies of five non-viable foetuses at Poundbury, all apparently miscarried around the fifth or sixth month of pregnancy – and the wealthier women would secure the services of a midwife at an early stage to see them through to labour and beyond. The training and skill of midwives varied, and many rural women will have combined midwifery with witchcraft and the preparation of herbal medicines. Soranus gave instructions as to the attributes of the ideal midwife, which included short finger-nails and long fingers as well as strength of mind and body. Some midwives were slaves but the majority were freedwomen and several of Italian or Gallic origin are known by name.[19] The most superior were well-read women, trained in many branches of female medicine, who treated various gynaecological conditions in addition to pregnancy.

Home deliveries were the norm and were rarely under the supervision of a physician unless difficulties arose. Soranus advised that the prospective mother should lie on a bed during labour until the baby was ready to emerge, when she should be transferred to a special midwife's stool which had an opening in the seat. The midwife sat on a lower stool in front with an assistant behind the patient in case restraint was needed. (Fig 9) Many of the contemporary medical writers' recommendations as to the correct procedures in complex deliveries might appal the modern reader, but it is impossible to generalise, as childbirth was an area where normal medical practices might be thrown to the winds to be replaced by magic and superstition. However, in Roman medicine the life of the mother was considered paramount, and in cases of difficulty the child was killed and dismembered in order to save the mother; evidence for this practice (embryotomy) in Roman Britain has been found at Poundbury cemetery.

Death in childbed may have been all too common – at Poundbury Margaret Cox has estimated that 51 out of 281 females (18 per cent) of child-bearing age had died shortly after childbirth; however, at the same site comparison between the Iron Age and Roman cemeteries indicates that neonate mortality had been halved by the improved birthing techniques introduced during the Roman period and it may well be that these new ideas had an impact on the death-in-childbirth statistics as well. Some problems may have occured as a result of poor health in the expectant mother; at Kempston in Bedfordshire one female skelton had a deformed pelvis due to osteomalacia (a vitamin D deficiency) which would have led to childbirth difficulties while the skeletons of two women from Poundbury showed them to have had particularly flattened pelvises which would also have led to problems during labour. Lack of sterilised equipment and limited techniques may have resulted in a prevalence of uterine haemorrhage and gangrene; however, the crowded unhygienic facilities which are known to have led to a high incidence of puerperal fever in Rome may have been less of a problem in Britain. In all cases, the level of the midwife's personal hygiene would have been of paramount importance and the ancient writers'

9. Tombstone from Ostia, Italy, showing a woman in labour assisted by two midwives (© Archivo Fotografica della Soprintendenza per i beni archeologici di Ostia)

comments about midwives washing their hands as a matter of courtesy may have saved many lives.

Multiple births would have led to a number of difficulties, both during the birth and in post-natal care. At Baldock a triple foetal burial with a young woman suggests that triplets were known, whilst the memorial from Chester, referring to two children called Atilianus and Antiatilianus, both aged ten, may record the death of twins.[20] In Republican Rome multiple births were not considered as a matter for rejoicing but a shameful and ill-omened event and Pliny reported that it had been common practice to choose one of the children and dispose of the other.[21] Whether parents from the provinces shared this view of multiple births is not clear.

A number of babies will have suffered trauma as the result of their rough treatment during birth and distressing malformations and deformities may often have resulted; for example, Calvin Wells identified the shoulder trauma on a male skeleton from West Hall, Munford as the result of a poor delivery. Clear evidence of congenital disease is rarely found in skeletal remains as major abnormalities of the foetus would have resulted in miscarriage, stillbirth or infanticide but there is some evidence that new congenital diseases may have made their appearance at this time; hydrocephalus has been identified at Arrington in Cambridgeshire, Poundbury in Dorset and Norton in Yorkshire, the latter in a young man who had survived into adulthood. The minor malformations of *spina bifida occulta*, as opposed to the grosser form, have been found at Cirencester and York but probably had little effect on the lives of those with the condition. The potentially painful condition of aphyseal aclasia, which leads to growths on the bones, has been noted in a girl from Poundbury whilst a female from Kingsholm, Gloucester was disabled with a clubfoot. Ralph Jackson has suggested that dwarfism was more common than today as a result of intermarriage in small communities – the skeleton of a female dwarf was found in one of the wells at Newstead, a skeleton at Dorchester shows evidence of the rare condition known as mesomelia which results in dwarfism, while a female from Gloucester exhibited the classic signs of pituitary dwarfism.

Tacitus praised German women for breastfeeding their own offspring and implied that wealthy Roman women preferred to pass the responsibility on to wet-nurses (Fig 10).[22] Soranus was of the opinion that breastfeeding by the mother was to be recommended, although he believed that she should be allowed to rest for three weeks in order to regain her strength and that the baby should be breastfed by a wet-nurse in the intervening period. His list of essential virtues for the perfect wet-nurse include clear specifications as to the shape and condition of her breasts, physical condition and moral character, and he particularly recommended that she be a Greek 'so that the infant nursed by her may become accustomed to the best speech'.[23] He also recognised the danger of baby battering, as his strictures about wet-nurses being 'self-controlled, sympathetic, and not ill-tempered' was based on his fear that 'angry women are like maniacs and sometimes when the newborn cries from fear and they are unable to restrain it, they let it drop from their hands or overturn it dangerously'.[24]

Wet-nurses were usually slaves or freedwomen and their period of nursing could last as long as two years, during which time they might either live in the mother's house or take the child into their own home. Wet-nurses often continued to look after the child after it had been weaned, and became respected members of the household. For nurse and mother alike Soranus was an indispensable guide, offering advice on weaning, teething, nappy rash and baby colds, and suggesting exercise by means of a 'little push-cart' and a chair on wheels to assist children in learning to walk.[25] Unfortunately his comments on potty training have not survived.

The evidence of tombstones suggests that Romano-British women did not produce large families compared with those in the medieval and post-medieval periods, who in similar circumstances and on a similar diet often produced as many as twenty or more offspring. The theory that the number of children a woman bears leaves identifiable signs on the pelvis, known as 'scars of parturition' once led a number of specialists to suggest that the skeletal evidence might indicate larger families, although few have suggested more

10. Tombstone of the wet-nurse, Severina, at Cologne, showing her tending her swaddled charge (© Römisch-Germanisches Museum, Cologne. Photo Ralph Jackson)

than five children for any individual woman. Recently this theory has been discredited and estimates of fertility based on these measurements shown to be meaningless. From tombstone evidence it is known that Carinus, a citizen of Rome who died at Dorchester, had three children: Rufinus, Carina and

Avita, as did Caesoria Corocca and her husband Rentius at Caerleon, while Sempronius Sempronianus at London had two brothers, and Vindicianus mourned a brother, Crotilo Germanus, and a sister, Greca, at Old Penrith, but these appear to be the exception rather than the rule.[26] The number of babies' skeletons found in excavations appear to confirm that the average number of children in a Romano-British family was two (see Fig 18).

While several natural causes for this small size of family in Roman Britain have been put forward, such as lead contamination in the drinking water or poor nutrition, these reasons were equally plausible in medieval and post-medieval Britain. The evidence indicates that social status and consquent living conditions did not affect the size of the families and thus it may be conjectured that some form of contraception was being practised in the province. Hopkins makes the sensible point that 'a general fall in fertility is a product of will plus technique, but the will is prior, if not to the discovery of contraceptives, at least to their use'.[27] If we accept that the women of Roman Britain had the will to limit the size of their families, what were the techniques available?

Aristotle, as early as the fourth century BC, had recommended cedar oil, white lead or frankincense smeared on the female genitals,[28] while Hippocrates suggested that women should drink *misy*, which was possibly dilute copper sulphate.[29] Pliny records 'a miracle: that is to rub it [cedar gum] all over the male part before coition prevents conception'.[30] He also recommended some antaphrodisiacs and treatments designed to cause impotence, but comments 'of all such preventives this only would it be right for me to mention to help those women who are so prolific that they stand in need of such respite'.[31]

Dioscorides in the first century AD put forward twenty prescriptions,[32] four of which are cautionary, three come under the heading of magic, such as asparagus used as an amulet, and seven are ineffective potions. Six of his recipes, however, contain elements which might have been effective to a greater or lesser degree. They are mostly mixtures applied to the genitals before coitus: peppermint with honey and water; cedar gum; axe-weed with honey; and alum, as well as two pessaries which may have hindered conception by blockage even though they contained no active spermicidal ingredient. Oribasius followed the same ideas as Dioscorides but added a pessary of cabbage to be applied after intercourse. Caelius Aurelianus, in the fifth century AD, endorsed an earlier suggestion that the woman should hold her breath on receiving the semen.[33] Lucretius mentioned that a prostitute to avoid conception withdrew 'from the man's passion with her buttocks, and receives the moist fluid with all her breast relaxed. For thus she drives the furrow of the plough from the true direction of the path, and turns aside the blow of seeds from the vital parts'. 'But', he added, 'nought of this is seen to be needful for our wives'.[34] The only clear reference to the use of *coitus interruptus* occurs when Augustine lists it amongst the sexual perversions of the Manichees, and there is no evidence to suggest that it was regularly practised as a contraceptive technique anywhere in the Roman Empire.

The best-known writer on the subject was Soranus, who appears to have researched contemporary practice with some thoroughness as he cited fifty-nine medical authorities in his treatise on gynaecology. His sensible advice indicates that contraception was widely practised throughout the Empire and was not confined to prostitutes and perverted foreigners. He recommended avoiding intercourse at 'those periods which we said were suitable for conception',[35] that is, just after menstruation, advice still being given by Western doctors in the nineteenth century. He continued, 'and during the sexual act, at the critical moment of coitus when the man is about to discharge the seed, the woman must hold her breath, and draw herself away a little, so that the seed may not be hurled too deep into the cavity of the uterus. And getting up immediately and squatting down she should induce sneezing and carefully wipe the vagina all round; she might even drink something cold'.[36] Among his more practical suggestions were the use of vaginal pessaries, particularly wool soaked in honey, alum, white lead, or olive oil; and applications to both male and female genitals before coitus of cedar gum, vinegar, brine, or olive oil. These methods, if strictly followed, may have offered a degree of protection. The use of olive oil was still being advocated by Marie Stopes in 1931; in 1947 E L Koos revealed that the lower classes in New York City were relying on douches of water mixed with vinegar, lemon juice or alum; and lemons were still being used in parts of Glasgow as recently as the 1970s. Alum, vinegar and brine are all highly spermicidal and as such were recommended by Marie Stopes.

If the women of Roman Britain followed these efficacious methods there would have been a noticeable effect on the reproduction rate. However, they had no way of knowing which methods would work and which were useless: even Soranus was able to suggest sneezing whilst also recommending blocking the cervix. Pliny put forward several old wives' tales, and no doubt Britain had its share of old wives offering the amulets and potions of which Soranus spoke so scathingly. In matters of family planning a bride's mother would invariably have had advice to offer based on personal experience, as would friends and neighbours. The efficiency of a contraceptive, however, is not easily observable, and an individual's own fertility would affect their view of the matter. A couple might be convinced that their childless state was due to the woman carrying the dried uterus of a mule when in fact one or both of them might have low fertility. Another might argue that alum was useless on the grounds that they had used this method yet had six children, unaware of their own high fertility or ignoring their failure to adhere conscientiously to the method.

This confusion arose through a lack of knowledge of the physiological principles involved, particularly the difference between contraception and abortion. Soranus was perfectly clear: 'a contraceptive differs from an abortive for, the first does not let the conception take place, while the latter destroys what has been conceived'.[37] St John Chrysostom, on the other hand, in his *Epistle to the Romans*, admitted not knowing what to call a contraceptive, for it is 'something worse than murder ... for it does not only destroy what is conceived but prevents it being conceived'.[38]

The Hippocratic Oath forbade abortion but eighteen of the medical writers mentioned it, of which fifteen gave methods. Soranus, for example, gave as much attention to abortion as he had previously given to contraception. His methods varied between being 'shaken by means of draught animals' to diuretic decoctions, poultices, baths in various substances such as a mixture of linseed, fenugreek, mallow, musk mallow, and wormwood; and vaginal suppositories of wallflower, cardamom, brimstone, absinthium, and myrrh in equal quantities with water. The *Digest* indicates no prohibition on abortion as such and although Septimius Severus passed a law which punished a wife who aborted without her husband's consent, it is clearly the deceit which is considered worthy of punishment not the act of abortion. In Roman law the foetus was seen as having neither a soul nor any individuality; its destruction, therefore, could not be murder, and although the sale of abortifacients was banned along with aphrodisiacs, it was under the law of poisons, because of the dangerous or lethal contents of some of the potions, rather than because of the moral issues involved.

In Rome abortion was an accepted form of birth control in fashionable circles but its use in the provinces is difficult to estimate. The Greeks dominated the medical profession throughout the Empire and all the medical men attested in Britain appear to have been of Greek extraction; so the methods of contraception and abortion described by Soranus and his fifty-nine sources are likely to have been familiar to their colleagues practising in Britain. There would also have been the backstreet practitioners who exist in every society to provide women with a way out of their difficulties. The methods listed above would all have been possible and available in Britain, particularly the use of bracken *(Pteris aquilina)*, which Dioscorides avowed caused both childlessness and abortion,[39] while Pliny considered it to have antaphrodisiac qualities as well;[40] more exotic ingredients such as pomegranate seeds may have been imported. No doubt there were other native methods which went unrecorded in the medical literature.

A third method of controlling the size of families was infanticide. Soranus, in his section on how to recognise which babies were worth rearing, implies that those who failed the test should be disposed of.[41] His reasoning appears to have been based on purely medical grounds: he was concerned with those babies which were sickly or malformed. The literary evidence, on the other hand, indicates that babies were also exposed on hill sides or local rubbish dumps if they were not wanted for financial reasons. Plautus referred to the exposure of infants as a common occurrence,[42] and it was this practice which led to the alimentary schemes, or family allowances, for poor families in Rome which Pliny mentioned in his letters. Not all the children who were exposed died, and there were complex laws regarding the legal status of children found and reared by other people, but any parent exposing their child would have been aware that death might result and that exposure was tantamount to infanticide. This method of removing unwanted children was not confined to the lower classes; as the Roman laws of inheritance divided an estate between the male children equally, a *pater familias* wishing to provide adequately for his offspring would keep his family small.

There are many references to infant exposure in the contemporary literature but this may be because it was a recognised dramatic device, much loved by playwrights. Infanticide by more proactive methods, such as smothering or strangulation, was also regularly practised in Italy; Tacitus' comment in *Germania* that 'to restrict the number of children, or to kill any of those born after the heir, is considered wicked', carries the implication that it was not considered so in Rome whilst Cassius Dio remarked that families in Scotland, like the Germans, reared all their children.[43] In his article on infanticide through the ages, Mays suggested that the number of infant burials found through excavations indicates that infanticide was widely practised in Britain.[44] However, the 'marked peak in deaths at around full term', which Mays noted, may have had a natural cause – newborn infants are at their most susceptible – while the ceremonies which accompanied the birth of a child in some tribes, such as those described by Soranus, must often have had tragic and un-looked for consequences.[45]

In respect of the argument that it was only the female babies which were disposed of, with its presumption that daughters were of less importance in Roman Britain, it is not usually possible to differentiate between male and female perinatal babies from the skeletal evidence alone, while the preponderance of adult male skeletons in the cemeteries of Ancaster, Cirencester, Colchester, Winchester and York may simply reflect a military population which had, perforce, to be male dominated, or even separate burial plots for men and women, rather than indicate that female babies were being disposed of at birth in an effort to produce 'designer' families.

In fact, the figures for infant deaths in Roman Britain may not be significantly high. Comparisons between the archaeological evidence for Romano-British infant mortality and the statistics for other periods is complicated by the inaccurate use of terms such as 'perinatal' and 'neonatal' in archaeological reports and the lack of statistics for stillbirths before the Second World War. We tend to be biased in our opinion as to what is an acceptable death rate by modern figures: in 1975, for example, the perinatal mortality rate for England and Wales was 9.8 per thousand: that is, stillbirths and deaths within the first week; the neonatal rate (deaths within the first month) was 5.9 per thousand live births, and the infant mortality rate (deaths within the first year) was 9.4 per thousand live births. This reflects the recent advances in antenatal and postnatal care, but in 1920 the infant mortality rate in Bradford was 93 per thousand live births with no record kept of the number of stillbirths. The London Bills of Mortality for 1762–71 show that 66 per cent of children died before their fifth birthday, with 75 per cent of those dying before the age of two. Brothwell has recorded that 49 out of 328 burials(14.9 per cent) at the Dark Age site of Cannington were under a year old at death compared with 23 out of 174 burials (13.2 per cent) in the medieval period at Wharram Percy. Boon compared an infant mortality rate of 20–25 per cent at Roman Silchester with the rate of 11.6 per cent in England and Wales in the 1970s, but if the archaeological evidence includes the bones of stillborn children while the early statistics exclude them then we might conclude that a Romano-British baby's chances of survival were not too bad.

Deliberate infanticide remains a possibility – in all societies there will be parents who, for one reason or another, kill their children and Roman Britain is unlikely to have been an exception – but there may be no more infants' skeletons than can be accounted for by natural events. With the wide range of contraceptives and abortifacients available, few women would have chosen infanticide as a preferred method of family planning, with its requirement to go through a full pregnancy and the dangers of childbirth.

It was the excavation of Hambledon villa which produced the most emotive report of infanticide.[46] A H Cocks recorded that 'the ground, roughly speaking throughout the northern half, was positively littered with babies. They number 97 and most of them are newly born, but an occasional one is rather older. A few were laid at length but the majority were evidently carried and buried wrapped in a cloth or garment, huddled in a little bundle, so that the head was almost central and the knee above it . . . As nothing marked the position of these tiny graves, a second little corpse was sometimes deposited on one already in occupation of a spot, apparently showing that these interments took place secretly, after dark. The majority of the babies lay in the yard, north of the third House'.

On the evidence of Barton Court Farm, where forty-one babies were buried in a separate area, we may now see the yard at Hambledon as the official infant cemetery. There is certainly no evidence for the burials being in any way illicit. The implication, made explicit elsewhere, is that the babies were illegitimate and were being disposed of by their mothers to avoid scandal. We do not, however, know whether illegitimacy carried any stigma in Roman Britain, nor is it likely that a girl could give birth in a rural community without the fact being widely known – that ninety-seven should do so stretches the imagination too far. S S Frere has suggested that the babies were the unwanted result of slave liaisons, but as slaves were marketable commodities it is more likely that an owner who did not wish to go to the expense of rearing a slave child would sell it on the open market. Mercatilla, for example, who died at the age of one year, six months, and twelve days at Bath, and is described as the freedwoman and foster-daughter of Magnius, may well have changed hands in this manner. Columella was of the opinion 'that [slave] women who are unusually prolific ... ought to be rewarded'.[47]

The discovery of an infant under the ramparts of the town at Winchester, as well as in the ramparts and ditches of other town sites, confirms that although Roman law forbade burial within city limits, children of less than forty days were exempt. The babies buried at Catsgore in stone-lined cists within the buildings or under the eaves had been interred with some ceremony and effort, and it can be argued that shaft burials were intended to help a child into the next world rather than that babies were sacrificed to sanctify the shafts or simply tipped down a handy rubbish pit. Several infant burials at Barton Court Farm, Winterton, Rudston and Catsgore were accompanied by animal skeletons, either dogs or sheep: further evidence that inhumation ceremonies were being carried out in a proper manner. It is more than possible that the funerary rites for a neonatal or perinatal child differed from those of an adult or even older children. The establishment of the infants' cemetery at Barton Court Farm might support this hypothesis, whilst the evidence at Trentholme Drive, York, which led the excavators to conclude that it was not the custom to inter neonates at all, may also indicate that such infants had their own burial plot so far undiscovered.

The tendency for archaeologists to excavate only the buildings on villa sites may have overemphasised the incidence of infant burials compared to those of adults, who would be more likely to have been buried further afield. It is not known how many years or how many fertile women the ninety-seven babies at Hambledon represent. It is possible that this is not an excessive number of natural fatalities given an establishment of reasonable size over a number of generations. At Bradley Hill a preponderance of female infants has been taken as proof that girls were not regarded as worth rearing, but Bradley Hill is unusual: the majority of sites show a closer correlation to the natural ratio of births between the sexes: 106 males to 102 females. The ratio of infant burials to adult burials tends to remain constant throughout the south of England.

The burial of babies in or close to a dwelling may be because there was no legal obligation for them to be buried elsewhere – there is, after all, no legal requirement in Britain today for a stillborn child to be given formal funerary rites – or because they were regarded as being in some way attached to the house. Soranus mentions that a new-born baby should be laid immediately on the earth, a ritual which implies that the child was being introduced to the household gods or dedicated to one of the fertility goddesses.[48] If a baby died whilst the mother was still lying in or before it was weaned it is conceivable that it was judged to belong to the spirits of hearth and home: the connection between infant burials and hearths at Catsgore and Rudston should be noted here, and it may have been considered detrimental to the household if the baby was buried elsewhere. The discovery of domestic infant burials in pre-Roman contexts at Kingsdown Camp, Rotherley and Baldock suggests the continuation of belief from the Iron Age. There is also a marked geographical bias: the settlement sites in the north of England and Scotland do not produce infant burials and the more northerly villas contain intramural infant burials from the first to the fourth centuries, while the southern sites show a gap between the first and the fourth centuries. This may confirm that tribal traditions were a major factor in infant burial practices. The resurgence of infant burial in the fourth century may reflect the changes in religious thought in Britain linked to the spread of Christianity.

If a couple remained childless other than by design they could adopt or foster a child. According to Roman law only men could adopt and if this was done by *adrogatio*, that is by a legislative act, then the child had the rights of a legitimate child, but this was not recognised as a procedure in the adoption of girls. If the child was taken into the household without legal arrangements being made then she retained her status at birth. A number of children are recorded as being fostered in Britain, for example Mercatilla, foster-daughter of Magnius; Hyllus[49] at York; Hermagoras in the household of the tribune Honoratus;[50] and Ylas, 'dearest foster child' of Claudius Severus.[51] Their names appear to attest to their slave or freed status.

Childlessness was regarded as grounds for divorce and, except in cases of obvious male impotence, a barren marriage was blamed on the wife. Divorce was permissible on specified grounds only, all of which involved an offence committed by one of the partners. In the case of a wife's adultery divorce was obligatory, otherwise her husband was considered to condone the act and so lost any claim to the dowry as well as making himself liable to prosecution as his wife's pimp. Insanity was not grounds for divorce; on the contrary, if a woman was declared insane she could not divorce her husband, nor could her family obtain a divorce on her behalf.

By the first century AD divorce was not a difficult procedure technically. As the marriage had been formed by the two parties consenting to the match, so it could be dissolved by either the husband or wife renouncing their commitment. The only exception was a freedwoman married to her previous owner, who could not obtain a divorce without his consent. The dowry reverted to the wife's family on divorce but the husband could claim for retentions; for example, he was allowed a sixth of the sum to compensate him for his wife's alleged misconduct. It was essential to the woman's chances of a second marriage for the dowry to be returned intact, and there were several cases in Italy of a *pater* dissolving his daughter's marriage in order to reclaim the dowry or to avoid paying the final instalment. If the original marriage contract had been vague or if claims were made by either side to the household property, each could resort to the courts and one imagines that in the ensuing legal wrangle the divorce lawyers did very well for themselves.

Any children of the marriage were the financial responsibility of the husband, including a child born after the divorce. It was possible, however, for a mother to claim custody and have the children live with her. In this case her former husband was expected to pay maintenance for the children. His *potestas* remained inviolable. The husband was not responsible for his former wife's maintenance as she reverted to being her *pater's* responsibility.

Loss of citizenship or enslavement resulted in the dissolution of a legal marriage without the need for divorce. If the husband joined the army the marriage was also regarded as null and void by the authorities although not necessarily by the partners involved (see below, Chapter 2). This latter stipulation will have affected a number of British families when the father was conscripted.

The majority of the medical writers state that the menopause occurred between the ages of forty and fifty, although Soranus extended the upper limit to sixty and Oribasius pushed the onset down to the early thirties. The latter recognised a correlation between the ages of menarche and menopause resulting in a set period of fertility for all women.[52] There was little written about the changes associated with the menopause, possibly because most doctors were more concerned with the problems of fertile women, or because many of the symptoms of menopause were seen as a continuation of earlier problems or as psychological disturbances. Galen, for example, considered that hysteria, in its original meaning of 'affections of the womb', might often have a psychological cause.[53]

There was an ancient belief in the Mediterranean world that the womb was a separate living entity which could move around a woman's body and cause illness and misey; a lead phylactery, found at West Deeping in Lincolnshire (Fig 11), inscribed with the command: 'Womb, I say to you, stay in your place........I adjure you, by Iaô, and by Sabaô(th) and by Adônai, not to hold onto the side; but stay in your place, and not to hurt Cleuomedes, daughter of A....', indicates that at least one woman in Britain held to this belief, although her name and the deities she invokes suggest that she was not a native Briton.[54] It is also not clear if Cleuomedes was simply suffering from painful periods or one of the female ailments discussed at length in the contemporary literature, such as inflammation of the uterus and vagina, prolapse of the uterus, closure of the womb and breast complaints. There were specialists in breast disorders, of which mastitis and tumours are likely to have been the most common. There is little evidence for cancer of the breast, cervix or ovaries being major causes of death in the Roman period but identifying specific diseases from ancient descriptions can be fraught with difficulties.

Medical problems might be treated by diet, medicines to be taken internally or applied externally, or by fumigation with the vapours being introduced into the nostrils or vagina. In many cases the treatment may have been worse than the illness. A number of medical instruments, such as the vaginal speculum and the uterine clyster, were designed specially to treat female complaints but few have been found in Britain.

One of a woman's duties was to look after the health of her family by maintaining a basic First Aid kit. In Letter 294 at Vindolanda, Paterna promises to bring 'two remedies', one for fever, when she comes to visit Sulpicia Lepidina. It is not clear, however, if she was intending to make these herself or if she was simply agreeing to collect the remedies from the nearest chemist, such as Albanus, the pharmacist known to have been plying his trade at Carlisle.[55] From the evidence it might be presumed that Albanus's most requested medication was for eye problems: over thirty oculists' stamps have been found in Britain

11. Cleuomedes at West Deeping hoped that this lead phylactery would alleviate her gynaecological problems (© The Collection, Lincolnshire County Council)

listing ingredients as diverse as 'metal scale', frankincense, myrrh, balsam, nard-oil and gall, all of which were listed as the active ingredients in a range of eye salves intended to cure trachoma, dim sight, running eyes and ophthalmia.[56]

The complaints of old age are most easily recognisable in bone assemblages and osteo-arthrosis was prevalent: over 80 per cent of the adults at Cirencester,

12. Pottery cup from South Shields, used for feeding infants and invalids (© Museum of Antiquities of the University and Society of Antiquaries of Newcastle upon Tyne)

for example, showed signs of osteo-arthrosis, with more women affected than men. The implication that women led an active life with a great deal of lifting and physical exertion which took its toll in later life is supported by the appearance of nodules on the vertebrae which are the result of using the spine in carrying out heavy tasks. The higher incidence of arthritis in the neck among the female population of Cirencester has been interpreted as the result of carrying heavy weights, such as water pots, on their heads, while 'squatting facets', that is the development of impressions on bones at the front of the ankle joint which develop in people who spend an appreciable amount of time in a squatting position, were more often found in the women at Trentholme Drive cemetery in York, suggesting that they spent long hours squatting over cooking fires or at their other work. Considering this evidence for an active lifestyle few female skeletons show fractures, although a woman at York with a badly healed right femur would have had a pronounced limp. This female showed a peculiar variation in her lumbar vertebrae which has tentatively, if improbably, been associated with her being a professional acrobat.

Osteoporosis will have been common among women of post-menopausal age but may not have become apparent in the skeleton unless they reached their sixties. The skeletons of the Lankhills cemetery, at Winchester, show variation in the survival rate of male and female skeletons which might indicate that the bones of elderly osteoporosis sufferers simply crumbled away, leaving few recognisable traces. So far only 45 individuals from eight sites in Roman Britain have been identified as having had osteoporosis.[57]

Identifiable fatal diseases are difficult to recognise. Tuberculosis and leprosy appear to have been Roman introductions but may not have been rife until the post-Roman period; so far only two skeletons, one at Poundbury and another at Cirencester, have provided evidence for leprosy in Roman Britain whilst twelve cases of turberculosis, all affecting men in the south of the country, have been discovered.[58] Poundbury cemetery also produced an example of Pott's disease, which is a result of tuberculosis, and other examples have been found at York and Cirencester. Venereal diseases, such as syphilis, may have been known, although the evidence is by no means convincing and descriptions of symptoms which might be identified as syphilis could be mistaken for other conditions, such as uro-genital tuberculosis. Certainly none of the classical writers warn the sexually active of potential medical dangers and it would appear that none were known.

Plagues regularly broke out in various parts of the Empire and are recorded as killing thousands of people. The movement of troops and merchants around the Empire would have helped to spread infectious diseases whilst the concentration of people into increasingly large urban conurbations would also have led to perfect conditions for the outbreak and dissemination of disease. The effect of such outbreaks on the population of Roman Britain escaped comment by contemporary writers, although John Wacher has attributed the breakdown of town life in the immediate post-Roman period to pestilence, among other causes. As there was little understanding of the mechanism of disease it is probable that any epidemic would take its toll, particularly of the very young and the elderly. Complaints which modern science takes in its stride would often have proved fatal.

Diet was a contributing factor to disease, particularly in the winter months when fresh fruit and vegetables were in short supply. The lavish meals and heavy consumption of alcohol among the upper classes would have resulted in their suffering from the 'executive' ailments of heart attacks, high blood pressure, ulcers and liver complaints. Twenty-three skeltons from Britain appear to indicate cases of diffuse idiopathic skeletal hyperostosis, a condition which is associated with obesity and diabetes. This is also the period when the first signs of gout appear. A diet rich with garlic, onions, wine and fish sauces would also have resulted in a high incidence of halitosis. At the other end of the social scale the diseases and deformities of the malnourished would have been prevalent; for example, night blindness due to a lack of animal fats and oils, and rickets and osteomalacia from a deficiency of Vitamin D in dairy foods and fish-liver oils. Chronic anaemia has been observed among the women and children buried in the Roman cemetery at Poundbury.

The rise in metabolic diseases and dental defects have been taken as evidence that some people's diet was less than adequate.[59] Only two individuals, however, are recorded as having had scurvy, a low percentage which may suggest that most people were managing to maintain a healthy level of Vitamin C. Poor diet would also have led to an inability to fend off diseases and fewer reserves to aid healing. At all levels of society hygienic storage would have been a problem and food poisoning a common complaint. Analysis of material from the sewers at York and Carlisle shows the inhabitants to have been riddled with worms and bowel parasites. One woman from Orton Longueville in Cambridgeshire had a hydatid cyst in her thoracic cavity, the result of a tapeworm infestation. Hers would not have been a unique case.

The use of stone to mill flour led, inevitably, to grit in the bread which wore down the teeth and exposed the pulp, but on the whole the diet was good for the teeth and dental caries was less widespread than today. There is, however, evidence that there was an increase in dental disease and caries, compared to the Iron Age, which may reflect the changes in diet brought about through Roman trade. Most skeletal assemblages indicate that the women's teeth were consistently in better condition than the men's.[60] This may reflect a practice, common in many primitive societies, of the women eating a plainer diet with fewer sugars – the choicer, less healthy food being reserved for the men.

The life expectancy of a Romano-Briton has been the subject of many papers. Unfortunately, recent research in forensic pathology has indicated that the age of many skeletons over thirty-five has often been wrongly assessed in the past and as a result the statistics for adult deaths are inaccurate whilst attempts to calculate life expectancy using demographic models have not been convincing. The suggestion that few women survived past thirty-five or forty is likely to be a considerable underestimate. Further discussion of this topic awaits the amassing of enough accurate data to be statistically significant. The evidence of the funerary inscriptions, however, shows a general spread of age groups with several women, such as Tadia Vallaunius and Julia Secundina from Caerleon living to sixty-five and seventy-five, while Claudia Crysis at Lincoln lived to the ripe old age of ninety. The evidence from Poundbury for a high death-rate among adolescent girls, however, may suggest that, contrary to natural expectations, some Romano-British women did not live as long as their menfolk and that there may have been geographical variations in female life expectancy.[61]

Chapter 2

Women and the army

The women with military associations came from every social stratum and every province of the Empire but the most important woman in Britain at any one time would have been an empress who accompanied her husband to the province. The number of emperors who brought their wives to Britain is uncertain but there is literary evidence to suggest that it was the norm for wives and children to be included in the imperial entourage: even Augustus had 'travelled to west and east with Livia as his companion'.[1] It is possible that Sabina was resident in Britain whilst Hadrian inspected the northern frontier, as his biographer seems to hint that an unsavoury incident between the empress and Septicius Clarus, prefect of the guard, and Suetonius Tranquillus, 'director of imperial correspondence', occurred in Britain.[2] It was, however, Julia Domna (Fig 13), the Syrian wife of Septimius Severus, who made the most impact during her state visit when the imperial court was established at York during the Scottish campaigns. For once Britain was the centre of the Roman Empire rather than on the fringes, and contemporary reliefs show that the empress's hairstyle, clothes and manners were carefully copied by British women. None of the other empresses are mentioned by name in connection with Britain, although it is reasonable to postulate that the governors of Britain who proclaimed themselves Emperor – Gordian, Clodius Albinus, Carausius and his finance minister Allectus, and Magnus Maximus – may have had their wives by their side. The part played by women in these rebellions is not recorded. In the later years of Roman rule several Britons became emperors of the Western Empire and the mothers, sisters and wives of Gratian, Constantine I and Constantine III may have had a considerable influence on the life of the province.

For 170 years after becoming a province of the Roman Empire Britain had a single governor who was recognised as a delegate of the Emperor with the rank of propraetor. The governorship of Britain was one of the most important posts available to an ambitious Roman and as such it was reserved for senior men of senatorial rank, ex-consuls. The post-holder was supreme commander of the army of occupation as well as the chief justice of the province, and in the absence of the empress his wife would be First Lady. There had been some debate in Rome in AD 21 as to whether wives should be allowed to accompany governors to provinces, as there had been some unfortunate incidents in the past. Aulus Caecina Severus had moved that 'no magistrate who had been allotted a province should be accompanied by his wife' as 'there was point in the old regulation which prohibited the dragging of women to the provinces or

13. Painting of the Emperor Septimus Severus with his wife, Julia Domna, and his children, Caracalla and Geta. Geta's face was erased after his murder by his brother in AD 212 (© Staatliche Museen zu Berlin – Antikensammlung/bpk Berlin/Johannes Laurentius)

foreign countries; in a retinue of ladies there were elements apt, by luxury or by timidity, to retard the business of peace or war and to transmute a Roman march into something resembling an Eastern procession. Weakness and a lack of endurance were not the only failings of the sex: give them scope and they turned hard, intriguing, ambitious. They paraded among the soldiers, they had the centurions at beck and call. Recently a woman [Plancina] had presided at the exercises of the cohorts and the manoeuvres of the legions.'[3] Despite this argument most governors continued to be accompanied by their wives, although a *senatus consultum* of AD 24 made a governor accountable for his wife's behaviour in the province.

One of the few governor's wives known to have resided in Britain is Pomponia Graecina, wife of Aulus Plautius, the leader of the invasion force of AD 43. She was accused years later of practising a nameless foreign religion which she was supposed to have discovered whilst in Britain, a slander which could hardly have become widespread if she had never been to the country. Domitia Decidiana, wife of Agricola, is not mentioned in connection with Britain, but

Tacitus records that in AD 84, that is after being governor for six years, Agricola 'suffered a grievous personal loss in the death of a son who had been born a year before',[4] so her presence might be presumed. Other wives may be assumed on similar tenuous evidence but they have not left their names; for example, we know that Pompeius Falco's wife had been the granddaughter of Agricola's predecessor, Julius Frontinus, and must have been familiar with Britain from childhood.

The first governors were Italian and had Italian wives, but over the years governors of Gallic, Spanish, Numidian and African origins were appointed who may have married in their home provinces or during the travels which were part of any senatorial career. A tour of duty could last up to seven years but the average was three. It was the Emperor Tiberius who extended the service period and by the end of his reign the governor's wife had become a recognised member of the provincial hierarchy. Her duties are unspecified but most will have accompanied their husbands on official visits and acted as hostess at functions. Of the wife of C Galenius, governor of Egypt, it was said that she would accept no petitions, would admit no provincials to her house, and was never seen in public – behaviour which was regarded as unusual as well as intolerably snobbish. Although unable to wield any official power a governor's wife with character might be able to influence her husband and political events; one only has to think of the great political hostesses of the eighteenth and nineteenth centuries. This possibility had already been recognised, as it was generally considered improper for a governor's wife to accept favours or presents from client princes, and she had to take care that her behaviour did not jeopardise her husband's professional impartiality. Juvenal criticised those women who 'with unflinching face and dry breasts' participated in male discussions of politics and military activities.[5]

A large building on the river terrace in the area of Cannon Street station in London has been suggested as the governor's palace, built about AD 80. It seems to have had a large central courtyard with a fountain and an ornamental pool, and small rooms or offices ranged along its east wing. None of the reception rooms or the living quarters of the governor's family have been uncovered. It has also been suggested that the palatial villa at Fishbourne, built at the same time, was not occupied by the native king Cogidubnus as previously thought, but was the summer residence of the governor's family. Both buildings would have been considered very old fashioned by the time Caerellius Priscus arrived with his family around 178 AD and may have been replaced. That the family was delighted at the new posting, a promotion from being Governor of Upper Germany, may be inferred from the inscription set up in Mainz to record the occasion by Caerellius Priscus, his wife Modestiana, his son Caerellius Marcianus and his daughter Germanilla; sadly, it is possible that Caerellius Priscus was the governor killed by invading tribes during the reign of Commodus.[6]

Around AD 197 Britain was divided into two provinces: Britannia Superior and Britannia Inferior, each with a governor, so there were now two 'First Ladies'.

London continued to be the capital of Britannia Superior while York is likely to have been the capital of Britannia Inferior, with the legionary legate promoted to governor. The governor's *praetorium* in York, or indeed the residence used by the Severi as the imperial court, has not been found although a large building under the Old Station Yard may form part of it.

The reorganisation of the Empire by Diocletian led to further subdivision of Britain into Britannia Prima, Britannia Secunda, Maxima Caesariensis and Flavia Caesariensis, all governed by *praesides* of equal equestrian rank, although Maxima Caesariensis may have been promoted later, as there is a reference to a consular governor in the *Notitia Dignitatum*. Lincoln and Cirencester have been suggested as the capitals of the two extra provinces. About AD 370 a fifth province was created, called Valentia, with a possible capital at Carlisle. Unfortunately, nothing is known of the wives and daughters of any of these later governors, few of whom, indeed, are themselves known by name.

A governor of Britain was in charge of the army and responsible for justice in his province but had no control over finances; this was in the hands of the imperial procurator. One of these, Gaius Julius Alpinus Classicianus, died in Britain and was commemorated by his wife, Julia Pacata. Classicianus was a Gaul who succeeded Decianus Catus as procurator in AD 61, during the Boudican revolt. His wife was the daughter of Julius Indus, a famous Treveran noble, who had distinguished himself fighting on Rome's side in Gaul in AD 21. Both were, therefore, members of the new provincial aristocracy which had begun to play its part in the administration of the growing Empire. It is to be regretted that we know so little about Julia Pacata as she was clearly a woman of some courage, accompanying her husband to a province in the throes of a major and very bloody rebellion. Possibly she returned to Gaul after her husband's death.

Under the command of the governor were the legionary commanders, known as legates, who were of senatorial rank. Of the 127 legates presumed to have been in office from AD 86 to 213, only twenty can be identified by name, and even fewer of their wives. At York the altar dedicated to Fortuna by Sosia Juncina is the only record of herself and her husband, Quintus Antonius Isauricus, legate of the VIth Legion. This has been dated to before AD 213, as after this date the legate would have been referred to as governor.

The legionary legates must have spent much of their time campaigning during the earlier decades of Roman rule, and their wives would have been expected to follow the drum and live in the *praetoria* of the legionary fortresses. Those at Caerleon, Chester and York must certainly have had legates' wives residing at various times, but even those installations which proved to be temporary, such as Inchtuthill, would have seen the families of legates in residence as the average tour of duty for a legate was three years, a long time to be separated from one's family. Of the legionary vexillation fortresses only Longthorpe has been excavated to any extent, but the discovery of ear-rings and other possibly female paraphernalia shows some women to have been living there in the first century AD.

14. Aerial view of High Rochester, home to the aristocratic Julia Lucilla and her husband, Rufinus. (© Lt Col R N Gross)

Anthony Birley has estimated that the number of equestrian officers serving in Britain at any one time must have been at least sixty, including prefects and tribunes. He has further calculated that more than five thousand men could have served as equestrian officers during the first two and a half centuries of Roman rule. Not all of these men will have married or have been married at the time of their tour of duty in Britain, nor of those married would the majority have had daughters, but the potential number of women of equestrian rank in Britain is still high. A few of these *equites*, such as Statius Priscus,[7] may have been born in Britain but the majority came from the other provinces. Equestrian officers were usually in their twenties or thirties, with either the necessary property qualification themselves or wealthy patrons to buy them commissions.

Two of the earliest fort commanders' wives to be known by name are Sulpicia Lepidina, wife of Flavius Cerialis, the prefect of the ninth cohort of Batavians, and her friend (or sister) Claudia Severa, wife of Aelius Brocchus. Cerialis was the senior officer at Vindolanda and we can be confident that Sulpicia Lepidina lived in the *praetorium* there as early as AD 100–05. This building was of timber and occupied a position on the eastern side of the south section of the *via principalis*. The lives of these women might be compared with those of the colonel's wives on the north-west frontier of India or the American Midwest in the nineteenth century. The picture is one of some discomfort, a certain amount of danger and a great deal of boredom and loneliness. There would be few other women living within a fort in the first century AD other than the domestic staff of the *praetorium* and some centurion's wives, and certainly none of these would have been of the same class as the commanding officer's wife, so a trip out of the fort to visit a town or to another military installation must have been eagerly anticipated.

Many of the females commemorated on tombstones or other inscriptions may have been the wives or daughters of commanding officers: Aurelia Romana and her sister Aurelia Sabina, for example, were probably the daughters of the prefect at Greta Bridge, while Anthony Birley has suggested that Vettia Mansueta and her daughter Claudia Turianilla were the wife and daughter of the commanding officer at Carvoran. Two women who are known to have been married to senior military men are worth discussing in some detail: Aurelia Eglectiane and Julia Lucilla. Aurelia Eglectiane was the wife of Fabius Honoratus, the tribune of the first Cohort of Vangiones, a large cavalry unit, at Chesters in the late second century. The family is known from a tombstone, possibly post-dating AD 161, mourning the death of their 'most sweet' daughter, Fabia Honorata. The age of the child is not given but the phrase 'most sweet' was usually reserved for the memorials of toddlers. The *praetorium* in which they lived was placed between the headquarters building *(principia)* and the east gate. Part of this building was excavated in the nineteenth century and found to have had a roughly built hypocaust heating system and a separate bath suite.

More is known of Julia Lucilla from her husband's tombstone and their freedman's altar to Silvanus Pantheus. She refers to herself as *clarissima femina*, that is, a woman of senatorial rank, although this was not strictly true as her husband was only an equestrian and she would have lost rank on her marriage. Her husband, Rufinus, had been prefect of the first Cohort of Lusitanians and also of the first Cohort of Breuci, before taking over the command of the first Cohort of Vardulli at High Rochester, north of Hadrian's Wall (Fig 14). The date of his command is not known but may have corresponded with the Severan campaigns at the end of the second century and the early years of the third. His career had also included the sub-curatorship of the Flaminian Way and Doles, as well as the sub-curatorship of Public Works, and it was possibly during this term of office in Rome that he met his wife.

Julia Lucilla's life at the outpost fort of High Rochester illustrates how the wives of officers often found themselves in the military arena, living in remote areas far from civilisation. The exposed position of High Rochester and the unsettled nature of the surrounding countryside would have meant that she would have been unable to venture far on her own. The difficulty of independent travel for such women may be seen in Letter 292 at Vindolanda, in which Sulpicia Lepidina comments that her acceptance of Claudia Severa's invitation was dependent on her husband giving permission. Whilst this might be interpreted as evidence for the level of control a Roman husband might expect to have over his wife, it is important to remember that in AD 100 the north of England was an unstable frontier zone and it is more likely that Sulpicia Lepidina was simply following sensible military procedure in asking permission of the fort's commanding officer to leave his jurisdiction.

In Julia Lucilla's case we know that her household included a slave called Eutychus, who may have been freed by her husband's will and who refers to his 'dependants' in his dedication to Silvanus Pantheus. The name Eutychus is

Greek, which may or may not reflect his origins, and it is likely that he and his wife and children had accompanied Rufinus and Julia Lucilla on their journey from Rome rather than having been inherited from the previous commanding officer. Little is known of the *praetorium* at High Rochester in which all these people lived except its probable position by the west gate.

When Rufinus died at the age of forty-eight he was buried in the cemetery outside the fort where other officers' stone-built tombs have been uncovered. Julia Lucilla will not have been the only soldier's wife to have buried her husband in a foreign land, nor Aurelia Eglectiane the only mother to have left behind a child buried in a military cemetery. It is probable that Julia Lucilla went back to her family in Rome when she was widowed but it is not known whether widows and orphans were usually expected to find their own way home or if the army made any provision. As the *praetorium* was a 'tied house' a widow would have had to remove herself and her household before the next incumbent took office, and this may have caused difficulties on occasion.

The best known of the fort *praetoria* is at Housesteads (Fig 15) although, unfortunately, none of the women who lived there are known by name. The building began as an L-shaped structure but was later extended to the more common courtyard plan. The kitchen, with a large oven, was in the north-east corner, and a bath suite was inserted into the north range some time in the second century. Several of the rooms were heated by hypocausts and there was

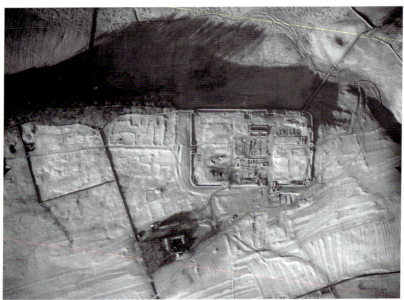

15 Housesteads fort from the air. The courtyard house of the Commanding Officer's family is just inside the south gate, while outside are the excavated inns and shops of the *vicus*. Houses and other buildings can be made out as rectangular marks in the ground outside the gates and above the cultivation terraces (© Cambridge University Collection (rights reserved): Unit for Landscape Modelling)

a lavatory in the west range. It has been suggested that the eastern end of the south range contained stabling with servants' quarters above. The courtyard form of *praetoria* was established throughout the Empire and reflected middle/upper-class housing plans in Italy. The *praetorium* at Housesteads seems to have been comfortable and the mistress of such a house would have had little to complain about as far as her quarters were concerned.

Both the legions and the auxiliary units relied on their centurions, each of whom was in direct command of eighty men. Most centurions had risen from the ranks although there were exceptions. The post offered a permanent job with no compulsory age of retirement and a steady, substantial salary. Centurions were, on the whole, intelligent men who had some education and were capable of dealing with paperwork. They were often transferred from legion to legion and province to province as situations developed which required men of experience, and as they had always been allowed to marry as soon as they reached the rank of centurion, their wives must have been among the most travelled women in the Empire. Several who visited Britain fleetingly are known by name: Claudia Marcia Capitolina, whose husband had served with the VIth Victrix at York before being transferred to Arabia with the IIIrd Cyrenaica and whose son had been born whilst they were resident in York; and Salviena Metiliana, whose husband, born in Cologne, died at Lambaesis in Algeria after a tour of duty in Britain, possibly at Housesteads. Such women thought little of packing their belongings and taking their children across continents. Papyri from Egypt suggest that it was common for centurions to go on ahead when they were transferred, leaving their wives to arrange for the transport of the goods and chattels. One can imagine that these were redoubtable women who stood no nonsense and could deal with any situation.

As the centuries of infantry were commanded by centurions so the twenty-four or sixteen *turmae* of a cavalry *ala* were commanded by decurions. Only one decurion's wife is known by name in Britain: Aelia Comindus, wife of Nobilianus, who died at the age of thirty-two at Carrawburgh. Luckily more information is available about the families of centurions. The most senior centurion's wife about whom we have any evidence in Britain may have been Januaria Martina, whose husband, Vivius Marcianus of the IInd Legion Augusta, may have been *princeps praetorii*, that is a centurion of senior rank who was the chief administrator in the governor's headquarters. Certainly his tombstone at London shows him to have been a man of some consequence. Aurelius Super, centurion of the VIth Legion, who died at York at the age of thirty-eight, may also have been a senior man to judge by the elaborate coffin paid for by his widow, Aurelia Censorina.

A woman of possibly African origins, Vibia Pacata, was married to Flavius Verecundus, centurion of the VIth Legion Victrix, whose own birthplace appears to have been in Pannonia (modern Hungary). How this couple of widely divergent origins met and what they thought of their posting at Westerwood, on the Antonine Wall, is unknown, but their story perhaps serves to emphasise the travels of centurial families and illustrates that foreign women were to be found as far north as the Antonine Wall. Other centurions, such as Gracilis, the husband of Aurelia from Piercebridge, came from Upper Germany to lead auxiliary units. He held a commission with the XXIInd Legion which was never stationed in Britain. The legion of Flavia Baetica's husband, Afutianus son of Bassus, is not recorded, nor is his place of origin, only that he was centurion of the second Cohort of Tungrians at Birrens.

The centurion resided in the suite of rooms at the end of each barrack block but until recently it was not clear whether his wife and family lived there as well or had accommodation outside the fort. However, the finds from the excavations of Barrack Block 13 at Housesteads make it evident that the centurions' families were present in the barracks. The centurion's quarters were not small, often measuring 20 to 30 feet (6–9 m) square internally, and would have been adequate for family housing.[8]

The tombstone of Marcus Aurelius Nepos, centurion of the XXth Legion Valeria Victrix, shows his wife as if standing a few paces behind him in an unusually subordinate position. Her name is not known – the space left for it was never filled. Possibly she remarried or moved away, and again one questions what happened to centurions' and decurions' widows. They would have been less able to finance their own transport back home than the wives of commanding officers and one wonders where they would feel home to be after a lifetime of travel. Possibly they gravitated to the *vici* or towns frequented by veterans and some will have remarried. Aurelia Censorina, whose husband died at thirty-eight, is likely to have been in the prime of life and could have faced a long widowhood.

Below the rank of centurion soldiers were forbidden by law to marry during their military career. Exactly when this restriction was first brought into effect is not clear but that it was in force before the invasion of Britain is indicated by Cassius Dio's statement that 'he, Claudius, gave the rights of married men to the soldiers, since in accordance with the law, they were not permitted to marry'.[9] The precise reason which led to the ban can only be conjectured but Herodian held to the theory that a soldier would be more disciplined, mobile and efficient if he was not hampered by a wife and family. The ban continued until the reign of Septimius Severus when, according to Herodian, 'to the soldiers he gave a very large sum of money and many other privileges that they had not had before; for he was the first to increase their pay and he also gave them permission to wear gold rings and to live in wedlock with their wives'.[10] The date of this edict was AD 197 and the phrasing can be interpreted in two ways: either that the soldiers were now allowed to marry legally or that they were being given permission to cohabit with the wives they already had. There had been no hindrance at any time to soldiers forming less formal arrangements with local women: Robin Birley has interpreted the term *contuberni*, in Letter 181 from Vindolanda, to mean 'concubine' rather than 'messmate', suggesting that the text refers to the *de facto* wife of Tagamatis, the flag-bearer.[11]

In Britain, several tombstones refer to married legionaries, such as Julius Julianus of the IInd Legion Augusta and his wife Amanda at Caerleon, or Flavius Agricola of the VIth Legion Victrix and his wife Albia Faustina at London; others mention foreign auxiliaries: Aurelius Marcus of the second Cohort of Dalmatians mourned his wife Aurelia Aia, who came from Salonae in Dalmatia (modern Croatia) but died at Carvoran, and Pusinna set up a tombstone on Hadrian's Wall to her husband Dagvalda, who was a Pannonian. These memorials set up by soldiers' widows or in memory of soldiers' wives have all been presumed to date to after AD 197, as theoretically there could be no soldiers' wives earlier. However, a tombstone is not a legal document: its inscription reflects how the couple saw themselves, not how the Roman legal system viewed the situation. It would seem improbable that the native Britons, with their strong moral values, would have allowed hundreds of their daughters to cohabit with soldiers without insisting on some form of wedding ceremony; if a woman had been married by native custom she, and her relatives, would regard her and describe her as a wife, even if the union was not recognised by Roman officialdom. Some of these tombstones, therefore, may predate AD 197, and the edict may simply have regularised a situation which the army was well aware existed already: it has been estimated that 40 per cent of military diplomas of auxiliary soldiers recognise an existing relationship with a woman – Amabalis, daughter of Firmus, for example, is specifically named as a soldier's wife in a military diploma found at Middlewich. A legal opinion given as early as the time of Hadrian presumed that soldiers would be married, as it 'decided that a son under paternal control, who is in the army, could be the heir of his wife'.[12]

Margaret Roxan noted that Britain was not unusual in having married soldiers in the ranks. Her survey of 904 tombstones from the Empire's frontiers revealed 102 military widows and 55 widowers who were still serving.[13] She also noted that the number of soldiers' families named in military retirement diplomas changed through time with a noticeable rise in the number of named families after AD 120.[14] Her conclusion was that the period of imperial expansion before AD 120 made it difficult for serving soldiers to form long-term relationships, while the more settled situation post AD 120 resulted in units being stationed at one fort for long periods, giving the soldiers in those units time to meet girls and marry them.

By refusing soldiers permission to marry legally the State simply avoided responsibility for their dependants. There was no legal requirement for the military heirarchy to provide food or accommodation for the women or children, or concern itself over their protection, yet there is evidence that many of the dependants of serving soldiers, particularly auxiliaries, followed them on campaign: Cassius Dio refers to 'not a few women and children' straggling behind the marching column of Varus,[15] and Caesar mentions carts filled with female luggage at the back of his convoy.[16] These camp followers will have walked or travelled in waggons, sleeping in tents or under carts, living off the country and earning money by performing services such as cooking or mending, or entertaining. The Roman army was not the only army in history to have had families with it on the march, and it is always a mystery how these families survived. As there were women and children at Waterloo, so there may have been women and children at Mons Graupius, the battle against the Caledonians in Scotland in AD 84. If one was attached to a military man one's only chance of continued support for oneself and one's children would be to follow wherever he went, although if a unit had permanent winter quarters the women may have felt it worth the risk to remain at the base.

In the case of installations with permanent garrisons, settlements grew up outside the gates and these were known as *canabae* at fortresses and *vici* at forts. There has been some argument as to whether these were provided by the military or grew up unofficially. Some show a formalised layout and may be housing for veterans, while others straggled along the roads leading to the gates. Some forts, such as Melandra and Ribchester, had fortified *vici* which may suggest that they grew in importance, attracting merchants and craftsmen until they were thought worthy of protection. This is a move which may have been associated with the legal recognition of *vicani*, the local councils.[17]

There is no uniformity in the size of the building plots nor in the type of house construction in *vici*. Many are long rectangular buildings varying from stone-founded wattle-and-daub dwellings to wooden shacks. Many of them were occupied by traders and these houses were open at the front with living accommodation at the rear. By AD 197 many of the inhabitants of *vici* will have been second or third generation: there are a number of inscriptions thoughout the Empire which refer to people born *ex castris*, although only Tadia Exuperata and her brother are convincing examples of such people named in Roman Britain.[18] The legal status of these people was very uncertain, as children born during their fathers' military service were illegitimate and could have no claim if their fathers died intestate. As a soldier could not register the birth of a child, even if his offspring were provided for in his will, they might have difficulty in proving their identity. Furthermore, a woman could not reclaim her dowry on the death of her husband if the State had not recognised her marriage, nor could her family prosecute for adultery. Even more unsatisfactory was the ruling that a marriage contracted legally was considered dissolved if the husband joined the army, and any subsequent children were considered illegitimate. This may have affected the 5,500 Sarmatians who were conscripted some time between AD 169 and 180 and sent to Britain, as well as units such as the *numerus Hnaudifridi* and the 'Tigris barge-men', and those raised in Britain.

In theory the removal of the ban on marriage should have affected the accommodation of the now legal wives and children. The discovery of individual buildings, referred to as chalets, which replaced the barrack blocks of many forts in the third century, led to their identification in the 1980s as married quarters, a theory strengthened by the apparent evidence that many *vici*, which could have provided alternative accommodation for the soldiers' families, were

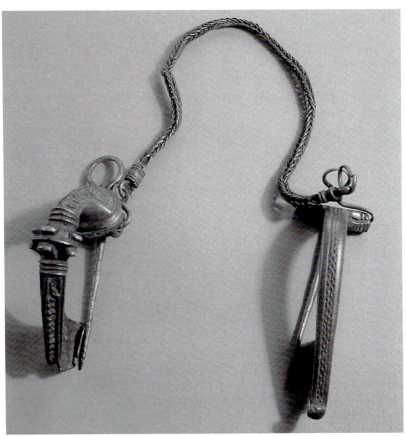

16. The dresses of Romano-British women were fastened by chained brooches like this unmatched pair from Newcastle upon Tyne. Finds of female accessories at such military sites indicate the presence of women in the forts at an early date. (© Museum of Antiquities of the University and Society of Antiquaries of Newcastle upon Tyne)

abandoned at about the same time. The analysis of the small finds, however, shows that female artefacts (Fig 16) appear in forts along Hadrian's Wall with some regularity in the second and early third centuries and appear to decrease in quantity at the time when the chalets were being occupied, which is the opposite of what might be expected. Finds of footwear also indicate increasing numbers of women and children in the military areas of the Empire during the second century, whilst the size distribution in the third century accords with a normal urban population. The chalets on Hadrian's Wall show few traces of female occupation, although at Malton, in Yorkshire, several infant burials found under the floors of possible chalets may suggest the presence of women. It is now accepted that the chalets are not married quarters but simply a variant form of barrack block. Furthermore, new survey techniques have revealed that the majority of *vici* were considerably larger than had previously been suspected and that the apparent abandonment of the civil buildings near to the fort walls may have been the result of official demolition by fort commanders wishing to have a clear defendable cordon in their immediate vicinity; the *vici* further from the fort walls may well have continued to be occupied by the families of the soldiers.

Wives were not the only female dependants: at Chesters Lurio, a German, lost not only his wife Julia and his son Canio but also his sister Ursa, who seems to have accompanied the family to Britain. Felicius Simplex, a legionary in the VIth Victrix at York, lost his ten-month-old daughter Simplicia Florentina, while Secundus of the IInd Legion Augusta at Usk was mourned by his mother. It is not clear how the army viewed female dependants who were not wives but who had a legal claim on their menfolk, such as sisters and mothers. Soldiers must often have found themselves in the role of *pater familias* on the death of their fathers and thus responsible for all their unmarried female relatives. Some may have considered that sending money home was an adequate discharge of their duties but others must have taken their responsibilities more seriously and preferred to have the women close at hand.

The pay of the average soldier, particularly if he was an auxiliary, was not overly generous and extra sources of income would have been required if he was the head of an extended family. The female relatives of soldiers must have had to earn their living in some way but no firm evidence of how they achieved this has come to light. Carol van Driel Murray's comparison of the women attached to the Dutch army in Indonesia with those attached to the Roman army suggests that many may have provided such services as laundry, clothes mending, and 'home' cooking.[19]

Not all the soldiers recorded by name were ordinary soldiers; many had specific duties, such as Vacia's brother, who was a staff-clerk at Great Chesters, and Gaius Valerius Justus, a record clerk of the XXth Legion at Chester, who mourned his 'most chaste and pure wife' Cocceia Irene. An *imaginifer's* daughter is recorded at Kirkby Thore while Julia Similina was the widow of a *beneficiarius* of the legate of the XXth Legion. There must also have been women married to sailors with the *classis Britannica* but none of their names have survived and it is possible that these women preferred to remain at the naval base at Bordeaux.

When a soldier retired he was granted certain privileges which were recorded on a diploma. A fine example was found at Malpas, Cheshire, in 1812 (Fig 17).[20] This is datable to AD 103, and grants Reburrus, a Spaniard of the ala I Pannoniorum Tampiana, among other soldiers serving in Britain under Lucius Neratius Marcellus who had served twenty-five years or more, Roman 'citizenship for themselves, their children and descendants, and the right of legal marriage with the wives they had when citizenship was granted to them, or, if any were unmarried, with those they later marry, but only a single one each'. This last clause highlights the interesting situation that, whereas the Romans were monogamous, many of the provinces of the Empire had a tradition of polygamy and many of the auxiliaries might well have had several wives before being

17. Military retirement diplomas, such as these examples, reveal that even before AD 197 many soldiers were married, some to more than one wife. (© British Museum)

drafted or have expected to marry more than one after retirement. This clause, of course, does not stop multiple marriages but ensures that only the children of one wife were recognised as legitimate and so entitled to citizenship.

The units referred to on the Malpas Diploma include Thracians, Pannonians, Gauls, Spaniards, Germans, Belgians, Dalmatians, and Portuguese. Not all of these will have returned to their country of origin after discharge, and some will have settled in Britain. Likewise veterans of British units serving abroad, such as *cohors I Brittonum milliaria*, will have settled in Dacia, Pannonia and Upper Moesia, marrying local girls unless their British wives had followed them abroad. Lucco, for example, was from the Cirencester area and married to a woman from the Brigetio region in Pannonia; he had served in Pannonia and then Moesia with the *cohors I Britannica* before moving back to Brigetio with his wife when he retired in AD 105.[21] Legionaries were originally granted land on retirement but by the time Britain was a Roman province this had been replaced by a cash bounty. There is evidence of land grants to some veterans at Colchester, Lincoln and Gloucester in the first century, as the State tried to establish official settlements, but this was rarely successful – the boorish behaviour of the veterans at Colchester, for example, was a contributory factor to the dissatisfaction which led to the Boudican rebellion. By the reign of Nero it was becoming clear that veterans preferred to settle near their old forts rather than be rehoused in 'new towns', and the population of *vici* swelled as a result.

Some veterans barely survived their discharge: Flavia Peregrina's husband Crotus, son of Vindex, died at Templebrough at the age of forty: he may have been invalided out because if he had served his full term he would have had to have joined up at the age of fifteen; possibly he lied about his age. Other veterans lived to a ripe old age: Onerata's husband Valerius Verecundus, at the age of seventy, was a young man compared to Cassius Secundus who died at eighty leaving a widow at Chester, or Julius Valens, who had passed his hundredth birthday when his wife Julia Secundina and his son Julius Martinus erected his tombstone. Julia Secundina's tombstone also survives, recording her death at the age of seventy-five. Clearly Julius Valens had married a much younger woman on his retirement and possibly had lived at Caerleon all his married life.

Marrying a veteran might be considered an excellent match for a girl, as veterans could be reasonably well off, having earned a good salary for over twenty-five years, as well as receiving a cash handout on retirement if a legionary. Their children also received full Roman citizenship and there were sundry other perks. This led to a number of families in *vici* and towns with young children whose fathers were in their forties or fifties whilst their mothers were only in their twenties. A typical, if rather sad, family is recorded on the tombstone of Flavia Augustina at York (Fig 18), whose husband, Gaius Aeresius Saenus, suffered in his retirement from the loss of his wife at the age of thirty-nine and his son and daughter, both in their second year.

18. Tombstone of Flavia Augustina at York, the young wife of a military veteran. Both of their children died before their second birthday. (© York Museums Trust (Yorkshire museum))

There is substantial evidence that ordinary soldiers could have slaves: Victor the Moor, for example, seems to have been the slave of a soldier of the *ala I Asturum*.[22] The majority of these slaves were male and possibly performed the functions of batman or groom, but female slaves were owned by centurions and other officers. The most interesting is an anonymous woman who was the slave of M Cocceius Firmus, centurion of the IInd Legion Augusta at Auchendavy. She is known, from a reference in the *Digest*, to have been condemned to cook for the convicts at the salt mines as a punishment for some unspecified crime.[23] Whilst serving her sentence she was 'captured by bandits of an alien race' and offered for sale. Cocceius Firmus presumably thought that, despite her criminal record, she was worth recovering and repurchased her but sued (successfully) the Imperial Treasury for the purchase price on the grounds that the State should have taken better care of his property whilst she was in its charge! One presumes that most of the slaves of ordinary soldiers lived in the *vici*, whilst those belonging to the commanding officer will have lived in the *praetorium* and those of a centurion's household would have shared the accommodation at the end of the barrack block, possibly sleeping in the attic.

Other women who were present at forts were the wives and daughters of the merchants and craftsmen or even merchants and craftworkers themselves who, attracted by the ready market provided by the army and the security offered by proximity to a military installation, set up in business in the *vici*. One of these merchants may have been Barates, husband of Regina, although it is not clear whether he was a maker of standards or a standard-bearer. Other traders, such as Antonianus at Bowness-on-Solway[24] and the possibly Jewish merchant Salmanes at Auchendavy,[25] may have travelled from *vicus* to *vicus* taking their families with them as Salmanes appears to have done, or made one *vicus* their home base. The women of these traders would have been expected to serve in the shop or assist in manufacturing, and it is regrettable that we know nothing of the butcher's family at Vindolanda, or the women who lived in the *mortaria* and samian shops at Castleford. Many women are recorded as living in *vici* but it is not always clear if they were the wives, widows, sisters, or daughters of soldiers or veterans or were members of the civilian population. Some of these women were British, for example, Verecunda Rufilia of the Dobunni, who is attested at Templebrough, but others are foreigners, such as Titullinia Pussitta, a Raetian (from modern Germany/Austria) who was at Netherby, an outpost fort of Hadrian's Wall (Fig 19).

Vici must have been noisy, bustling, cosmopolitan places, teeming with people of all nationalities. It was in the *vici* that travellers would have found overnight accommodation and where soldiers would have come in their off-duty hours. Taverns and cafes have been identified at several sites, one inn at Housesteads revealing the seamy side of *vicus* life as excavation revealed the skeletons of a murdered man and woman buried in the floor.[26] Prostitutes, acrobats, singers, dancers and jugglers would also have inhabited a *vicus*, entertaining the troops as well as the locals who flocked there on market days

19. The tombstone of Titullinia Pussitta, a Raetian, who died at Netherby. (© Carlisle Museum and Arts Services)

to sell their produce. A *vicus* will have offered a focal point for a wide range of people living in its neighbourhood, both military and civilian, male and female, honest and dishonest, as well as providing a target for travellers from further afield.

Chapter 3

Women of town and country

It may seem to be an obvious comment that the life of an urban woman differs from that of a rural woman but in Roman Britain the differences were fundamental. The initial impact of the Roman invasion on the life of a country woman outside the battle zone appears to have been minimal. In most areas she would have continued to play her traditional part in the agricultural and social life of her community and the cultural changes experienced by her urban sisters would have been only slowly assimilated, if at all. The rural population's hesitancy in accepting the Roman lifestyle is reflected in its domestic architecture: in the first century, while the townswomen were settling into their Continental rectangular houses, the women of the country continued to live in the traditional, often circular, huts of the Iron Age.

These huts were made from the building material most readily to hand: boulders or rough-hewn blocks where stone was plentiful, timber, wattle-and-daub or cob in other areas. The roofs would have been thatched with straw, reeds or heather, or covered with turves (Fig 20). Most early reconstructions included a central hole in the roof to allow smoke to escape, but experiments at Butser in Hampshire show that this arrangement, coupled with Britain's windy climate, results in roof fires. It is now known that the roof covered the whole house and smoke escaped as best it could through the thatch, which may have led to respiratory problems amongst the inhabitants.

It is easy to imagine these buildings as small, rather squalid dwellings, but many were as large as 40 feet (12.19 m) in diameter, covering an area greater than a pair of modern semi-detached houses. Such a house would probably have been occupied by an extended family or several related families, with similar groups living in other huts in the compound, surrounded by a ditch-and-bank, wooden palisade, or stone wall.

These settlements were based on a self-sufficient agricultural economy, and aerial photographs have revealed the majority to have had associated field systems. Women living in the rural settlements would have been fully involved in growing crops and tending animals. Indeed, the distribution of decorative finds such as armlets and beads, and domestic items, such as querns, in the settlements, compared with the spearheads, arrowheads and other military objects which dominate the hillfort assemblages, may hint at a tradition of a predominately male warrior class living separately in army camps, with food production almost entirely in the hands of the women living in extended family groups with their children and the elderly. Women may also have

20. Reconstruction of an Iron Age settlement at the Cat's Water site, Fengate (after Pryor). Circular huts in small compounds continued to be built and inhabited into the second century in some parts of the province (© British Museum. Drawn by S James)

been responsible for gathering food as well as growing it, not only harvesting wild crops but also hunting and fishing. This picture of the pre-Roman rural economy is, however, speculation based on anthropological parallels rather than firm archaeological evidence.

After the invasion life in some of the more remote settlements may have continued as before with little immediate change, but for those rural populations living close to the areas of intense Roman activity there may have been considerable disruption to every aspect of their lives. Some settlements will have been destroyed by enemy action whilst others, such as Milking Gap in Northumberland, may have been demolished to make way for forts and military zones. One wonders what happened to the occupants of these settlements; evidence from Egypt is beginning to suggest that the army occasionally offered some degree of compensation, and there may have been an official rehousing programme which moved the displaced rural population into the towns and *vici*. It is possible that other settlements may have been incorporated into imperial estates, as has been tentatively suggested for areas such as Salisbury Plain and Cranbourne Chase. If there were imperial estates in Britain, the men, women and children who lived in these areas would have been enslaved and their lands confiscated to provide food for the military.

The surviving farmers would have been expected to concentrate on providing food for a greatly increased non-productive population, both the army and the new town-dwellers. Farms which had previously been worked to provide just enough for the family's annual needs, with some surplus as insurance against a bad year, started to expand. With the breakdown of the Iron Age warrior class there will have been a shift in the gender roles in agricultural work, and as increased yields led to greater prosperity, despite corn taxes and other dues, women may have become further removed from the day-to-day sowing and harvesting although on some farms women may have been needed more than ever to replace the young men who had been recruited into the Roman army or to provide for the increasingly non-agricutural section of society. In the more remote upland areas, however, where it was difficult to scratch a living from the soil, many subsistence farms must have continued to be run by owner-occupiers or tenant farmers with every member of the family expected to work from dawn to dusk from a very early age.

In the military zones, particularly the northern frontier, the small Iron Age type settlements were occupied into the third century at least, and there are indications that some of the population diversified into industrial production, supplying the military personnel with small items of metalwork, jewellery and other craft goods. Analysis of the finds from settlements around the northern frontier, compared to those from the forts, has shown that this was a one-way process. Few artefacts of 'Roman' manufacture were purchased by the native population, either because they were not to native taste or because they were too expensive. The native goods, however, found a ready market among the soldiers and *vici* inhabitants. How involved the women were in these industrial processes is unknown; possibly they continued to concentrate on the production of food and left it to the men to supplement the family's income, but most of the artefacts could have be made by a person working alone, and there is no reason to suppose that the women were not as skilled as the men, particularly if the numerous spinning and weaving accessories imply a cottage industry rather than the provision of home needs.

In the lowlands, villages in the more modern sense of the word began to be built, with rectangular houses of timber or timber-framed wattle-and-daub being later replaced by stone structures. Some of these buildings apparently housed people of some affluence: at Park Brow in Sussex the houses had glazed windows and lockable doors. In both town and country locks and keys became more common at this period: either house contents were now considered to be of some value or the population, which now included many travellers and incomers, were becoming more suspicious of their neighbours. The smaller villages tended to replace earlier Iron Age habitation but a number of the larger ones were on new sites. The village below Thundersbarrow hillfort, for example, may represent the enforced removal of members of the local Regni tribe from their fortified enclosure into an undefended, less troublesome village. Other villages grew up in mining areas or pottery production centres and, although most villages continued to have associated field systems, many of them had a mixed population of farmers and industrialists and were no longer totally reliant on agriculture.

Individual families prospered in the lowlands away from the military areas and as they grew financially more secure, so their houses developed from the purely functional to the more elaborate. These new farms were known as villas, an ambiguous term used by Roman writers to cover all rural buildings from small farmsteads to palatial establishments, with only the slightest connection with agriculture, owned by aristocrats and officials who used them as summer retreats from the pressures of town life.

The variety of villas built throughout the four centuries of Roman occupation makes it impossible to describe an 'average' villa. In an attempt to give some idea of villa life, therefore, an example of a basic agricultural villa, Sparsholt (Fig 21), might be compared with the more palatial site at Bignor (Fig 22). Excavations at Sparsholt, near Winchester, have indicated that the occupants in the early second century lived communally in a large aisled hall made of flint with stone bonding courses. The thatched roof was supported by wooden posts and the building was lit by a clerestorey in the nave. As the residents became more prosperous partitions were built to provide some privacy and two of the new rooms were embellished with mosaic floors. The influence of Roman standards of civilisation resulted in a bathroom being made, although initially this only had a portable bath and the hypocaust heating system appears to have doubled up as a corn dryer. It was some years before a brick-built bath suite was erected.

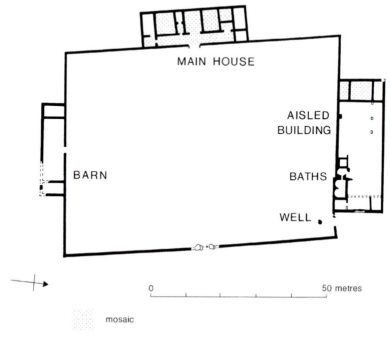

21. Plan of Sparsholt Villa showing the original aisled building to the right (after D. E. Johnston). The later house provided more comfort and privacy for its inhabitants. (© D A Welsby)

In the third century a second house was built at right angles to the first, which continued to be occupied. This building was a single-storey dwelling in the Continental manner, with a verandah running along the front and windows placed near the tiled roof. Inside, the house was divided into separate rooms with the central front door leading into the main reception room.

The plan of Sparsholt reflects the changes in agricultural life throughout the first two centuries of Roman rule. The lack of privacy in the original aisled building suggests a communal life with few noticeable differences between the life of the farmer's family and his workforce, or perhaps a family-run establishment relying solely on its members for labour. The development of separate rooms points to a new class distinction between the farm-workers and their employers, whilst the family's increased prosperity can be seen in the provision of wall-paintings, mosaics and a bath suite. The building of the main house may be an extension of this development, with the family living in separate quarters and the labourers living in the aisled building, or an expansion into two nuclear families, possibly different generations working together, or even a new owner or tenant with more Romanised ideas requiring a more modern house. Despite these concessions to modernity, Sparsholt seems to have remained a reasonably prosperous farm well into the post-Roman period but never rose to the ranks of the wealthy. The mistress of such a farm would have been fully occupied, as were the female occupants of small medieval manor houses, supervising the kitchen garden, managing the house, providing meals for the immediate family and the farm-hands, and rearing her children. The more her house expanded, the less involvement she would have had in the farm. Her daughters will have been expected to help in the house and on the farm from an early age, training for their later role as wives on similar farms in the neighbourhood. These women will rarely have visited towns, except on occasional market days, and will have lived restricted but busy lives.

The owners of Bignor, by contrast, may have led a leisured life of culture and travel. The villa was built on a south-facing slope commanding extensive views, and the lack of other villas in the area has led to the assumption that it eventually formed the centre of a large estate, possibly farming 2,000 acres (810 ha.) of arable land as well as pasturage on the Downs.

Little is known of the timber-framed house destroyed by fire in the early years of the third century, but the first stone house, built around AD 250, was a simple rectangular building, probably housing a similar family to the contemporary occupants of Sparsholt. The Bignor family, however, was more successful and as their financial situation improved so the house was enlarged (Fig 22). At first the extensions were modest: a portico along the east front and two projecting rooms (numbered 2 and 3) which turned the cottage into a middle-class winged corridor villa, complete with a private bath suite and piped water from two adjacent streams. The villa at this stage, although large, was not palatial and it may have been a change of ownership or a sudden increase in wealth which led to the installation of the impressive fourth-century mosaics,

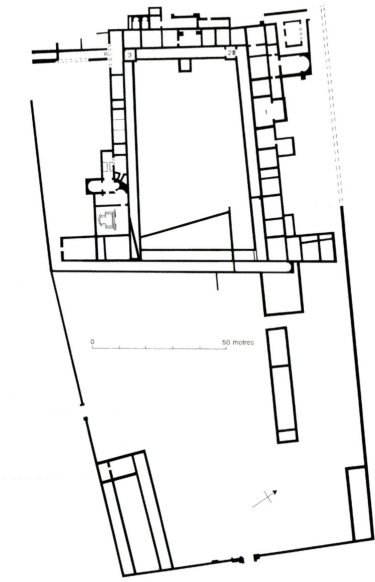

22. Plan of Bignor villa (after S S Frere). Bignor was one of the largest and most elaborate of the British villas but it still retained an agricultural role, the buildings in the outer courtyard being used as barns and byres. (© D A Welsby)

whose subjects point to the owner's high level of education, and the provision of such luxuries as a summer dining-room with a central hexagonal fountain (Room I).

The building was always of one storey although the slope of the ground led to a split-level plan with short flights of steps in some of the corridors. The number of small rooms as well as the quantity of reception suites indicates that a large number of people were housed here and, no doubt, an extensive staff was required to run the establishment. Both in the house and on the farm slave women will have been used for various tasks. Literary sources describing life in similar large villas in Italy indicate that these tasks would have been very specific and limited in their scope: a woman would have been responsible for doing the laundry, or looking after the hens, or peeling the vegetables, and she would have had a clearly defined place in the hierarchy of servants, both slave and freed.

The women of the owner's immediate family would have had little to do with the day-to-day running of Bignor other than issuing orders to the housekeeper or steward. In fact, the mistress of the house may rarely have been in residence, dividing her time between her town and country houses, and supporting her husband in the political and administrative duties of a provincial aristocrat.

In its final form Bignor was one of the largest villas known in Britain, covering 4.5 acres (1.8 ha). The size and the quality of the interior decoration point to a more substantial income than could be accounted for by agriculture alone, although it is clear from the buildings in the outer courtyard that agriculture was still important to the economy of the villa. The owners of Bignor are unknown, as are most of the villa dwellers of Britain, but there is a tentative suggestion that the fifth-century owner was Ambrosius Aurelianus, the antagonist of Vortigern in AD 437.[1] A woman known to have owned similar vast estates in Britain was the heiress Melania, although it is not known if she ever visited them or where they were located.

The lack of inscriptions from rural sites at any time in the Roman period has meant that few women living in the villages or villas are known by name, except by graffiti on pottery, for example: Matugena, Secunda, Bellicia and Vitia. An exception is Aurelia Concessa, 'a very pure girl', whose tombstone was discovered near Flixborough. The inscription records that she was buried 'on the estate'. Most villas had burial plots nearby but tombstones are rare: Sulicena buried at Wotton-under-Edge and Julia Ingenuilla at Nailsworth were also country dwellers, while Candiedinia Fortunata, Titia Pinta and Cosconia Mammiola appear to have been wealthy women dividing their time between York and their northern villas at Adel, Eastness and Sutton-under-Whitestone Cliff.

The Roman was an essentially urban being: political activities, social life and commerce all revolved around the town. Iron Age Britain, by comparison, was agricultural and the majority of people lived in small groups. A few larger settlements existed, which Latin authors referred to as *oppida*, but this term was not accurate, simply the nearest equivalent title for a phenomenon which was alien to Roman life: the *oppida* of Iron Age Britain were not towns in the sense of administrative centres. As her empire expanded Rome made the establishment of towns a priority, not only because towns were seen to be a vital factor in civilising primitive people, but also because they simplified the administration of a new province. By breaking up the tribal strongholds and evacuating the defendable hillforts potential centres of rebellion were dispersed and the people more easily taxed, educated and policed. The effect on the population, particularly the women, must have been extensive. The status of an individual woman was no longer dependent on her own, her husband's or her father's social standing in an agricultural community but was affected by the status of the town in which she lived, as well as the standing of her male relatives within that town.

To establish towns more was required than merely rehousing the population in larger groups. Urban living demanded a completely different lifestyle which had to be learnt by example. Model towns known as *coloniae* were established, populated by legionary veterans, the earliest of which was Camulodunum (modern Colchester), founded in AD 49. This town, according to Tacitus,[2] was provided with all the main official buildings of a Roman town: a forum, a theatre and a temple to the Deified Emperor. Other *coloniae* were placed strategically at Lincoln and Gloucester so that the maximum number of native Britons could witness the benefits of urban living.

The classical accounts of the Boudican revolt give some indication of how rapidly towns had been established in the first seventeen years of Roman rule. During this time the female urban population had grown as the womenfolk of veterans, merchants and traders as well as camp-followers moved in. It was against these women that much of the hostility of the Boudican troops was directed: those who were of Roman origin were seen as the enemy, while those of native origin were regarded as collaborators and traitors. Cassius Dio relates that: 'the worst and most bestial atrocity committed by their captors was the following. They hung up naked the noblest and most distinguished women and then cut off their breasts and sewed them to their mouths, in order to make the victims appear to be eating them; afterwards they impaled the women on sharp skewers run lengthwise through the entire body'.[3] Some of the milder atrocities perpetrated on these women bring to mind the humiliations meted out to female collaborators in post-Second World War France. It clearly took more than seventeen years for the intermarriage of Roman veterans and native women to be accepted.

The inhabitants of *coloniae* would have been regarded as the elite. The majority were full Roman citizens, although many of their wives would have been provincials, and a number of non-citizens, known as *incolae*, would also have been residents. One of the urban upper class, and the only Roman knight recorded by name from the province, was Macrinus or Macrinius. His tombstone was erected at Colchester by his widow Valeria Frontina and two men who may have been his freedmen. According to Anthony Birley, his name and that of his widow indicate that they were both descended from first-century veteran colonists.

As well as the 'new towns', existing settlements were promoted to the rank of *municipium* by grant. A *municipium*, and thus its inhabitants, could have either full Roman rights or Latin rights, and might retain some native by-laws in addition to the civil law of Rome. A town whose inhabitants were not Roman citizens would only qualify for Latin rights, although citizenship with all its privileges would be conferred on the town's magistrates and their families. *Municipia*, like *coloniae*, would have had *territoria*, that is land surrounding them over which the council would have jurisdiction and which the townspeople would farm. For some women therefore, the difference between living in a town or a village might be largely social, as their livelihoods might still be based on agriculture.

Each *colonia* and *municipium* was governed by a council called an *ordo*, which was nominally made up of a hundred councillors referred to as 'decurions'. Decurions were appointed from the men of the town who were over the age of thirty and satisfied the property qualifications. Peter Salway has pointed out that if one subtracts those not eligible to be decurions, such as women, slaves, children and freedmen, the numbers involved indicate that, although they were the elite, the decurions were by no means a tiny minority, and over the centuries a high proportion of free families would have been able to boast a decurion among their members, although few are known by name. An exception is Aurelius Senecio and his wife Volusia Faustina at Lincoln (Fig 23).

By the second century grants conferred citizenship on all the members of the *ordo* and their families, not just the magistracy, and by the third century the intermarriage of Roman and native must have meant that the majority of decurions would have been of mixed ancestry. The honour of serving on the *ordo* was shared by the whole family and a decurion at York is presumed from the fact that his widow, Aelia Severa, described herself as *honesta femina*, 'honourable lady', a title which women of the curial class adopted unofficially.

New decurions paid an entrance fee on joining the *ordo* and the expenses of holding a magistracy could be heavy. The *ordo* was responsible for collecting local and national taxes and Diocletian made the individual decurions personally responsible for the payment of these taxes to the Treasury; if any money was outstanding members of the *ordo* had to make up the deficit out of their own pockets. Few wives would have encouraged their husbands to enrol as decurions, fearing reduced housekeeping money if not bankruptcy. Their rise in the social scale of the town would have brought few benefits to compensate.

There was a third class of large town called *civitas* capitals, which were based on Iron Age tribal areas and were established to act as administrative centres for these areas. Of the twenty-three known tribal areas of Britain, sixteen became self-governing *civitates peregrinae* and their capitals included the old tribal names in the new titles, for example Venta Icenorum (Caistor-by-Norwich), Noviomagus Regnensium (Chichester) and Isaurium Brigantium (Aldborough). They were set up by the provincial administration as areas were freed from military control, and were established by mutual agreement between the government and the local leaders. As a result the same level of society which had led the tribes continued to dominate the new *civitates* so,

23. Tombstone of Volusia Faustina, a citizen of *Lindum* (Lincoln) and the wife of a decurion. (© British Museum)

except for a few troublesome elements, the arrangements would have had little immediate effect on most people's social status. There is every possibility that the traditional native by-laws relating to female matters – marriage, inheritance and the control of children – may have continued to regulate life in the *civitas* capitals, while the stricter Roman legal code was followed in the *coloniae* and *municipia*, where the inhabitants led a more Romanised lifestyle.

The only *civitas* decurion known by name is Flavius Martius, a councillor of quaestorian rank in the *civitas* of the Carvetii, who was buried by his daughter Martiola at Old Penrith. A woman also thought to have been of the same class was Flavia Victorina, wife of Titus Tammonius Victor, who lived and died at Silchester.

The houses of the urban upper classes resembled rural villas in many ways. The more elaborate ground plans of both took some time to be adopted and the earliest town houses tended to be simple rectangular structures with timber frames and wattle-and-daub walls, often with the area nearest the street front given over to trade. In the mid-second century the corridor house, with a single range of rooms flanked by one or two passages, developed into an L-shaped building, or into a three-range plan by the addition of two wings, and then into the courtyard house. Urban architecture, however, does not appear to have been a series of chronological developments from strip house to courtyard house, and most towns by the mid-second century will have had a mixture of all the house types. It has been suggested by Walthew that the courtyard house was particularly favoured by veterans' families and that the peristyle in several British courtyard houses had derived from military architecture; recent surveys, however, have shown that the fully developed peristyle house in the Mediterranean manner did not dominate domestic architecture in Britain. A typical house at Caerwent, a town populated by a large number of veterans of the IInd Augusta, formed a square block looking inwards to the central courtyard or garden, rather than out to the street. The peristyle was supported by columns, and rainwater from the roof was collected in a drain around the edge of the courtyard and piped away to flush the latrine. Drinking water was piped by wooden and lead pipes through the main entrance: the better houses in towns were attached to the main water supply on payment of a fee. Private latrines were commonplace for town houses as well as villas, with seats of wood or stone. Latrines were usually incorporated into the house but the Gorhambury excavations have revealed a two-seater establishment at the bottom of the garden. Urban latrines could be plumbed into the main sewer system or, as at Silchester and many rural sites, rely on cesspits.

We have no evidence to indicate whether the sexes shared rooms in either town houses or villas, or whether the women had separate quarters. It is difficult to identify the purpose of individual rooms in any house other than bath suites and occasionally kitchens, both of which were used by women. Bedrooms, nurseries and living rooms, other than the main reception rooms, are particularly difficult to identify. The allocation of space within the house

24. A town house as excavated at Verulamium (© Allason-Jones)

may well have depended on the ethnic origins of the occupiers as well as their financial status. It is probable, following the evidence from Italy, that slave women were expected to share their accommodation either with each other or, in the case of nannies and maids, with their charges or their mistresses.

Many of the houses of the curial class were large (Fig 24). A number at Colchester and Leicester had cellars below for storage and some may also have had upper storeys to accommodate servants. So far, however, there is no evidence for the apartment blocks which were such a feature of Italian cities. The main alternative to a householder in search of more space was to move outside the town walls. A decurion, whilst serving on the *ordo*, was legally required to reside in a house of a specified minimum size within the town, although this could be interpreted as including the *territorium*. Some decurions would run two homes, a town house and a villa on his country estate, and his family would either commute between the two with him or make one of the houses their main base.

Roman towns were laid out in a grid pattern of streets with the official public buildings dominating the centre. The domestic buildings were democratically arranged: there appear to have been few neighbourhoods regarded as better class or as slum districts; the large curial houses shared blocks with small shops and simple strip houses, and the dwellings of craftsmen and merchants jostled together. Some of these people were Roman citizens: a man called Carinus is proudly referred to on his tombstone at Dorchester (Dorset) as *civi Romano* by his grieving widow Romana, his son Rufinus and his two daughters, Carina and Avita, who would also have been citizens; but a large proportion of the urban population would have been non-citizens, including freedmen and slaves set up in business by their masters.

According to Caesar 'nobody except traders' travelled to pre-Roman Britain 'without good cause; and even traders know nothing except the sea-coast and the districts opposite Gaul'.[4] The effect of the Claudian invasion was to open Britain up as a new market and merchants flocked to the province to take advantage of the opportunities. Some of these men married local girls, while others brought their wives and daughters with them. Flavia Ingenua was the Greek wife of a Greek trader, Flavius Helius, who died at Lincoln, while Emilia Theodora, a Greek who had married an Italian from Noventum, lived with her son Valerius Theodorianus at York until his death at the age of thirty-five. Rusonia Aventina, a tribeswoman of the Mediomatrici from Gallia Belgica, may have been a member of the merchant class resident in Bath or simply on an unsuccessful visit to the healing shrine of Sulis Minerva, while the tombstone of Carssouna's husband may record another Gallic merchant family living in Lincoln. The cosmopolitan nature of most Romano-British towns is attested by inscriptions, as at Silchester where several were set up by the 'guild of immigrants resident at Calleva'.[5]

Few of the merchants have left references as to the nature of their trade, merely describing themselves as *negotiatores* or *mercatores*. We have, therefore, no idea as to what M Verecundius Diogenes, a tribesman of the Bituriges in central Gaul, and his Sardinian wife Julia Fortunata were shipping between Gaul or the Upper Rhineland and York. The majority of these merchants trading across the English Channel and the Irish Sea were freedmen, and as the doubtful privilege of being elected decurion was denied to them many will have become wealthy men: at York, for example, L Viducius Placidus of the Veliocasses (Rouen) paid for an arch and a temple to be built in the city.[6]

A healthy merchant trade, confirmed by the number of harbours, the amount of imported goods available and the discovery of a number of shipwrecks such as the ship found off the Pudding Pan Rock full of samian, would only be possible if there were sailors to man the vessels. None of these men or their families have left any record, but the ports of Britain, both on the coast and on inland waterways, must have been teeming with the wives and children of the merchant fleet as well as those of fishermen, boat-builders, ship's chandlers and sailmakers. Warehouses at Sea Mills, London, York and Bawdrip extend the trading population to include stevedores, warehousemen and carriers.

A town's population of craftworkers included people who worked in metal, glass, wood, stone, tile, leather, ceramics and reeds. A number of these men are known because they signed their work but less is known of their womenfolk. Domitia Saturnina may have been the wife of a mason, as her tombstone, which leaves a space for her husband, has an adze, punch, pick and plummet in relief down one edge; but the wives and daughters of Lucius Aebutius Thales the shoemaker,[7] Bonosius the blacksmith,[8] Vertissa the cooper,[9] or Cabriabanus the tiler[10] remain anonymous. Although David Peacock has put forward a theory, based on anthropological parallels, that women were employed in the production of black-burnished ware, the only fragment of evidence which seemed to name a female potter, a piece of mortarium from Brockley Hill, apparently bearing the name Catia Maria, was dismissed by Kay Hartley as graffiti rather than a potter's stamp; a recent re-analysis has now shown it to be a copy of a stamp of a male potter, C Attius Marinus. Analysis of pottery stamps has, however, revealed dynasties of potters who occasionally moved their factories to new production areas, uprooting their families and workforce in the process.

Evidence from Pompeii reveals women working as weavers, waitresses, money lenders, tavern owners, bakers and laundresses, while at Ostia female poultry sellers, vegetable sellers, shoemakers, doctors, nurses and barmaids are attested. Abudia Megiste is known to have sold grain and pulses at the Middle Stairs in Rome, Atinia Tyrannis sold seeds at the Porta Triumphalis in Praeneste, and Aurelia Nais was a wholesale fish seller at the warehouses of Galba. Sellers of purple dyes,[11] ointments,[12] beans,[13] bottles[14] and resins[15] are also recorded from Italy, and inscriptions and sculpture provide a similar picture of female endeavour in those other provinces where such records survive.

A bronze stamp found at Carrington with the name of Tullia Tacita in retrograde, was thought by Curle to have been used 'for stamping stoppers of wine jars, loaves of bread and suchlike objects', and may indicate a woman working in one of these trades, but the otherwise complete silence about the female workforce is likely to give a completely erroneous impression of town life in Roman Britain. The number of craftsmen who have left their names is very small compared to the thousands who must have existed, so the lack of inscriptions for female workers may not be so surprising. At the lower end of the social scale funerary inscriptions, if they existed at all, may have been more commonly of wood than stone, and it is also conceivable that the names recorded on artefacts are those of the factory owners rather than the individual workers, male or female. The only two career women in Britain who are known by name are Verecunda, the actress, and Diodora, the priestess, but between these two extremes there must have been multitudes of midwives, wet-nurses, bath attendants, agricultural workers and craftswomen.[16] A beaker from Water Newton depicts a female acrobat and, while there is much doubt about the identification of a cremation in London as having been that of a female gladiator, it takes no stretch of the imagination to accept that the woman found murdered in the tavern at Housesteads was a barmaid.[17]

Apprentice documents from Roman Egypt and Italy suggest that children, including girls, could be handed over to a master craftsman for a specified period of time in order to learn a trade.[18] Most of these children were twelve or thirteen at the time of their indentures but it is noticeable that their parents were all of freed or slave status: freeborn girls, even from the poorest families, do not appear to have trained for a career in a formal way. None of the provinces of the Roman Empire have produced conclusive evidence for freeborn women working, except within the family circle.

One profession which must have been practised in Britain was prostitution. Much was written about prostitutes in the ancient world but nothing about those in Britain. Nor can any building be confidently identified as a brothel, although the finds from a timber building at Holditch may suggest such a use, whilst the suitability of its architecture and its prime location next to the baths may make another building at Wroxeter a possible candidate. Brothels were often sited next to public bath-houses[19] and as a result were not normally allowed to open before 3 pm, so that the female clients of the baths should not be troubled on their way to their morning ablutions. Prostitutes in Italy were often of Syrian or Egyptian origin, and were identifiable by their heavy make-up, the lack of bands in their hair, and their short tunics and brightly coloured togas.[20] Some were independent operators who rented rooms in inns (most inns had a dual purpose) or a brothel, while others were employed by pimps and madams. Hadrian tried to stop the large brothels from trading by banning the sale of a male or female slave to either a pimp or a gladiatorial trainer without cause being given, but it is unlikely that he was successful.[21] Streetwalkers also plied their trade in most towns. No matter at what level they operated, all prostitutes had to be registered with the authorities and, from the reign of Caligula, had to pay a tax equal to the sum which they might expect to earn from a single client on any one day.[22] This tax continued to be payable even after retirement, and pimps and madams were also liable. Prostitution was, therefore, a financial fact of life in the Roman Empire and prostitutes likely to be found in every town or *vicus*.

Even if the women of Britain have not left any evidence for their involvement in trade or industry they would have had difficulty avoiding it, as many of the working class lived 'above the shop', or, more accurately, behind it. At Silchester the shops were rectangular buildings with their narrow frontage to the street. At least a half or two-thirds of their floor space was used for selling or manufacture, with living accommodation at the rear. Several had open fronts which could be closed by shutters or blinds after hours. More spacious shops have been excavated at Verulamium and Wroxeter. All the shops would be limited as to stock, as each would sell only a specific type of commodity, often made on the premises; department stores were not known, although the small rented premises in the forum and the markets might have resulted in facilities similar to those of shopping centres. Some were owner-occupied, whilst others were erected as investments by local businessmen and rented out or run by slaves.

Evidence from Rome leads to the supposition that middle-class and upper-class women did not do their own shopping but relied on their husbands or servants to do the marketing. In Gaul and Germany, however, reliefs indicate that provincial women regarded shopping as part of their daily duties or entertainment.

Some of the smaller towns were established to provide housing for workers in specific industries. Mancetter, Chesterton and Water Newton, for example, were pottery towns, as was Congresbury, whilst others, such as Braughing, were metalworking centres. Mining towns were built in lead, tin and iron areas, and life in such towns might be compared with life in the nineteenth-century mining or factory towns of America or Europe, where the women were relegated to either non-skilled work such as packing or sorting, or domestic or entertainment roles. In the country districts, market towns such as Godmanchester and Bourton-on-the-Water provided a focus for the surrounding countryside, holding weekly markets and seasonal fairs. Again we can look to more recent parallels to create a picture of unsophisticated small-town life. Other towns seem to have grown up around posting stations, at major river crossings and road junctions, or around temple complexes, providing services for travellers.

The impression given by most descriptions of town life in the Roman Empire is of spacious, well-organised streets, water on tap, an efficient sewerage system and well-stocked shops; but this may not be the whole picture or even an accurate one. Little is known, for example, of what effect the uprooting of agricultural communities and their resettlement in towns had on a native population. Modern parallels might suggest that such an upheaval might have had profound social consequences, particularly on the women. If one was used to living in small family groups where one knew everyone, where life was geared to seasonal changes, where buildings were circular and where the community grew, made, hunted and cooked all that the family needed, it must have been a shock to the system to find oneself in a town full of people from all parts of the Empire, with different colours of skin, different traditions and different languages, where there were enormous public buildings built of dressed stone with lavish interior and exterior decoration but where the houses were often smaller than the native huts, and where one could not grow food or hunt but was expected to shop for one's daily needs using coins, and could even buy bread ready baked. Towns would have been crowded, noisy, smoky and smelly: a number of trades such as fulling, tanning, and dyeing were particularly unpleasant, although butchers' shops and markets may not have been much better. The streets would have been full of people and carts, and traffic accidents must have been everyday occurrences – the council at Aldborough finally built a by-pass! Women who had married away from their families, such as Regina (see Fig 6), a St Albans woman married to a Syrian, Verecunda Rufilia, a woman of the Dubonni who died at Templebrough, and Ved.. ic.. (see Fig 4), who also died a hundred miles from home, and foreign immigrants like Rusonia Aventina from Metz in France and the Greek Flavia Ingenua, must often have felt displaced and confused: psychological illness and suicides may well have been the result.

It is also possible that the high standard of engineering has been overrated. The great civic bath-houses, unless kept scrupulously clean, would have been hotbeds of disease. Some were provided with a constant supply of running water from aqueducts but most were not and relied on regular draining and refilling in order to function. Aqueducts also supplied water to the larger houses and public fountains, but most housewives would have had to carry water from the public water tanks or draw it from a well for all the family's daily requirements. Even a housewife with the luxury of mains water would not have been able to rely on a regular supply: at Wroxeter the aqueduct provided two million gallons daily, but the system was organised so that in times of drought the supply was automatically cut off from the private subscribers.

We have seen that the houses of the curial class had their own flushing latrines, but the majority of homes did not, relying either on pots, often literally broken *amphorae*, or on public lavatories. These were often private enterprises: at Verulamium a shop ran a public lavatory as a sideline, complete with attendant and flushing system, seating ten people at a time. Most of these public facilities made separate provision for the sexes but were not divided into private cubicles: their use was a social activity. A basin was provided for washing the hands. The literary references to the use of sponges instead of paper has been confirmed recently by the discovery of spicules of marine sponges in the York sewers. Regrettably, these sponges were for general use rather than individual possessions, and one can only hope that the non-recyclable moss found in sewage deposits at Bearsden was commonly preferred.

Sewerage systems have been uncovered in many Romano-British towns, and possibly the best were provided at Lincoln. However, the rough sides of the main drains at York would have been difficult to flush clean and in the summer the amount of water available may well have been inadequate. The sewers, like the aqueducts, were often open or built very close to the surface, leading to unpleasant smells and the spread of disease, while their contents invariably emptied into the nearest river or stream on which another community might rely for its water supply. Dysentery, diarrhoea and internal parasites were rife, as were the other diseases of overcrowding and pollution: London, for example, may have been decimated by plague in the second century. Without our modern knowledge about the transmission of disease, mothers would have been unable to protect their children from the dangers which a truly efficient water and sewerage system might have controlled, but even without this knowledge many women may have been aware that country living was healthier, even if it lacked the sophistication and convenience of town life. Faced with the mental and physical stresses and strains of urban life, the women who looked back longingly on their country roots may not have been in the minority.

Chapter 4

At home

Most women's lives would have centred around their homes, and keeping these buildings clean must have kept the houseproud fully occupied. At Cirencester the occupants of houses at the west corner of lnsula XXIII must sometimes have despaired of ever having clean floors. The houses had been built with porticoes on the roadside, but the surface of the road was continually ground to dust by the passing traffic and every time it rained this dust was washed down the camber into the porticoes. This led to a continual renewal of the portico floors and, no doubt, a constant trail of muddy feet into the house. This is unlikely to have been an isolated incident. The rural housewife would have found it easier to protect her home from traffic pollution but the predominantly agricultural way of life would have brought its own cleaning problems.

Some householders considered the difficulties of cleaning at the design stage. At Colliton Park, Building I had been built so that the floors of four of the rooms were progressively lowered with communicating drains so that when washing the floors one would have started at the top and worked down. The kitchen floor at Frocester Court also has a drain in one corner to enable it to be swilled down, as have several mosaic floors in other villas.

Few domestic appliances, such as brooms or scrubbing brushes, survive, nor can dusters be easily identified from scraps of textile. Furniture and wooden doors would have needed dusting and polishing with cedar oil, juniper oil or beeswax, and oil would also have been needed for shale furniture. The illustration of the Colliton Park table leg (Fig 25) shows the splitting which occurs when Kimmeridge shale dries out; the careful housewife would have had to keep her shale furniture well oiled to keep it intact and retain its black sheen, and it would have been advisable to keep shale tables away from underfloor heating systems.

In the more elegant houses silver and pewter would have had to be cleaned with solutions of acid and polished with chalk applied on leather cloths, or simply by regular rubbing with bare hands. The high relief on some plates must have made cleaning a laborious and complex operation; if one could afford silver tableware, however, one would also have had slaves to keep it clean. As in the Victorian era, when even quite modest establishments had a maid-of-all-work, there would have been few Romano-British households without slaves to do the housework and cooking, look after the children or mend the clothes. The female head of the house would have had her work cut out supervising her staff, unless the establishment was large enough to have a steward to keep everything

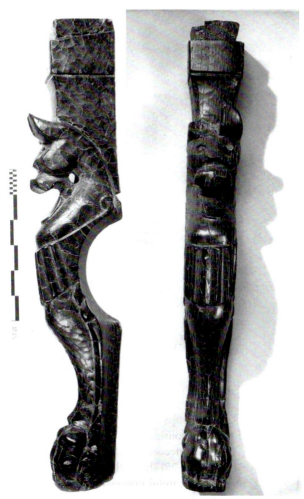

25. Shale table leg from Colliton Park, showing the splitting which occurred if a housewife failed to keep her shale furniture well oiled (© The Dorset Natural History and Archaeological Society at the Dorset County Museum)

running smoothly. The larger the household the more specific the task which each slave had to do, but in the smaller houses the women of the family would have had to do their share with one or two slaves for the heavy work.

One aspect of housework which we know little about is laundering clothes and household textiles. It is to be presumed that clothes were washed in rivers or lakes where possible, or alternatively in large bowls or buckets in the backyard or kitchen. Again some houses will have had a slave whose sole task it was to do the washing but in most homes washing would have had to be fitted in with the other chores. Fullers, who dressed newly woven cloth, also washed clothes professionally and some town-dwellers would have been able to send their laundry out. Justinian's *Digest* refers to several cases where clothes left for washing with fullers were lost, stolen, damaged or returned to the wrong customer: all situations familiar to modern dry-cleaning establishments.[1] Washing would have been draped over bushes and from trees to dry and then the creases rubbed out by friction with a stone or a glass smoother. Several linen smoothers are known from such sites as South Shields and the method was still in use in Scotland and Ireland at the beginning of the twentieth century. There is no evidence for ironing fabric by applying heat.

Windows were either glazed, shuttered or barred. The methods of producing glass resulted in panes of varying thickness which were translucent rather than transparent. Moulded glass will have been opaque if the mould was sanded or had a rough surface: one would not be able to look through these glazed windows (nor tell if they were clean!) and the light entering a room would be diffused. Most of the window glass found is the pale green of 'uncoloured' glass, although excavations at Gorhambury have revealed fragments of blue window glass, implying that one family at least had an elegant 'designer' bath suite.

Sliding shutters and folding shutters were used on glazed as well as unglazed windows, and elaborate window grilles of iron have survived complete at Duston, Hinton St Mary and Wall, with fragments from many other sites. The grilles were intended to deter intruders and keep out birds and animals.

Artificial lighting would be needed in most rooms and was provided by oil lamps (Fig 26), candles or torches. The lamps were made of bronze, pottery or iron and consisted of a circular well for the fuel, one or more spouts to take wicks, and a handle. They could be suspended from a wall or beam, and the more common lamps would have burnt oil, presumably olive oil, which was poured in through a small hole. The lamps, on the whole, were very small and would have had a limited efficiency in terms of light given out and the man-hours involved in their servicing. They would have required continual attention, such as refilling and wick trimming: a tablespoon of oil would only burn for about two hours and if the flame was too high it would give off oily smuts.

The evidence from London suggests that pottery lamps were not used much after AD 170 – 200, and it has been suggested that a disruption in the supply of fuel oil from Spain may have been responsible. An alternative was the candle, either used on its own or in groups in candelabra of pottery, bronze or iron. Pottery examples were either tubular with a wide flat base, or shallow saucers with a central ring to hold the candle, surrounded by a drip tray, as found at Verulamium. The evidence for candlesticks is by no means as great as for oil lamps, but wooden holders may also have been used, or candles may have been stuck on to table tops or potsherds with molten wax. The evidence for torches is even slimmer, as they only appear in artistic depictions.

A circular hut had no windows to let in light or air, so controlling the temperature was a matter of keeping the door shut and stoking the open fire. Keeping a villa or town house warm was a more complex matter. Tiled open hearths were placed in the centre of some rooms, following the native pattern; other rooms had fireplaces set into a wall. At Bignor the fireplaces were made of

26. Oil lamps gave a variable amount of light depending on the number of wicks they held. These examples from Great Chesters and South Shields are of copper alloy and pottery. (© Museum of Antiquities of the University and Society of Antiquaries of Newcastle upon Tyne)

three large tiles set on tiled hearths. Fire-dogs were of iron, and wood was the principal fuel, but coal may have been more commonly used than can be proved from the current evidence. The coalfields of the Forest of Dean, Redesdale and Somerset were worked in the Roman period and there is evidence that they supplied local villas and military establishments. Fire shovels and pokers have been discovered but only in industrial or religious contexts. Braziers were widely used, burning wood or charcoal. These are thought to have been made of iron although none have survived, and their existence is only surmised from scorch marks on the floors of villas and town houses.

The principal rooms in villas and the better town houses were heated by the underfloor system known as a hypocaust. By this method the floor was raised on low pillars of tile or stone, or on dwarf walls, and hot air passed through from an outside stoke-hole heating the room above. Hollow tiles set in the walls carried the fumes to air vents and heated the walls at the same time. This system was efficient but could be expensive in fuel and man-hours as a slave had to be on duty full-time to keep the fire suitably adjusted. Like modern solid fuel heating, it was more economical if it was kept going continually so that the room did not have time to cool down, but some householders may have relied on braziers, lighting the hypocaust only when visitors were expected, as most houses only had the system installed in the dining-room.

It was in the dining-room that the most elegant interior decorations in the form of mosaics and wall-paintings were to be found. The status-conscious woman would have wanted the latest fashions in her home to show off to her friends. Mosaics were first introduced into Britain around AD 75–80, and although it might be thought that only the most lavish establishments had mosaic floors, even timber-framed wattle-and-daub dwellings at Colchester and Verulamium and basic aisled farmhouses were provided with them.

Mosaic, made from small cubes of tile or coloured stone, makes a very hardwearing floor covering which is also decorative, and has the added advantages of adapting itself to uneven surfaces and of being resistant to the damp which will rot wooden floors. In the first century AD mosaics were more often found in urban dwellings than in villas, although early examples were installed at Eccles, Angmering and Rivenhall. In the second century mosaics became widespread, particularly those with geometric motifs, and British mosaicists set up in business: David Neal has suggested that a customer would pick a design from a pattern book and the mosaicist would adapt the general pattern to fit a particular room. Although the work of David Smith has demonstrated that different schools of mosaicists were working in Britain, and that designs changed throughout the centuries, few buildings show any indications that their floors were often replaced. Many women will have spent their lives with the mosaics laid down by their predecessors and would rarely have had the opportunity to choose a new pattern. When there was a choice this was almost bewildering, with black-and-white or red-and-white geometric motifs as well as multi-coloured patterns and figural scenes. Some of the geometric floors were very effective: a mosaic from a courtyard house at Silchester, dated to AD 140–60, has an all-over maeander design which incorporates scattered squares, each containing a different motif. Some floors had very 'busy' designs, such as the Blackfriars mosaic at Leicester, in which nine octagonal panels separated by plaited borders contain multi-coloured complex patterns, the whole contained in a stylised foliage frame. Designs centred on figured panels were popular but more expensive: Dionysus was a favourite subject but Cupid, Venus (Fig 27) and Orpheus were also popular, as were scenes of hunting, gladiatorial combat, marine life and mythological incidents. In the fourth century, Christian symbols and busts of Christ began to appear, as for example at Hinton St Mary.

It is always possible that if one did not like the mosaic one had inherited, and could not afford to replace it, one could cover it with rugs or mats. No textile floor coverings survive but some mosaics appear to follow textile designs, and rugs and carpets may have been widely used. Rushes, either scattered loosely or woven into mats, were also a possibility – fragments of matting have been found at Newstead and Vindolanda.

Mosaic was not the only available flooring. Wooden floors have been found in houses at Carmarthen, Colchester and Leicester, and Piddington villa had yellow and red tiles laid in a herringbone pattern. Floors could be laid in the *opus sectile* technique where stones were cut into geometric shapes. A more prosaic flooring was *opus signinum*, where broken tiles were mixed with mortar to produce a tough waterproof surface – particularly useful in a bath-house – while the most basic houses would have had no applied flooring, just beaten earth.

27. Diana, goddess of hunting and the amphitheatre, portrayed on a mosaic at Bignor villa (Reproduced with kind permission of the Tupper family, Bignor Roman Villa, West Sussex)

Marble and other stones were imported for floors and wall veneers and enough fragments survive to indicate that there was a thriving trade providing exotic stones as well as the cheaper native materials. Frances Pritchard's work on Roman London produced an impressive catalogue of imported marbles of various colours used for wall veneers, but if these were beyond one's purse, 'Forest' marble from Alwalton, Purbeck marble, Rutland and Oxfordshire oolites, and Collyweston slate could be used effectively. A few householders adopted the Italian method of stuccoing the walls, as at Gorhambury, where the designs include female figures, but the technique does not seem to have been widely accepted.

Almost every civilian building of any size had the walls plastered and painted inside and out. Even quite simple wattle-and-daub or wooden houses of first-century date at Colchester, London and Verulamium had plaster, which was either monochrome or painted with motifs. The most common design of wall-painting divided the wall into three horizontal bands. It was in the deeper middle zone that the principal decoration occurred, taking the form of two-dimensional panels from the first to the fourth century, with architectural schemes giving an illusion of depth appearing in the mid-second century. Large-scale scenes involving figures typify the interior design of the third and fourth centuries.

The most popular colour scheme for flat panels was deep red with black areas forming frames, but yellow and green colour schemes were also used. Architectural illusion panels attempted to enlarge or make more impressive the basic shape of a room by providing mock niches, apses, windows, and projecting columns. Most of these schemes are realistic but the grasp of the rules of perspective was sometimes shaky, as at Caerwent, where a 'niche' fails to suggest more than a pattern of geometric shapes. A motif which appears to be confined to Britain is imitation mosaic: at Sparsholt the double band of *guilloches* on the floor is repeated in paint on the wall above, blurring the edges between floor and wall and making the room seem larger. Landscape painting is rarely found in Britain, although an example, so far unique in the province and dated to about AD 75, adorned a wall at Fishbourne.

The majority of the figured scenes are mythological with later depictions of Christian significance. A female bust on the walls of the baths of Sparsholt (see frontispiece) may be a mythological or religious figure or a member of the family. Still-life scenes also appear in British houses: at Verulamium one building had a painting of a lyre with a quiver and a bow against a red ground, whilst at Fishbourne a fragment shows a red plate holding yellow fruit. Bowls of fruit also appear at Brading and Dover. Animals and birds, either individually or in inhabited foliate scrolls, abound, while fish were a favourite subject in bath suites. Floral designs usually appear in a stylised form and lettering was used where it was felt necessary to label or embellish the scene.

Painted wall-plaster appears all over the province from Hadrian's Wall to Cornwall, although the greatest concentration is in the 'villa belt'. It is found on urban sites in houses, shops and public buildings, as well as in rural villas and temples. It was clearly a status symbol which reflected the civilised Roman outlook of the household and as such was often confined to the one room in which guests were entertained. The number of painted rooms might indicate the financial standing of the family – even in the fourth century the villa at Iwerne Minster had only one painted room, whilst the main house at Winterton had eleven of its sixteen rooms painted. Even in the homes of those in the upper income bracket the quality of the painting was graded, so that the more elaborate treatments were in the dining-rooms and the bath suites as well as the corridors leading to them, while the less public rooms were less impressively decorated. Again, few walls show more than one layer of paint and most homes will have looked the same for generations.

Although few ceilings survive, enough fragments have been found to indicate that some were highly decorated. Some treatments could be restrained, for example a white ground with coloured rosettes was found at Fishbourne, whilst others were more overpowering. Many are painted in octagonal or square shapes to give the impression of a coffered ceiling, an architectural technique popular in Italy. Others have stylised garlands breaking up the expanse into smaller compartments. In bath-houses a random scattering of fish and marine plants on a blue-green ground continued the theme of the walls and floor to give the bather the impression of being in the sea or in an aquarium.

On the whole the ceilings and floors were lightly coloured to balance the rich colouring of the walls, but even then the general effect must have been overwhelming, not to say crowded, to modern taste. The use of deep plush reds and many clashing patterns resembles the late Victorian era of interior design, particularly as the furniture, although sparse, was also highly decorated.

Most of our information about Romano-British furniture comes from tombstone reliefs. Those depicting funerary banquets have as their centrepiece the figure of the deceased reclining on a couch with food laid out on a small table in front. The couches were made in a variety of materials, either with backs, like the couch on which Curatia Dinysia rests, or without, as preferred by Julia Velva (see Fig 5). The finest depiction of a Romano-British couch is on the lavish tombstone of Victor, a soldier's freedman who died at South Shields,[2] but the final resting places of Aelia Aeliana (Fig 28) and Candida Barita also show a high degree of decoration.

There is no evidence that the bulk of Romano-British furniture was upholstered although it may well have been. Loose covers in textile or leather

28. Tombstone of Aelia Aeliana at York. She is seen reclining with her husband on a wide couch with a funerary meal laid out on a small three-legged table in front of them. (© York Museums Trust (The Yorkshire Museum))

are also a possibility, with cushions and mattresses providing the padding. Although one relief from Chester shows a child asleep on a couch,[3] it is unlikely that the couches were comfortable enough, or long enough, to be used as beds and most people will have slept on a mattress laid on a chest or platform or even the floor. A pipeclay model from Bordeaux, however, shows a couple snugly tucked up in a double bed with a high back and sides, supported on 'lathe-turned' legs and covered by a sheet or rug. A fountain head from Bath appears to be in the form of a bed rather than a day-couch, as the high headboard has additional upholstery but not the low footboard. The reclining figure in this instance has been identified as a water god.[4]

Although both men and women are shown lying on funerary couches in Romano-British sculpture, it is rare for a man to be depicted sitting on a chair, and many chairs appear to have been solely for the use of women. One type, preferred by a mother goddess from Bewcastle, is a smaller version of a couch with undulating arms and high back. The more common chair, as seen on sculpture and in models, however, is the basket chair, which had its origins in Iron Age Britain. Pipeclay models of mother goddesses show them seated in such chairs, possibly reflecting their popularity with nursing mothers (Fig 55). Unlike the Lloyd Loom chairs which they resemble, these chairs usually have semi-circular bases rather than feet, although the elaborately woven chair used by the lady from Neumagen does have feet (Fig 29).

Footstools were used in conjunction with chairs. The deity from Bewcastle rests her feet on a low box, as does one of the harassed mother goddesses from Cirencester. A similar box stool, probably of wood, can be seen on Candida Barita's tombstone with a small boy standing on it. Proper footstools with legs do not appear on British sculpture nor do they survive in the archaeological record, although an iron leg from Mansfield Woodhouse has been tentatively identified as part of a low stool.[5]

Roman Britain has produced two folding stools, from Bartlow Hills and Holborough, and fittings at several other sites. Both of the complete examples have a split front bar and leather strip seats, recalling the recommendations of Soranus for a midwife's stool (see Fig 9). Traces of a chaff-filled leather cushion decorated with bronze ribbons found with the Holborough stool suggest that these stools were not as uncomfortable as they first appear.

Sculptural evidence from the Continent suggests that large, solidly made wooden tables with a rectangular top and four legs were common articles of furniture, particularly in the kitchen. In Britain they do not appear on tomb-stones nor have any fragments been recognised, although the stone uprights in the kitchen at Spoonley Wood may have had a wooden worktop. Tripods of metal or wood were used to support bowls or braziers or a flat tray forming an occasional table for use in the dining-room or bedroom. Fragments of small circular tables, similar to those seen in funerary banquet scenes, have been found in wood and marble but the majority were of shale from the Kimmeridge area in Dorset. The legs of the more elaborate are carved with a griffin's or lion's

29. Relief of a lady from Neumagen, Germany, having her hair dressed by her attendants
(© Rheinisches Landesmuseum, Trier)

head at the top and a clawed foot or hoof at the base. The complete leg from Colliton Park, Dorchester, is typical of the type (see Fig 25).

An item of furniture also peculiar to the villas in the south-west is the stone 'sideboard' or serving table. These solid rectangular slabs of stone, usually limestone, have elaborately carved geometric patterns along one or more edges which probably reflected the carving or inlay on wooden furniture. They butted against a wall or fitted into a niche as permanent additions to a room and were supported by one or two legs or brackets.

The Simpelveld sarcophagus (Fig 30) from Holland depicts more everyday furniture including a couch, a chair and two types of table, as well as shelves and cupboards, for which we have little evidence in Britain. Cupboards and wooden chests for the storage of clothes, blankets and kitchen equipment were probably to be found in every home, and cupboards under the stairs, as at Chalk, and other built-in cupboards are also likely to have been common.

We have already seen that mattresses and cushions were used and were probably of textile or leather, stuffed with wool, flax, feathers or straw. The evidence from Victor's tombstone and the Holborough barrow indicates that cushions were decorated with tassels, embroidery and appliqué, while leather

30 The inside of a sarcophagus from Simpelveld, Holland furnished with cupboards, tables and other comforts which the deceased might need in the afterlife. (© National Museum of Antiquities, Leiden)

from Billingsgate Buildings in London shows traces of an embossed lattice motif. Fragments of a purple wool cushion decorated with gold ribbon, found at Colchester, indicate that these household accessories could be very elegant and expensive. A number of reliefs from other parts of the Empire show customers buying rugs, curtains and other hangings and there are references to rugs in the writing tablets from Vindolanda and Carlisle, although it is unclear if the textiles are floor coverings or soft furnishings. The majority of rugs and bedclothes would have been locally made: the British *tapete* was considered to be of very high quality, although Lucretius seems to have preferred 'Babylonian coverlets of rich beauty'.[6] Textile hangings as decoration are seen on wall-paintings from Italy, as well as curtains hung in doorways; window curtains, however, rarely appear although it is possible that the curtains of scarlet, green and purple listed in one of the Vindolanda writing tablets were intended to be used as window curtains. Linen table clothes were used after the time of Diocletian and there are several literary references to the correct use of table napkins.[7] Napkins, towels and linen are all mentioned in writing tablets from Carlisle and London.

Although there were some male cooks, the feeding of the population was the responsibility of the women, and most will have spent a high proportion of their working day in their own or their employer's kitchen. This is an essential part of any house but one which is surprisingly difficult to identify through archaeological excavation. In the native huts stone hearths are usually found in the centre, suggesting that the fire was used for general heating as well as

31 Reconstruction of a Roman kitchen. The charcoal for cooking was stored under the stove. On the left are several *amphorae* and a storage jar for flour. (© Museum of London)

cooking, and as such formed the focal point of the dwelling. The hearth would have been kerbed and may have had a cauldron suspended over it or a spit for roasting meat. In the poorer houses pot-boilers, heated until red hot and then dropped into the mixture to be cooked, may still have been used. Small domed clay ovens have also been found.

In many Roman town houses and villas a room was set aside for preparing and cooking food. At Newport villa a tiled hearth was found built against the wall of a room next to the baths: a popular position which may have been intended to take advantage of the handy supply of hot water. At Folkestone two tiled hearths had been raised above floor level, one in the centre of the room and the other against the wall. This had not been a tidy kitchen, as food remains and potsherds were found all over the floor and in the small backyard. A second kitchen was found in the same building with a corner hearth of stone and a rubbish pit full of food remains behind it. There was also a large masonry platform with two upright stones to support a water tank heated by a fire placed in the space beneath. Spoonley Wood villa boasted a fitted kitchen with a stone-paved floor, a stone-lined well and two stone table supports.

Not all kitchens had a hearth. Tripods and gridirons have been found, indicating that much of the cooking was done over a charcoal fire. A reconstruction of a kitchen at the Museum of London (Fig 31) shows a gridiron supported on a tile-and-clay platform with a raised edge. Fuel was stored in the cavity underneath. In simpler houses the gridiron (Fig 32) may have stood

32 Iron gridiron from Icklingham, used to support cooking vessels over heat. (© Museum of London)

on a single large tile or stone on the floor. Tripods were also used to hold metal washing-up bowls.

The hazards of solid-fuel cooking were ever present and at Greta Bridge a fourth-century house burnt down when a fire started in the kitchen. At Binchester one householder had taken the precaution of keeping the charcoal in a separate room to the oven. Other families preferred to have their food cooked in an outhouse or an annexe: a small building near House IV.I at Verulamium contained a brick hearth and pottery debris and may be interpreted as a cookhouse, as may a thatched building, 20 feet (6.1 m) square, found at Lullingstone, which contained three ovens cut into the floor.

Domestic ovens have been found in other rural dwellings, such as Atworth and Bourton-on-the-Water, but are less common in town houses. This reflects the tendency for town-dwellers to buy their bread from professional bakers, while the country housewife had to provide for her family's needs by baking her own. The third-century oven at Bourton-on-the-Water was an oval structure built of the local oolite with a narrow mouth and a natural clay floor. To use it, a fire was lit inside and the ashes raked out when the required temperature was reached. Such ovens need regular maintenance to ensure that cracks are filled in as soon as they appear and in the winter it may often have been difficult to reach and maintain a temperature high enough to bake the dough.

Few houses had water pumped to the kitchen and water for cooking and cleaning would have had to have been transferred from a well or cistern by wooden buckets. Most kitchens would have been hot and fuggy with the aroma of oil lamps, burning charcoal and cooking food mingling with the smell of stored food. They would also have been untidy and overcrowded by modern standards, with joints of meat, bunches of herbs, and drying vegetables hanging by iron hooks from the rafters, and other fresh produce stored openly on shelves or in baskets, barrels or sacks on the floor. Liquids would have been kept in their transport containers.

Amphorae are the best surviving of the storage vessels and of particular interest in the study of Roman trade, as they were usually made in the area of their contents' manufacture, and not only carry a maker's name but sometimes an indication of the quantity and quality of their contents. A full *amphora* would have been extremely heavy and the contents were probably decanted for convenience. They were used to transport small fruit, such as figs, dates and olives, as well as liquids, but were reused for a variety of purposes such as storage and even as urinals and seed trays.

The housewife would have had a wide choice of cooking equipment but two basic requirements were a quern and a *mortarium*. In the early Iron Age grain was ground on a saddle quern, that is, a rounded stone rubbed backwards and forwards by hand over a flat lower stone, but in the later Iron Age the rotary quern became the more common form and continued to be so, with some slight design changes, throughout the Roman period. The native quern had a high-domed upper stone with a handle of wood fixed into a hole in the side. The Roman quern, introduced by the military, had flatter upper and lower stones with the handle fastened on by an iron band (Fig 33).

The lower stone was either bedded into the floor or fixed on to a work bench, the upper stone held in position by a spindle and the grain fed into a central hopper. Some of the larger villas may have had donkey-driven mills.

Many recipes required the ingredients to be pulverised before cooking and this was done in a *mortarium*: a pottery bowl with grits scattered over the inner

33 Quern for grinding corn, from Chesters (© English Heritage)

surface and a pouring lip. The wide overhanging rim could be fitted over a metal frame to stop the bowl moving while the contents were pressed against the sharp grits by pestles of stone or wood. There was a wide variety of colours, forms and grits available, and one can imagine that individual cooks would have held firm views as to which were the best. Large stone mortars have also been found.

Pottery was used extensively for storage and cooking, and would have been ranged around the walls of the kitchen on shelves and in cupboards. Flagons were predominantly cream, white or buff, while jugs, jars and bowls came in a variety of wares, mostly red or grey, and varied in size from tiny examples, which may have held spices, to enormous storage bins. Lids were either of wood or flat discs cut from broken pots or stone, or specially made with lifting knobs. Flat bowls and dishes were inverted and used as lids for the larger jars and casseroles. Early pots tend to be lighter in colour and follow Continental designs, while late vessels are darker and hark back to the Iron Age tradition. The housewife would have had a wide choice as pottery which had to be transported over great distances was usually as readily available as local products.

Pottery vessels are easily broken and need to be replaced continually, although some Romano-British pots have been found repaired with lead rivets or clamps (Fig 34).

The *mortaria* shops at Castleford and Lancaster and the general pottery shops at Wroxeter and Colchester will have done a brisk trade, while the many kilns

34 Broken cooking pot from South Shields mended with a lead clamp (© Museum of Antiquities, Newcastle)

scattered throughout Britain supplied both the military and civilian markets. Unglazed earthenware is difficult to keep clean and pots with large inclusions of shell or grit must have become rather unpleasant quite quickly unless there was a method of 'proving' them, such as boiling in sour milk – a method used in the Shetlands until the twentieth century.

Metal may always have been preferred to pottery for cooking purposes because, although more expensive, it was longer lasting and more easily cleaned by rubbing with sand. The majority of bronze saucepans in Britain have been found in military contexts but they were used by civilian households as well: a relief from Arlon in Belgium shows a family at dinner with a handled pan on the shelf behind them. The most common form has a deep body with thin-bellied walls, a flat rim and lathe-turned concentric rings at the base to allow the contents to heat quickly whilst protecting them from too much direct heat. Incised lines on the inside of some examples may be level markers, those on the outside are purely decorative. It has been suggested that the saucepans were used for heating an alcoholic mixture resembling *Gluhwein* but their appearance in some numbers in the camp kitchen found at Prestwick Carr (Fig 35) in association with well-used cauldrons must indicate that they were primarily for general cooking purposes. Many seem to have been used by several generations of cooks. Oconea, a resident of Bath, was so upset at the theft of her pan that she asked for divine intervention in an attempt to recover it, cursing the thief in the process. As the Vindolanda writing tablets indicate that these could cost up to 5 *denarii* each, this would have been a significant financial loss as well as a culinary inconvenience.

35 A selection of pans and cauldrons from Prestwick Carr showing extensive repairs (© Museum of Antiquities of the University and Society of Antiquaries of Newcastle upon Tyne)

Colanders found in Britain are invariably of the elegant type which echo the shape of the saucepans and are pierced by holes arranged in elaborate patterns (Fig 36). They are thought to have been used for warming or cooling wine, by filling them with ice or hot coals and pouring the wine through, a service which the mistress of the house performed for her guests. Plainer versions must have been used for straining vegetables: the wide pots with perforated flat bases found at Silchester may have served the purpose. For straining liquids a piece of cloth would have been fastened to a wooden loop, like a jelly bag. A pottery funnel with a built-in strainer, found at Richborough, would have been a particularly useful piece of equipment, as would the bronze bowl from

36 Colanders and jugs were used for serving wine. The small tin cup from High Rochester is a rarer find (© Museum of Antiquities of the University and Society of Antiquaries of Newcastle upon Tyne)

Aldborough which has a series of holes pierced in its narrow base. Small pots with concentric ribs around perforated bases are thought to be cheese presses rather than strainers.

Large cauldrons for making stews and soups were used in both military and domestic kitchens. They were of copper alloy, either beaten from a single sheet or made in strips riveted together. The Prestwick Carr cauldrons show signs of heavy usage as they have been repaired several times with patches. Cauldrons were suspended by iron chains of some complexity.

To serve out the contents of cauldrons ladles were used. An example from Great Chesterford has a large hook at the end so that it could be hung up or used to fish large joints of meat out of hot stock. The ladles of silver are more likely to have been used for serving mulled wine.

Iron frying-pans are known which are oval or circular with a pouring lip at one end and a folding handle at the other, making them easier to store. Copper-alloy examples seem to have been less common but were included in the metalwork hoards from Wotton and Sturmere and an single pan has been found recently at Great Lea in Berkshire. Other metal vessels which have been found on Italian sites include fish kettles, roasting tins and moulds in the form of suckling pigs, hares or hams. A flat iron disc with a long handle found at Housesteads has been identified as a baker's peel, used for moving loaves in and out of a hot oven. Peacock has suggested that the large bowls of Pompeian red ware found in London were used for making bread.

Lead was also used for cooking vessels, and analysis of human bones from Poundbury has indicated that significant amounts of lead were absorbed as a result. This cannot be accounted for purely by the use of lead water pipes, as the skeleton of one child revealed traces of lead thought to have originated in Attica. Lead pans were recommended for reducing wine, which must have added to the incidence of lead poisoning.

Glass vessels were little used in the kitchen except for rectangular or cylindrical bottles. These were mould-blown in the first and second centuries and used for transporting and storing liquids. Many have a geometric pattern or the maker's name in relief on the base. The wide strap handles do not project beyond the width of the vessel so that they could be tightly packed together in transit. Large glass jars have been found reused as cinerary urns but are likely to have been domestic storage vessels originally.

We know a great deal about cooking in Rome from the Latin writers, in particular Apicius, who wrote a book on sauces in the first century AD. The collection of recipes known today as *The Art of Cooking*, which has been attributed to Apicius, is probably a fourth-century collection of recipes by a number of authors, including Apicius.[8] This is not a book for beginners: there are few indications of quantities or cooking temperatures, and much is left to imagination and experience. Many of the recipes have long lists of ingredients and as such resemble modern Indian cookery. There seems to have been a dislike for the plain taste of meat, fish or vegetables, and herbs, spices and sauces were used extensively. This may have been due to the difficulty of storing fresh food, leading to a need to disguise slightly jaded produce, but could be taken to extremes: after a recipe called 'A Patina of Anchovy without Anchovy' Apicius says 'at table no-one will know what he is eating'.

The Art of Cooking has preserved many recipes which use both ordinary and exotic ingredients, and many that are listed would make a modern cook think twice: testicles of capons, sow's udder, lights of hare, and entrails of fish. Modern scientific analysis of animal bones, pollen and seeds have revealed the extent to which some of the ingredients were available to the Romano-British housewife. It has often been suggested that the population of Roman Britain was practically vegetarian, with the consumption of meat confined to the wealthy, but this has been disproved by the amount and variety of meat and fish bones found in excavations. Ox (beef and veal), sheep (lamb and mutton), goat, pig (both joints and suckling pig), red deer, roe deer, fallow deer, boar, frog, and hare bones have all been found with butchery marks (despite Caesar's assertion that the Britons would not eat hares).[9] The bones of butchered dogs have been found at Abingdon and Vindolanda whilst elk bones have been found at Newstead and South Shields. No doubt in Scotland if one caught a bear one ate it. At York and Lincoln animal scapulae have been found with holes cut thorugh to allow the joints to be hung over fires for smoking; the meat would then be shaved off the bone for serving. At Insula III at Verulamium a pile of horse bones led the excavators to surmise that horse meat had been used for making sausages. Beef bones found on several sites had been broken to extract the marrow and it could be said of all animals, not just the pig, that the only bit which was not used was the squeal.

Animal bone analysis by Tony King has indicated that unromanised civilian sites of first-century AD date have produced a much heavier representation of sheep/goat bones than military sites, while the villas, *vici* and smaller *civitas* capitals show less sheep/goat and more ox. The implication that the people who lived in Romanised houses inclined more to a Romanised diet was attributed by King to the influence of the army, its veterans and associated personnel. He also discovered that on the high-status sites in the area north of London there was a marked preference for pig or beef with sheep/goat as a third choice, but by the later period the diet across the province had changed and the proportions of ox to pig to sheep/goat were almost equal.

Julius Caesar was of the opinion that the Britons had a taboo banning them from eating fowls and geese[10] but the quantity of fowl bones found in excavation suggest that he was mistaken. Indeed, the variety of fowl eaten is extensive: swan, coot, crane, raven, redwing, avocet, thrush, water-rail, golden plover, jackdaw, crow, herring gull and even stork, no longer a native bird, have been found in domestic contexts, along with the more familiar gamebirds. Doves were reared in *columbaria* to supplement the meat supply of the families at Caerwent, Fisbourne, Waddon Hill and Silchester, and there is a suggestion that pheasants may have been hand reared at Barnsley Park. Ducks, geese and chickens were eaten in quantity and there is some evidence from Caerleon to suggest that birds were served with the heads cut off but their feet left on.

Eggs of domesticated fowl and wild birds, particularly sea birds, were used both as a main ingredient – either boiled or fried and accompanied by a sauce – and as a secondary ingredient to thicken stews or make sweet or savoury puddings. Eggs were preserved by soaking them in olive oil.

The list of edible fish is equally long and includes both river fish and sea fish such as perch, trout, salmon, dace, eel, bass, black sea-bream, and grey mullet. There appears to have been an efficient transport system for getting fish to inland customers as grey mullet and herring have been found at Silchester, sea bream at Uley and flounders, herring, bass, and horse mackerel at Great Bedwyn in Wiltshire. At Shakenoak the estate included three fish ponds for breeding coarse fish and many villa sites may have bred fish for their own table as well as for profit. Pike was eaten by the British but was apparently not to Roman taste and there are no recipes recorded in *The Art of Cooking* for its preparation. At Waddon Hill the remains of the very bony Great Wrasse were found, possibly eaten because it resembled the Parrot Wrasse which was considered a great delicacy. Tunny-fish in oil was exported from Provence in pottery vessels as well as from North Africa: an inscription on an amphora fragment from Carlisle advertises 'Old Tangiers tunny relish, 'provisions' quality, excellent top quality'.[11]

The latter may have been a form of that essential ingredient to successful Roman cookery, *garum* or *liquamen*. This was a sauce made from the entrails of large fish and whole small fish, which were salted and then left in a warm place to ferment before the resulting liquid was drained off. It was used as a seasoning like soy sauce or Worcestershire sauce and was mostly made in factories, one of which has been identified at the Peninsular House site in London. This traded from the first to the fourth century, allowing London housewives to buy the sauce freshly made. It was also imported from Italy, Libya and Spain. An *amphora* found at Southwark is inscribed 'Lucius Tettius Africanus's finest fish sauce from Antipolis': Antipolis (Antibes in France) is known to have produced a sauce made from tunny, which Martial stated was cheaper than sauces made from mackerel.[12]

From the quantity of shells found it is likely that edible crabs as well as cockles, periwinkles, scallops, and whelks were staple foodstuffs for those people who lived near the coast and were also enjoyed by those living as far inland as Silchester. Caerleon Baths, where snacks were sold ready cooked, did a brisk trade in edible shellfish, both the common mussels and whelks, as well as the more unusual prickly cockle, otter shell, peppery furrow shell, carpet shell, razor shell, and purple top shell. The edible snail *(Helix aspersa)* is known to have been eaten at Silchester and at many other town and villa sites, while the escargot *(Helix pomatia)* has been found at Shakenoak. There is a possibility that frogs' legs were enjoyed at York and Silchester.

The earliest reference to British oysters dates from shortly after the expeditions of Julius Caesar but it was during the administration of Agricola that the gourmets of the Empire became aware of the superiority of this export; Constantine the Great in the fourth century is said to have returned from Britain having acquired a taste for Kentish oysters. The original beds were natural but as demand outstripped supply artificial beds were introduced. Oyster shells appear on sites all over the province – military and civilian, urban and rural – clearly a taste for oysters was not confined to emperors. Oysters can survive up to ten days out of water as long as they are kept shut, and can also be taken great distances by boat if continually doused with sea-water, so housewives all over the country would have been able to rely on a regular supply. They were also sold ready pickled.

Vegetables were available in a lesser array than we are used to and in a strictly seasonal capacity, although it is believed that the Romans introduced carrots and leeks, amongst other vegetables, to Britain. The carrot at this period would have been a creamy white in colour, like a parsnip. Many ingredients that we today associate with cold salads, such as lettuce, endive and cucumber, the Romans preferred to braise. Green vegetables, such as cabbage, lettuce, cornsalad and cornspurry, would have had to be eaten immediately when available, while the root vegetables, such as the newly introduced radishes, turnips and parsnips, could be stored for some time. Beans, lentils, peas, vetch, and other pulses could be eaten fresh or dried, as could the many native varieties of edible fungus. The Romano-British housewife must also have used potherbs and wild crops more intensively than is the modern habit: for example, elder, dandelions, Good King Henry, and sorrel. *The Art of Cooking* gave a recipe for a *patina* (egg custard) based on nettles and Pliny recommended the nettle as a green vegetable, adding, 'the root, too, of the wild varieties makes more tender all meat with which it is boiled'.[13] Edible seaweeds would also have been harvested where possible.

Few recipes for puddings are included in *The Art of Cooking,* but fruit was eaten either by itself, fresh or stewed, or was added to stews and stuffings. Many of the exotic fruit, such as lemons, melons, pomegranates, peaches, dates, and figs, will only have been available as imported luxuries, although there is evidence from some southern sites of solitary fig trees struggling to survive. An amphora sherd from Carlisle provides evidence for the importation of doum palm, which has been described as looking 'like a shrivelled banana' and tasting 'like a glucose door mat'; Roger Tomlin has suggested that the fact that it was imported from Egypt to the northern frontier 'is an index of how starved they were of sugar'.[14]

Some fruit trees were introduced by the Romans, for example, the cultivated cherry, which was an improvement on the native variety. Soft fruit, such as the black mulberry, plum, strawberry, raspberry, currants, gooseberry, elderberry, and cranberry, were much appreciated in their season or were preserved in honey or pickled in vinegar: the autumn would be a busy time for the skilful housewife as she bottled fruit or picked hips and haws, blackberries, bullace, and elderberries from the hedgerows. Seeds of mulberries and medlars, fruit too fragile to be transported any distance when ripe, have been found in the south west as well as London, indicating local production. Nuts were also gathered from the wild or were imported: almonds are only known from Wiggonholt bath-house and London, but hazelnuts, walnuts and stone-pine nuts are common finds. The sweet chestnut is thought to have been a Roman introduction.

Mention has already been made of the use of herbs and spices in Roman cookery. British sites have revealed coriander, rue, savory, borage, celery seed, dill, poppy seeds (for sprinkling on bread), black and white mustard, horseparsley, fennel, and mint, although care must be taken not to presume that these were intended for culinary uses as they all have medicinal properties as well. Thyme, garlic and chives were also available as native species. Other herbs and spices, such as aniseed, asafoetida, cumin, and ginger, would have been imported luxuries. Three types of pepper were imported and played an important role in Roman cuisine in both sweet and savoury dishes.

Bread and various forms of porridge were part of the staple diet. Spelt, emmer, barley, oats, breadwheat, clubwheat, and rye were all grown in Britain during the Iron Age, but in the Roman period rye and clubwheat appear with greater frequency, while spelt became a principal crop. Apicius mentioned the use of spelt in soups, stuffings and vegetables, as well as in puddings. Oats, during the Roman era, were mostly relegated to animal fodder. Lentils and field beans, as found at Bearsden, may have been other important sources of carbohydrate.

Although many towns had professional bakers most households, particularly in the villages or in villas, would have baked their own bread. At The Poultry, London, a dough trough was discovered and a *testumus* (a pottery cover used whilst baking bread) was found at Castor, near Peterborough. Literary sources reveal that both white and brown bread were baked, and the digestive benefits of wholemeal bread were already recognised by Petronius.[15] Some bread was unleavened but yeast and sour dough were used and Pliny mentions soaking grain in unfermented wine to make leavened bread.[16] The loaves were circular and either shaped like cottage loaves or flat discs. The twisted bread referred to in a Vindolanda list would have been made with milk, pepper and oil or lard.

Salt was required for seasoning food and pickling. This was produced in large coastal salterns and inland salt springs, and transported in jars sealed with pitch or in barrels. It has often been suggested that a common agricultural practice was to slaughter and preserve in salt a high proportion of the stock in the autumn because of the difficulties in providing winter fodder. This practice would have resulted in a high proportion of young animals being represented in bone assemblages but this has not proved to be the case. We must presume that, although meat was salted as a regular method of preservation, few families had to survive on salted meat throughout the winter, although the seasonal limitation on supply would mean that a cook would have had to plan her meals carefully.

The other essential for cooking, medicine, lubrication, lighting, and a thousand and one other uses was olive oil. Most of the oil imported into London came from southern Spain, particularly the province of Baetica, as did the oil used at Sheepen, Verulamium and Skeleton Green. In the third century, however, the Spanish trade was overtaken by suppliers from North Africa and customers would have had to adjust their palates to a slightly different taste. Olives were also transported whole: a complete *amphora* from northern Spain was found off the Pan Sands near Kent still full of olives, and black olives preserved in wine are recorded, as are salted and unsalted olives.

The only sweetener which was readily available was honey and most country people would have had their own hives. Pottery hives are known from Casterley Camp (Iron Age) and Rockbourne villa, but wooden and straw hives would also have been used. Honey was further used as a preservative for meat and fruit, to sweeten wine and to make mead. Butter was rarely used for cooking, being regarded as of mainly medicinal use, but cheese was popular. Pliny mentions cheeses from Nimes (France), the Alps, the Apennines, Umbria, and Etruria,[17] but most farms produced their own using rennet of lamb or kid. Hard and soft cheeses were made as well as smoked varieties.

The milk of cow, goat or sheep was drunk but poor hygiene must often have counteracted the food value to the extent that milk was a dangerous liquid, full of bacteria leading to dysentery and diarrhoea. The adult population regarded it as a poor substitute for wine or beer, suitable only for invalids and small children.

In Rome the day's meals would follow a regular pattern. Breakfast *(jentaculum)* would be bread and cheese or just a glass of plain water. Lunch *(prandium)* might be simply bread, cold meat, vegetables or fruit, and was, according to Seneca, an unceremonious meal which did not require the table to be set or the family to wash their hands. The serious eating was done at dinner *(cena)*: a meal divided into the hors d'oeuvre *(gustatio),* the main course *(mensae primae)* and the dessert *(mensae secundae).* No doubt the upper and middle classes who followed the Roman way of life would keep to this arrangement of meal times but the ordinary household would be more likely to have just one or two meals a day. The time of the main meal varied but it might reasonably be presumed that most people would eat when their day's work was done rather than waste valuable daylight hours eating. It is also unlikely that the average family had an elaborate three-course meal with several removes, but based their diet on one course of stew, soup or joints of meat, with fruit when available. The excavation of Caerleon Baths suggests, however, that there was a tendency to nibble between meals, and shops at Cirencester and Wroxeter also supplied snacks of seafood or cooked meats.

Country dwellers would have been largely self-sufficient, growing their own vegetables, fruit and grain, and killing their own meat, with supplements from the wild. Their colleagues in the towns would have had to rely on purchasing their food in shops or from street pedlars. Butchers' shops have been discovered at Verulamium, Gloucester, London, Vindolanda, and Braintree, with a meat market at Cirencester; a seafood shop at Wroxeter and an oyster seller at Caerwent; a fruit shop and a spice seller at Colchester and a possible dairy at Silchester; bakers at London, Canterbury, Verulamium, and Silchester; and wine merchants at York, London and Verulamium. None of these have left any indication of the price of their commodities but in AD 301 the Emperor Diocletian issued an Edict freezing prices throughout the Empire, and this gives some fascinating details. If we take an elegant three-course meal, based on recipes from *The Art of Cooking*, of eggs and oysters, followed by pork cooked with figs and barley, plus chicken with vegetables, and finishing with stewed plums, we can estimate the possible cost from the Edict. Eggs and oysters were 1 *denarius* each, pork 12 *denarii* per Italian pound, figs 4 *denarii* for 25 or 40 depending on the quality, barley 100 *denarii* per modius (15.3 pints), chickens 60 *denarii* a pair, lettuces and leeks 4 *denarii* for ten, and a bunch of 25 kidney beans 4 *denarii*. Plums were 4 *denarii* for 30 or 40 depending on size. On this reckoning the meal for four would cost 114 *denarii*, excluding the sauces which would be made from ingredients already in the store cupboard: honey, wine, herbs, *liquamen* and spices. To put this in its context, the Edict also stated that a stonemason – one of the better-paid craftsmen – should be paid 50 *denarii* per day, while a linen weaver got 40 *denarii* and a sewer cleaner 25 *denarii* (all with maintenance). The housekeeping money of few women would have stretched to 114 *denarii* per meal.

The majority of the Romanised population would drink wine with their meals. Rhodian wine was inexpensive and may have been the *vin ordinaire*, while the most expensive came from Gallia Narbonensis; other sources were Spain, Italy, Africa, the Aegean, and Gaul. There is some evidence for grapes being grown in Britain at Boxmoor and Brockley Hill, and possible vineyards have been suggested for the sites at North Thoresby and Wollaston, but it is unlikely that the British wine industry ever offered a threat to the other producers.

As well as being drunk either neat or diluted with water, spiced or warmed, wine was also used in varying degrees of reduction for cooking. Some of these wine products, like *defrutum* and *passum*, were imported already prepared but some will have been made in the home. Wine was also mixed with honey for drinking and cooking.

Although there is plenty of evidence to suggest that considerable quantities of wine, from a wide range of sources, were being imported into the south-east of Britain before the Roman invasion, the native tribes seem always to have preferred beer to wine and continued to make and consume vast quantities. Corn driers for malting barley for home-brewed ale have been found on several villa sites and the inclusion of Celtic beer in Diocletian's Edict, at 4 *denarii* per Italian pint compared with Falernian wine at 30 *denarii* and *vin ordinaire* at 8 *denarii* suggests that beer was also brewed commercially and may have been an important British export. Athenaeus, quoting Poseidonius, referred to the

Celts flavouring their drink with cumin and drinking beer made from wheat prepared with honey.[18] There is evidence from Frenchfield near Doncaster which may point to the production of cider.

The Romans had very firm views on the subject of women drinking and several writers declared that no woman should ever be seen the worse for drink.[19] This was not due to a dislike of social embarrassment but because heavy drinking was associated with loose morals. Cato was not the only one to attribute the custom of men kissing their female relatives when they met to the necessity of checking if they smelt of drink.[20] There is every possibility that alcoholism, with all its associated social and medical consequences, was a problem for both men and women, even if the majority took their wine diluted. Diodorus Siculus commented on the amount drunk at Celtic feasts[21] and the size of the tankards found suggests that beer was drunk by the quart rather than by the pint. It is not known whether women shared this thirst for beer. Spirits appear to have been unknown.

The bulk of the drinking took place while entertaining friends in the dining-room and, as the use of fancy tableware was a favourite form of display among the wealthier classes, it was in this room that the best crockery was used: red Samian ware from the workshops of Italy and Gaul, pots from Spain and Gaul dusted with shiny mica, colour-coated and glazed wares and vessels decorated with rouletting, barbotine, 'marbling', and black slip. Pots for the table were often designed for specific purposes, for example, for the first course, bite-sized pieces of food would be served from an hors d'oeuvre dish; an example from Gadebridge Park is divided into four compartments by vertical walls while one from Colchester has a central circular bowl with compartments around it.

Glass was very much a material for the table, with jugs, bowls, beakers and plates of all colours imported from the Continent. Drinking beakers could be elaborate, with faceted, moulded or painted decoration, and in the fourth century a group of vessels with engraved decoration was imported from the Cologne area. Tin, silver, gold, and gilded vessels would have been used in upper-class houses or displayed on a sideboard, and many will have been given as presents. In particular, pewter – a metal used for canisters, bowls, cups, plates, and spoons – was given as wedding or betrothal gifts in the third and fourth centuries and examples are known from mid-second-century contexts. One dish found at Verulamium was owned by a woman called Viventia, the wife or daughter of Victoricus, who had her name scratched on the base; lightly incised numbers may suggest that the vessel was one of a set.

A grave uncovered at Winchester contained a rectangular shale tray with a typical place setting for a meal: a Samian cup and platter, two knives and a spoon. Forks were entirely unknown, as food was first cut up and then eaten with the fingers even in the politest society. A wide variety of knives was used (Fig 37), mostly of iron with bone or wood handles or with looped ends. As guests were expected to bring their own cutlery, there were also elaborate folding knives with ivory handles in the form of gladiators or animals, and one would take care, as did Flamma at Colchester, to have your name on the handle of your personal knife, even if it wasn't very elaborate. Spoons, some of which could also be folded, were made in metal, bone or wood and had circular, oval or lute-shaped bowls varying in size from tiny 'salt' spoons to large servers; spoons used by individuals at table could also be folded. A number which have sharply tapering handles might be identified as *cochleare*, small spoons used for eating eggs and shellfish – the pointed ends being used for winkling snails or other delicacies out of their shells. Pliny referred to the superstitious habit of piercing the shells of eggs or snails with the end of the spoon immediately after eating them,[22] a practice which indicates that, however busy women were with their housework and cooking, the spiritual side of their lives played a part in their most mundane tasks.

37 A folding knife with an iron blade and ivory handle in the form of a gladiator (© Museum of Antiquities of the University and Society of Antiquaries of Newcastle upon Tyne)

Chapter 5

Fashion

The women of the household were responsible for keeping the family clothed. Most clothes would be made at home – even the Emperor Augustus was reported to have had his clothes made for him by his female relatives,[1] and it was regarded as a womanly occupation, carrying no social stigma, to spin and weave the cloth oneself. Indeed, Columella was very scathing about those women who were so 'inclined to luxury and idleness that they do not deign to undertake even the superintendence of wool-making', preferring to buy clothes ready made 'for large sums and almost the whole of their husbands' income'.[2] In Roman Britain spinning wool was probably a daily chore for most women if their households were to remain clothed. Several women appear on their tombstones carrying spindles and/or distaffs, for example the wife of M Aurelius Nepos at Chester; and Regina (see Fig 6) has balls of wool neatly stacked in a basket by her side as well as a spindle and distaff in her left hand. Spindles of wood and bone and segmental distaffs of shale, jet, bone, and amber have been found with whorls made from discarded fragments of pottery, stone, bone, lead, shale, and jet. Some homes would have had slaves to spin (*quasillariae*) and weave but most women were capable of producing plain cloth as well as fancy braids. An embroidery frame found at Pompeii has not been paralleled so far in Britain but no doubt 'fancy work' was carried out as a relaxation as well as a duty, using sets of needles of the type found at Cirencester and Vindolanda.

If the family did not produce its own cloth it is likely that they bought their clothing ready made as most garments were woven in one piece on the loom with only the most minimal tailoring afterwards. It was very rare for plain woollen cloth to be sold as a strip 'by the yard' for home dressmaking.

The basic item of women's clothing in the north-west provinces is known today as the 'Gallic coat'. This was a wide unfitted tunic with sleeves which were either sewn into place or woven in one piece with the body of the garment. Sleeveless examples are also known. The coat was a unisex garment worn knee-length by men and ankle- or calf-length by women, with the hem curved to avoid sagging at the sides. Examples of Gallic coats have been found at Les-Martres-de-Veyre in France and Reepsholt in Ostfriesland, but in Britain we are dependent on tombstone evidence for proof that the coat was worn.

Alternative dresses were available but appear to have been indicators of tribal origins rather than fashion changes. A costume, now named after a woman called Menimane from Mainz-Weisenau, was worn in the northern provinces in the pre-Roman Iron Age and the Roman period up to the end of the first century AD and then reappeared in the fourth century when German units on active service were accompanied to Britain by their womenfolk. The ensemble involved a closely fitting bodice with long tight sleeves ending in turned-back cuffs. The front of the bodice was fastened by one or more brooches. Over this a loose tunic was worn, in the form of a simple tube of cloth with the back and front held together at the shoulders by a pair of brooches and, occasionally, at the breast by a third. Menimane's tunic is shown slipping from her left shoulder. Around the waist a girdle took some of the weight but the garment is literally pinned together and the many finds of chained pairs of brooches in Britain may suggest that this was a common form of dress (see Fig 16).

Tunics had regional variations across the Empire and may have been worn in the tradition of their homelands by foreign women in Britain, such as Javolena Monime (a Greek), Titullinia Pussitta (a Raetian) and Ursa (a German). The dress of the women of the Ubii from Germania consisted of a series of tunics worn one over the other, and John Peter Wild has suggested that this dress, with its enveloping cloak and accompanying large bonnet, was common throughout Lower Germany.[3] Altars at Domburg dedicated to Nehalennia show the goddess in a tunic and cloak similar to that of the Ubii but with a smaller bonnet and shoulder cape. One of the inscriptions names a merchant from York trading between the Walcheran and Britain, so this costume may have been familiar to the inhabitants of York.

Tunics were also indicators of class and age: the small figures seen hovering in funerary banquet scenes are often dressed in tunics and it is difficult to say if some of these are the children of the household or servants. The three-year-old Vacia from Carlisle is shown in a girdled long tunic with three-quarter-length sleeves, either covered by a shorter tunic or caught at the waist in a heavy overfold – all the better to grow into! At Great Chesters the young Pervica, in a shapeless calf-length tunic with long sleeves, is clad similarly to the four-year-old Ertola at Corbridge, who wears a sleeved tunic with a tuck at the waist, while at York Mantinia Maerica's tunic is worn very short. Clothing appears to have been the same for boys and girls, any differences in appearance on tombstones being possibly the difference between winter and summer clothing. Such evidence for children's dress, however, should not be taken too literally, as they are often shown far older than their age at death. Flavia Augustina's children, for example, at the age of one year and three days, and one year, nine months and five days, stand sturdily in front of their parents fully dressed in Gallic coats and ankle boots (see Fig 18). Gypsum burials at York have revealed that small babies were swaddled, as recommended by Soranus.[4]

Deities were also shown in tunics with girdles tied below the bust, particularly mother goddesses, and many of these costumes appear to have been based on copy-book representations of the dress of the Italian matron. Women such as Julia Pacata in London and Julia Lucilla at High Rochester may well have continued to wear the sleeveless or short-sleeved tunic known as the *stola* in which they would have been comfortable in Rome, although there is evidence that the *stola* had largely fallen out of favour by the late first century AD.

38 Tombstone of Aurelia Aureliana who died at Carlisle showing her wearing a Gallic coat with a cloak thrown over her shoulder, and holding a bunch of flowers. (© Museum of Antiquities of the University and Society of Antiquaries of Newcastle upon Tyne)

Over both the coat and the tunic a cloak was worn, usually rectangular in shape although the Ubian costume included one of semicircular shape with the straight edges rolled back on the shoulders and fastened at the waist by a brooch. The rectangular cloaks were worn in various ways: either over the head, or across the shoulders, or folded lengthwise and wound around the neck and shoulders like a scarf with the ends thrown back over each shoulder. Aurelia Aureliana's cloak has fringed ends (Fig 38).

Cloaks are the only form of female outer garment shown in British sculpture, but a curse tablet has revealed that at Bath Lovernisca lost a *mafortium*[5] which has been identified as a short cape covering the neck and shoulders and resembling the *pallium simplex*, described by Varro as worn by women, particularly those in mourning. The fringed herringbone twill hood with decorative tablet woven bands, known as the Orkney Hood, which has recently been dated to AD 250–615, may be such an article of outdoor clothing.[6] We cannot be confident that in rough weather women did not wear the hooded cape seen on men's tombstones or even the *birrus britannicus*, the long wet-weather garment of heavy wool or skin which was one of Britain's more famous exports. Severus Alexander, when banning the use of a type of cloak known as the *paenula* in Rome, did concede to its use by both men and women when travelling, 'since that sort of clothing has always been for journeys and wet weather'.[7]

Small shawls were also worn and examples can be seen on a relief of the three mother goddesses from Midlothian, drawn tightly across the shoulders and pinned centrally by large circular brooches. The figure in a funerary banquet scene from York (York I) preferred to fasten her mantle at the left shoulder with the other end drawn forward. The mother goddess from Bewcastle has her shawl crossed over in front and fastened by invisible means (Fig 39).

Scarves were worn either crossed at the neck with the ends tucked into the top of the coat or folded like cravats.

Under the coat was worn an undertunic: Regina has a long full shift which is invisible at the neck except for the fastening brooch, the close-fitting sleeves end just above her bracelets (see Fig 6). Fragments of material adhering to a bracelet worn by a female skeleton of fourth-century date at Castor indicate that shifts were made of linen. Regina's shift hangs below the hem of her outer garment and, as so many respectable ladies are portrayed with their undertunics visible, we must presume that they were intended to be seen, Marcus Aurelius Nepos's wife going so far as to hold up the front of her dress in her left hand.

References from the ancient writers indicate that a linen band was worn around the bust as a brassière, although no examples have been found.[8] The long strip was wound several times around the body in order to keep it firmly in place; by wrapping it under the breasts it would have been possible to achieve some uplift but the breast band's purpose was more to provide comfort rather than to improve the figure. Briefs, when worn, are also likely to have been of linen, although six pairs made of leather are known from London. The pair from Queen Street had been cut to an hour-glass pattern from a single piece of leather and hemmed at the edges (see Fig 7). The garment was worn with the grain outwards for comfort with reinforcing pieces at each corner of the original shape to take the laces which were tied in a 'granny' knot. The briefs were described by Tony Wilmott as 'well worn, with deeply defined stretch marks across the front, the pattern of which would appear to preclude a male wearer'. Allowing for leather shrinkage he estimated that they had been worn by a slim woman with a hip measurement of 31 inches (78.74 cm). The date of the deposit was Flavian (AD 69–96) or earlier, while a similar pair of goatskin briefs from Shadwell came from a third-century context. These are more ornate with openwork decoration at the front and frilling around the legs, fastened with three integral laces at each corner. Figures wearing such garments are known from a mosaic at Piazza Armerina in Sicily and statuettes from Rennes, Hamburg, Dougga, and Pompeii, and are identified variously as acrobats, athletes and dancers and it is known that ordinary women often wore briefs

39 Relief of woman, possibly a mother goddess, from Bewcastle (© Carlisle Museum and Arts Services)

whilst doing their warming-up exercises in the bath-houses.[9] It is possible that leather briefs, which must have been uncomfortable for day-to-day wear, were worn only for energetic pursuits. Alternatively it has been postulated that they may have been connected with monthly protection, used in association with moss or wool in cloth pads, and it is noticeable that all come from domestic rubbish on purely civilian sites.[10] The discovery of the well-worn lacy briefs in a water storage tank at Shadwell, with broken laces suggesting violent removal, does not assist in identifying their precise function although it does exercise the imagination.

Corsets *(capitus)* were worn at Rome but a leather article found at London, which was initially identified as a corset, is now no longer thought to be an article of clothing. Excavations at Micklegate, York, have produced a stocking made in the sprang technique, whereby woollen threads are stretched between fixed rods and interlaced. This (if Roman) is the only known example of sprangwork from Roman Britain although fragments are known elsewhere in the Empire. The stocking is fringed at the top and stops short of the knee so could be more accurately described as a sock. The foot is missing. A pair of stockings found at Les-Martres-de-Veyre in Central Gaul were of heavy woollen twill with a back seam and the feet attached at the ankle. Again, the tops, one of which was embroidered with the letters PRI, were fringed and held up by a string garter which passed through the holes in the fabric. Les-Martres-de-Veyre also produced a pair of ankle socks which were fastened with a strap which crossed the instep.

Head-dresses are not commonly seen in sculpture of provincial women, possibly because having spent time arranging their hair they may have seen no reason to cover the result. However, enough representations survive to suggest that there were many types of bonnet, snood or hat available which may have varied according to fashion or tribal origin. There is no evidence to indicate whether the wearing of a head-dress was related to a particular period of a woman's life, for example marriage or widowhood, although Joachim Garbsch identified life-stage variations in the costumes of the women of Noricum and Pannonia in central Europe. The women of the Treveri in Gaul sometimes appear in a close-fitting bonnet like a bathing cap, fine enough for the contours of the hairstyle underneath to be discerned, which resembles that worn by Mantinia Maerica. The mother goddesses of the Ubii are depicted in enormous, almost spherical, bonnets, a smaller example of which might be seen worn by the woman seated in a basket chair on Julia Velva's tombstone (see Fig 5). A remarkable cap is worn by a head from Birrens which completely covers the hair and is drawn into two 'wings' on either side of the head by two bands or 'fillets', like a Dutch bonnet (Fig 40).

The form of the silk head-dress on the skeleton of a small child from Holborough is not known but the weave was a simple geometric damask of different colours giving a tiny check pattern.

A stylised mother goddess from Caerwent has a hood which fits snugly around the head with a raised edge framing the face, and tied under the chin, and Macdonald has suggested that the mother goddesses from Midlothian are also wearing hoods which cover the neck. A *capitularem* lost at Bath[11] may have been a garment of this type.

It has been suggested that gloves were not worn but that long sleeves were used to cover the hands in cold weather. Excerpts from Palladius and Ionas indicate that leather gloves were worn for rough work,[12] and a curse tablet from

40 Bonneted head from Birrens (© Dumfries Museum)

Bath seems to bemoan the loss of a pair of men's gloves.[13] It would seem odd, considering the British climate, if some sort of mitten was not worn by men and women alike.

The most popular material for clothing was wool and the fragments of woollen cloth found in Britain indicate a surprising variety of weaves: herringbone twill, two-over-two weave with weft chevron pattern, two-over-two diamond twill (the most compact weave and suitable for outer clothing), and half basket, as well as plain weaves. Linen was of secondary importance but was used for tunics and undergarments, in plain weave or basket weave. Fragments of silk are rare but are known, for example at Holborough and London, and silk and linen tunics with tapestry woven decoration may have been worn in the later period. A piece of silk cloth from Colchester was made from cultivated silk, not the wild variety, and both silk thread and woven fragments were exported from China or India. The only identifiable piece of cotton in Roman Britain, so far, is a piece of thread from an early fourth-century well near Chew Stoke, although cotton is known to have been exported to the Roman world from India and Sudan. It is always likely to have been an expensive rarity.

Very few of the sculptural representations of clothing from Britain retain traces of colours but there is no reason to doubt the bright colours to be seen on the Lullingstone wall-paintings. Evidence of fabric samples from excavations has revealed black cloth with a single tapestry woven band in a lighter colour inserted into the weft, from London; a band of red ribbed or purple cloth from Clementhorpe, York; wool dyed russet brown from Caerwent; and fragments of a tartan cloth of light yellowish brown and dark chocolate brown from Falkirk. Dyestuffs available at the time would have created blue,[14] black,[15] yellow,[16] green,[17] brown,[18] scarlet red,[19] red-purple,[20] and red-purple-brown.[21] The use of madder is well attested as a dye and would have been imported in dried root form, but analysis of some of the Vindolanda textiles has revealed the use of the local bedstraw to achieve a similar red colour. Lichen in the Vindolanda area also produces a purple dye similar to that of orchil.

Literary evidence gives us an idea of the colours used throughout the Empire, from Tacitus' reference to the black-robed women on Anglesey[22] and Ovid's many references to 'wool that blushes with Tyrian dye' as well as sky-blue, golden, green, grey, saffron, amethyst, white, chestnut brown, pink, and yellow.[23] He advised women to 'choose those that are sure to please, for not every one suits every woman. Snowy white skins like dark grey colours ... those of dark hue like white'.[24] The dyes could also be controlled to create designs: Tacitus, when describing the Germans, says 'women often wear outer garments of linen ornamented with a purple pattern', which was probably achieved by overdyeing woad with madder – a practice well known in Egypt at this time.[25] Tertullian, the early Christian writer, was against display and this included dyeing cloth, his attitude being that if God had wanted people to wear purple and sky-blue clothes He would have created purple and sky-blue sheep.[26] It was possible to create attractive designs in white, cream and shades of brown using the natural hues of the full fleece, but the majority of women preferred bright clashing colours. A female figure in a Claudian family group at Ingelheim (Germany), for example, wears a light-green undertunic, a red overtunic and a cloak and scarf of dark grey, while a female figure on the Lullingstone wall-paintings is more tastefully attired in mauve with purple bands.

Where these garments are confined it always seems to have been by a fabric band. Metal buckles have been found in numbers in Britain but mostly in military contexts and it is unlikely that women wore buckled belts. Vacia at

Corbridge tied her girdle at the back, while a woman from Castlesteads has hers neatly tied in a bow at the front. A woman from Bowness-on-Solway has her girdle slung loosely round her hips and a *maenad* at Corbridge wears a band with a chequered design. Such decorative belts could have been produced by tablet-weaving and the number of bone and bronze tablets, both square and triangular, found throughout the province shows this to have been a common technique. By using different coloured threads and turning the tablets individually or in groups, complicated patterns could be achieved. Another method was to use a rigid heddle, only one example of which is known from Britain at South Shields (Fig 41). This could take eleven threads and would produce a fine braid 10 mm wide for use as decorative edging or hair ribbons. Gold thread was also incorporated as decoration on clothing and soft furnishings as has been found in a female burial at Spitalfields in London (see Fig 48).

Fastenings for clothing, other than brooches and girdles, were known but not common. At Caerleon Baths small hooks were discovered which resembled modern hook-and-eye fastenings and may have been used to secure cuffs. More ambiguous are the button-and-loop fasteners found throughout Britain. These are of bone or metal and consist of a head (the button), which can be of various shapes and is occasionally enamelled, and a triangular loop set back from the

reverse of the button and intended to be sewn on to leather or cloth. It has been suggested that these were used to fasten capes but those seen on sculpture seem to be fastened on the inside, while the *birrus* was fastened by clasps and the military cape by thongs. Two button-and-loop fasteners were found in toilet boxes at York but Wild has expressed an opinion that they were used to fasten horse blankets rather than human clothing.

Pockets of textile have been found but not as yet in circumstances which make it clear whether they were attached to male or female garments or were, in fact, horn covers from horse bardings. Women are known to have carried

41 Bone weaving heddle from South Shields used for making hair ribbons or braids for decorating clothing(© Museum of Antiquities of the University and Society of Antiquaries of Newcastle upon Tyne)

coins and personal belongings in purses of various types. On her tombstone one woman from Ilkley is shown carrying a wedge-shaped purse which may have been formed by two pieces of leather sewn together and held at the top by a metal ring or a gathered cord; another (Chester 2) appears to carry a 'Dorothy bag', probably similar to the two piece example found at Angel Court, London, while her neighbour (Chester 5) holds a semicircular object like a clutch bag. In a barrow at Holborough a purse made of leather with a linen lining was found in a child's grave but unfortunately no details survive of its form, while the bag found 'quite decayed' with a small coin hoard at Husthwaite was entirely of linen. The bronze arm-purses found in the north are thought to have been a military accessory only worn by men.

The use of fans is known from sculpture; the woman from Murrell Hill, Carlisle, holds her fan unfurled and shows it to be circular with spokes radiating from the sticks (Fig 42). One of the women from Chester (Chester 2) holds what may be a folded fan in her right hand, as it resembles the ivory sticks of a fan found in a grave at York. No trace of the material has survived on the York fan but it may have been of textile or fine leather although there is evidence that chicken skin was used elsewhere in the Empire. An ivory catch held the sticks together when not in use. York has also produced the ivory ribs of a parasol with the ends protected by silver sheathing. Comparison with examples from Italy suggest that this was covered with light green material.

Shoes in the Iron Age were simple pieces of hide tied by thongs: not always very attractive nor particularly serviceable, but with a surprising number of variations, so that the *carbatina* found at London and Bar Hill differ in style from those from southern Germany and the Lower Rhine. So marked are these differences that the variations may be seen as reflecting regional costume. They were worn by all age groups and sexes in early Roman London. Examples survive which retain their uppers, many of which had openwork designs, and the effect must have been very pleasing with coloured stockings showing through the gaps.

Single-piece shoes found at London and Vindolanda show Roman features at a very early date and suggest that, whatever the populace thought of the invasion in general, they were ready to welcome Roman footwear with enthusiasm, particularly the nailed sole, which was specifically Roman and whose spread across the known world was in direct relation to Rome's political expansion. Unfortunately, the introduction of solid, well fitting closed shoes led to the earliest known cases of bunions and similar afflictions being visible on female skeletons.

Sandals, initially, had naturally shaped soles and were only worn by women and children but became acceptable male footwear after AD 180 when male and female modes were developed. Women's sandals became narrower and more pointed through the third century, while men's sandals became rounder and blunter until they were triangular in shape. Around AD 100–120 there was a short-lived fashion for women's sandals to have a single notch to indicate the

42 Tombstone of a lady from Murrell Hill, Carlisle. She fans herself whilst watching her child play with a bird seated on her lap. (© Carlisle Museum and Arts Services)

big toe, although some had extra notches for other toes. It has been suggested that sandal shapes were made by tracing round the customer's feet so that each pair was bespoke. Rhodes has commented that, if this was so, then the female owner of one sandal from Billingsgate, London, suffered badly from bunions, as the first three toes are displaced.

The soles of early sandals consisted of several layers of leather held by stitching with a line of nails round the edge. At London it would appear that only sandals have this stitching, which makes even small fragments easily recognisable. Towards the end of the second century the stitching became more closely spaced and set further in from the edge, and this appears to have been seen as a decorative feature as by the third century stamped or incised lines imitate the pattern of slits originally left in the sole by stitching. The sole of a woman's shoe from the Bank of England excavations in London was decorated with flowers and the figure of a bird. Wooden soles are also known.

Few sandals retain their uppers but the principal thong invariably started between the big toe and the second toe. One sandal from London has traces of an upper margin, suggesting that only the toes were left exposed, whilst another appears to have had a wide band of leather over the instep, as have sandals found at Vindolanda. Sandals were regarded as *de rigueur* in Rome but were probably only worn out of doors in the summer in Britain. Men wore them as house shoes, politely removing them when reclining to dinner. In London sandals were less common than one-piece shoes and rare in comparison with the more solid nailed shoes.

Calcei covering the entire foot were worn out of doors by men and women and could be brightly coloured. At London the nailed shoes with closed uppers fall into two types: those with intricate openwork decoration, which would not have been suitable for manual labour, and plain ankle boots, seamed at the front with a series of holes for thongs at the instep. The largest range of nailed shoes found in Britain are the military *caligae* and from their size appear to have been worn by men only, although some of the adolescent sizes may have been worn by women of military families doing active work.

A form of ankle boot with an elaborate lacy openwork upper was popular and has been found in military and civilian contexts of the late first century AD. It was an expensive item of footwear. A later type from a burial at Southfleet (Fig 43), of purple leather with gilded decoration, represents a late second- or early third-century development when openwork with embroidery and gilding became more common. After the AD 130s it was largely replaced by the latchet shoe which was worn by men, women and children throughout the Western Empire. These were shaped like children's shoes in Mabel Lucie Attwell illustrations: round at the toe with sensible straps fastened across the instep and with occasional openwork decoration on the uppers.

Another type of boot, worn in the third century, had a front fastening and integrally cut laces. Examples are known from London and Usk. The nailing on this type was often arranged in a tendril motif, although nailing became sparser in the third century and had all but died out by the end of the fourth century. At Lankhills the women and children gave up nailed shoes before the men, although the native population in general continued to affect the nailed shoe for longer than the possibly Germanic immigrant population. A woman's shoe which incorporates most of the features of late Roman footwear – a low vamp with an openwork top and an ankle strap made from an asymmetrical pattern – has been found at Low Ham.

Slippers were worn by women only and an example from St Magnus House, London, has gold leaf decoration which would have been familiar to ladies all over the Empire. These slippers have a raised cork sole as has an example from Inveresk. From Vindolanda a 'Persian' slipper has a single strap emerging from between the toes to fasten to the decorated instep strap. Other slippers found at Vindolanda have thick wooden soles and wide leather straps across the instep, and appear to have been intended for use in the bath-house, where thick soles were needed to protect the feet from hot concrete floors.

Joan Liversidge suggested that women's shoes were generally of softer leather and brighter colours than men's but recent discoveries appear to contradict this. Indeed, Carol van Driel-Murray has commented that the richest decoration on shoes from Saalburg, Cologne and Vechten is to be found on the men's shoes. Naked footprints on tiles from Leicester and Silchester, however, show that some people, at least in the summer, went barefoot.

From the amount of jewellery found in excavations it is clear that Romano-British women, whatever their station in life, were fond of bedecking themselves with precious metals and semi-precious stones. However, their jewellery may well have represented a woman's independence as, under Roman law, a woman's dowry was not considered as part of her husband's assets and jewellery often made up a substantial proportion of that dowry.

Solid neckrings, known as torcs, had been seen as symbols of power and status in pre-Roman Britain and as such had magico-religious significance. Dio Cassius tells us that Boudica 'wore a great twisted golden necklace[27] when she led the Iceni into battle and, as torcs were not normally worn at this time by women, it is to be presumed that in donning a torc Boudica was symbolically investing herself with the authority of an Iron Age warrior chieftain (see Fig 3). During the early Roman period torcs were awarded to soldiers for acts of bravery but later came to be regarded merely as good luck symbols. It is in this guise that Regina and a lady from Chester (Chester 3) appear to be wearing their torcs; the woman from Chester adds a crescentic pendant, another lucky amulet.

43 Shoe found in Southfleet, London (© British Museum)

Necklaces worn for purely decorative purposes were lighter and more delicately constructed. Thin gold chains set with emerald crystals, or green glass copies, are known from Wincle, Canterbury, London and Thetford, while a similar chain with double links from Richborough incorporates small sapphires. Amulets and religious symbols were hung from some necklaces, as at Backworth, where two chain necklaces and a matching bracelet all have wheel pendants thought to have been associated with a sun cult such as that of the Celtic god Taranis (Fig 44).

A necklace from the Aesica Hoard at Great Chesters comprises three silver chains of double loops held in a rectangular box at each end and supporting, in the centre, an oval cornelian set in a cable-edged mounting. The fastening and back section is missing. A similar necklace in gold, with a central crosspiece instead of a mounted stone, is known from Newtown in Cumbria.

Necklaces were more commonly made from beads, particularly of glass, strung on leather thongs, copper alloy wire or fibre string. The relief of Volusia

44 A gold bracelet and two necklaces from Backworth decorated with wheel and crescent symbols: these are amulets to ensure good luck (© British Museum)

Faustina shows that beaded necklaces could be worn around the base of the neck rather than hanging on the chest, although some necklaces from graves at York and Lankhills seem to have been longer. Some examples were made from matching beads but at Lankhills the majority were of mixed beads: Grave 199, for example, had a rope consisting of 108 beads of cylindrical, biconical, globular, and hexagonal shape, and green, blue, reddish amber, and yellow coloured glass, as well as double-segmented beads of clear white glass enclosing gold foil. This necklace includes examples of nearly all the glass bead types common in the late Roman period, the gold foil segmented beads being the most exotic as they are thought to have been manufactured in Egypt and imported into Britain from the second century AD. Beaded necklaces had either hooked fastenings or were continuous strands.

There is some evidence for gold armlets being male accessories in the Celtic world and it is now clear that men as well as women wore bracelets throughout the Roman period. Two massive gold armlets in the form of serpents from Dolaucothi may have been worn as symbols of the warrior class in the same manner as torcs. The two silver bracelets in the form of snakes from Castlethorpe, however, and the many copper-alloy bracelets with snake's head terminals are more delicate and more representaive of female jewellery, although they may still have had religious significance as snake's head motifs have been found in association with the worship of Bacchus.[28]

Finds from graves suggest that women wore several bracelets at the same time, although sculpture suggests rather that one bracelet on each forearm was the preferred fashion, as shown by Regina (see Fig 6).The Rudston Venus also has a single bracelet pushed well up on each forearm (see Fig 57).

Bracelets could be very expensive, such as the late Roman pierced-work gold bracelet belonging to Lady Juliana at Hoxne, or very elaborate, such as a first century hinged gold strip bracelet from Rhayader, which has plaited designs of applied beaded wire, with Celtic motifs on the end plates filled with green and blue enamel. Some were elegantly simple, such as a broad silver strip bracelet from Great Chesters which has a single cornelian as decoration (Fig 45). The majority of bracelets found in excavation are of copper alloy and are based on narrow strips, either decorated by incised or stamped motifs or twisted together to give a cable effect.

Three main types of annular glass bracelet have been recognised, the earliest having bands of chrome yellow, dark crimson or dark blue over translucent glass, while the other two types are based on opaque white, yellow or translucent coloured glass with blue-and-white cable mouldings or inlaid scrolls. Analysis seems to suggest that Roman vessel glass was recycled to provide the raw materials for the bracelets, which appear most commonly on the military sites and civilian settlements of the north.

Balsdon considered anklets to have been worn only by the less respectable women and the few examples known from Britain do not provide enough evidence for this to be proved or disproved. A decapitated female skeleton from

45 Bracelets and finger-rings of copper alloy, silver and jet from sites on Hadrian's Wall. Semi-precious stones were set into the costlier pieces, such as the wide hinged bracelet from Aesica (Great Chesters) at the top.(© Museum of Antiquities of the University and Society of Antiquaries of Newcastle upon Tyne)

Wroxton St Mary, for example, wore a twisted wire circlet on her left ankle and a skeleton from York wore two jet anklets as well as a jet bracelet and a bone and silver bracelet. The skeleton of a man wearing an anklet at Catterick has been identified as a *gallus* or priest of Cybele, which may suggest that anklets may have had religious significance. The only real evidence in the western provinces for anklets being 'respectable' everyday wear comes from Neumagen, where the hairdresser on a relief is seen wearing an anklet on her right ankle (see Fig 29).

Finger-rings were worn by both men and women as decoration and as a convenient way of carrying seals. Some rings are very small and may have been worn on the top joint, although children are known to have worn finger-rings at a very early age. In some families rings were exchanged on betrothal and the late fourth-century gold rings from Richborough and Thetford, which show pairs of clasped hands, could have been made for this purpose. The Aemilia finger-ring from Corbridge is also likely to have been used as a betrothal ring (Fig 46). A custom, thought to have come from the east and popular in aristocratic circles in Rome, was the placing of an iron ring on the third finger of the woman's left hand by her fiancé at the betrothal ceremony. This was based on the belief, explained by Aulus Gellius,[29] that this finger was directly connected to the heart by the nervous system. In Britain the majority of iron finger-rings are solidly made, of large size and mostly hold intaglios, and are usually considered to have been worn by men of some status, despite the tradition amongst some of the German peoples that an iron ring denoted slavery. Skeletal evidence does not reveal a bias for a particular finger for the wearing of rings, so it would appear that the Roman betrothal custom was not widespread in Britain. Nevertheless, the frequent mention of rings on curse tablets suggests that many finger-rings were of sentimental value to their owners.

46 Aemilia's gold finger-ring from Corbridge with possible Christian motto (© Museum of Antiquities of the University and Society of Antiquaries of Newcastle upon Tyne)

Finger-rings came in various forms from simple annular strips to the elaborately decorated, inlaid with semi-precious stones, applied wire or granulation. A narrow band with a small circular cup holding a bun-shaped inset of green glass was a popular trinket ring in the second and third centuries, while in the fourth century an openwork design running around a wide gold band might include a name or a motto. A gold ring set with a cornelian from Vindolanda inscribed *Anima Mea* ('my life') is one of many inscribed rings which were probably presents from husbands to wives or between lovers.

Ear-rings are now known to have been worn by many women in various forms, all designed for a pierced ear. There is no evidence as to how the ear was pierced nor if there was any significance in the operation, bar a passing comment by Tertullian which implies that a girl had her ears pierced when still a baby.[30] Roman writers made derisive comments about the eastern habit of men wearing ear-rings and in Britain it appears to have been a form of adornment largely confined to women. The most common type is a plain penannular ring of gold, silver or copper alloy, sometimes with pendants of glass or stone. A form found in third- and fourth-century coffins has the ends overlapped and intertwined, so would have been permanent or semi-permanent, with pendants ringing the changes. Elaborate gold ear-rings with semi-precious stones in box settings with rilled flanged borders are known, as well as the pendant type known as 'Hercules' club' ear-rings, which Jack Ogden has suggested may have been given as love tokens alluding to the legend of the love-lorn Hercules, who gave Omphale, Queen of India, the trophies of his labours. This type has a wide distribution in Britain from Birdoswald to London and a wide date range from AD 50–150 at Ashstead to the fourth or fifth century at Thetford. It is possible that some of the many studs found on Romano-British sites were worn in the ear, as was the fashion in Egypt, but proof is sadly lacking.

Many of the simpler ear-rings are of similar manufacture to some of the bracelets and finger-rings, being based on decorated single strips of metal or several strands twisted together. This similarity suggests that women wore matching sets of jewellery. It is clear from some of the Egyptian panel paintings that parures were being worn in other parts of the Empire at the same period, although some women clearly preferred to wear a great deal of jewellery whether it matched or not. The individual from Rome who was praised because 'she wore her jewellery without drawing attention to herself' may have been the exception rather than the rule.[31]

Brooches do not appear to have been included in parures but this may have been because brooches were largely utilitarian, and their aesthetic qualities may have been regarded as secondary to their usefulness in holding garments together. The majority of brooches were made of copper alloys: brasses, bronzes and 'gunmetals' with a number tinned or silvered to give a silvery finish. A lack of native sculpture and grave-goods of first century date makes it difficult to envisage how the early brooches were worn by the British and if they were worn by both men and women. Even later in the Roman period it is difficult to assign specific types to male or female wear. It has been suggested that the use of brooches had become less popular by the end of the second century, particularly in female fashions, and at Lankhills it is noticeable that the brooches – all massive crossbow brooches – are confined to male graves. Pairs of brooches linked by a thread or chain appear to have been exclusively female, worn to fasten dresses of the Menimane type. A pair of chain-linked simple silver brooches is known from Great Chesterford in a very early context and a pair of bronze bow brooches from Red House, Corbridge, found complete with a length of bronze chain, may well have belonged to the wife of the Commanding Officer of the Agricolan supply base. Two copper-alloy brooches from the River Tyne at Newcastle are linked by a typically complex chain even though the brooches are not matched. The chain would be fastened to a head loop, which is a feature found rarely on the Continent but a common element of first- and second-century British brooches. There has been some argument as to which way up Roman women wore their bow brooches and much evidence has been put forward to suggest that they were worn 'head' down in a way which looks very odd to modern eyes. However, there is also evidence for the brooches being worn horizontally and it may have been a matter of personal taste.

An unusual item of jewellery, found at Hoxne, Suffolk is a gold body-chain, which consists of four loops of chain which passed over the shoulders and under the arms and were joined in the middle of the back and chest by a plaque, one of which was a gold coin known as a *solidus*, whilst the other had nine gem settings for amethysts, garnets and pearls. It is noticeable that this chain is quite small and could only have fitted a teenager or a slender woman. The chain would have been very costly as it contains nearly 250 grams of gold and it is possible that it was only worn for special occasions or in religious ceremonial.

So far we have concentrated on jewellery of gold, silver, copper alloy and glass but many other materials were used. Iron, for example, does not always survive but is known to have been employed for the manufacture of brooches until about AD 55. The fourth-century Lankhills cemetery has produced nine iron bracelets, all from female graves, and there is an expanding iron armlet from Thameside, London, dated to the first century AD. The Colchester iron armlets are plain, except for one which seems to have been bound at regular intervals with plated copper alloy and carries an annular bead.

More exotically, ivory was also used for bracelets. Lankhills, again, has yielded eighteen, two of which are annular and made from transverse sections cut across the tusk. The rest have bronze or silver sleeves joining two semicircles. Armlets of bone were cheaper and the forty-two from Lankhills are mostly plain with only a few aping the incised decoration of the copper-alloy bracelets. Plain bone bracelets have also been found, but finger-rings and beads of bone are rare finds compared to those of other materials.

Coral may have ceased to reach Britain in any quantity as early as the third century BC, but some necklaces have been found at Heslington Field, Cirencester and Walmgate, York. The necklaces found at Lankhills are either made solely from coral or from both coral and glass beads. They were only found in rich graves and coral is likely to have been an expensive commodity. The Romans regarded it as having magical properties and, when fashioned in the form of a phallus, a powerful charm to ward off the Evil Eye. The British coral objects, by comparison, seem to have been purely decorative.

Amber, also, was more popular in prehistoric Britain than during the first to fourth centuries AD, and it did not enter the Empire from the Baltic in any great quantity after the late second century. The few pieces of amber jewellery which have been found may all be associated with Pliny's comment that amber was very expensive and of special appeal to women.[32] Both Pliny and Artemidorus in the second century noted that for women to dream of amber rings signified benefits to come:[33] it has even been suggested that amber was only worn by women when asleep. Amulets from Fordington Hill, Dorset, and Butt Road, Colchester, have been identified as fertility symbols. Plain amber beads have been discovered at Walbrook in London, South Shields, Lankhills and Icklingham while a fine finger-ring with a relief carving of Minerva was found at Carlisle. A grave group from Walmgate, York, has produced a bracelet of amber and pearl beads.

Pearls were valued for their exactly spherical shape, as well as for their size and white colour; consequently, Tacitus thought little of British pearls, regarding them as undersized and of poor colour but this was probably because the majority were fresh-water pearls rather than by-products of the Richborough oyster beds.[34] They were worn in groups hanging from ear-rings to make a clacking noise like castanets but as pearls dissolve in acid soils they rarely appear in the archaeological record. Only one British ear-ring, from Gloucester, retains its four pearls. As beads they were normally mixed with other materials to make necklaces or bracelets, as at Fordington Hill, where a necklace was made of beads of glass, bone, and both seed and blister pearls.

Apart from pearls, emerald crystals, jasper, sapphires, chalcedony, amethyst, and garnets were used in decorating jewellery, but not in the quantity found elsewhere in the Empire. Cornelian beads, in particular, were rare in the later period and Margaret Guido has suggested that a cornelian necklace from Lankhills was imported from Hungary. The use of jasper was confined to intaglios in finger-rings, while sapphires and emeralds tend to appear as beads well separated by lengths of chain. Garnets are more common and a notable example of a pear-shaped garnet dominates a gold ear-ring from Bath. Many semi-precious stones only appear cut as intaglios, but the Thetford hoard contains amethysts, chalcedonies, garnets, and emeralds used purely for their colour. Rare stones include the use of variscite for a finger-ring from Gadebridge Park and a few beads from York, and chrysoprase beads on a necklace fragment from Colchester. Alternatives to these luxury stones were glass, often used in place of emeralds, and enamel, which was particularly favoured by the northern craftsmen in the second century.

An important group of jewellery in the third and fourth centuries was made of jet and shale. The best-known centre for Roman jet-working was at the Railway Station site at York, where beads and bracelets are known to have been made, but other workshops in the city made pins, finger-rings and pendants. The pendants are either in the form of animals such as bears, or flat ovals with relief decoration of Medusa heads, portrait busts of betrothed couples and family groups (see Fig 8). Necklaces and bracelets were made of beads, or were solid and annular, either plain or decorated with chevrons, continuous spirals or faceting. Finger-rings of jet are found in the same shapes as metal rings, but one type, with a sinuous s-motif running across the centre panel, seems to have been made in jet only. Hairpins adopted the decorative motifs of bone pins with faceted cubes, urn shapes, spheres and male and female heads.

As well as jewellery, spindle whorls, spindles, knife handles, and a few fragments of inlay were also made of jet, and it is noticeable that the majority of items are for female use or found in female graves. Even when one includes the jet artefacts found in Germany only one exclusively male artefact, a scabbard chape from Bonn, is known although on rare occasions male skeletons at Catterick, Brougham and Cirencester have been found wearing jet jewellery. The reason for this bias may be religious as the British finds have mostly been from religious contexts, or because jet, like amber, had a particular significance for women. Pliny related that 'the kindling of jet drives off snakes and relieves suffocation of the uterus. Its fumes detect attempts to simulate a disabling illness or a state of virginity. Moreover, when thoroughly boiled with wine it cures toothache, and if combined with wax, scrofulous tumours'.[35] These comments do not fully explain why jet should be worn or used mostly by women and there is a noticeable lack of fertility amulets among the finds. In Britain the distribution of jet artefacts is largely confined to the east, although there was a major sales outlet at Silchester. This distribution appears to be related to transport constraints rather than tribal preference.

Shale had been worked in Dorset, and in particular at Kimmeridge, without a break since the fourth century BC and continued to be popular even when jet was not in demand. The Kimmeridge factories were very productive, with an emphasis on tables, trays and lathe-turned armlets, the latter following the shapes and motifs of their jet counterparts. At some time in the third century AD a rival factory was established at South Shields using a wide range of black materials, such as torbanite, cannel coal and detrital coals as well as shale, which were gleaned from all over Britain; the output again aped the products of the York factories. This was on a smaller scale and catered to the needs of the women of the military along Hadrian's Wall who wanted armlets, spindles, spindle whorls, pins, gaming counters, and figurines. Shale was not a suitable material for the manufacture of finger-rings but a few were successfully produced, as were some beads.

Jet must always have been more expensive than shale or cannel coal by reason of its limited accessibility, and it is possible that shale, well oiled to give it a good rich polish, was passed off as jet and sold at inflated prices. Yet the shale-working tradition in Britain was older than that of jet and required different techniques to avoid the splitting which occurs when shale dries too rapidly. Shale is only known to have been used regularly for jewellery in Britain and was never popular on the Continent. It is thought to have been referred to by its Celtic name as no Latin term or description has been discovered.

To keep all this jewellery safe a casket was needed. Regina is shown holding open the lid of a solid box with binding at the corners, a decorative crescentic handle and hefty lock, and at York a wooden trinket box was found in a grave, bound with copper alloy, with a lock, leaf-shaped mountings and studs, and containing jet armlets and glass perfume flasks. Strips of ivory, bone and bronze inlay were used to decorate wooden jewellery caskets. An unusual lathe-turned circular shale box with a raised lid seating and a turned ridged lid was found with the Thetford Hoard; a fragment of a similar lid comes from Verulamium. Boxes of shale could not have been locked but the wooden and bone examples usually have lock plates. It is probable that the keys worn as finger-rings were used to secure jewellery caskets and document cases, as well as the toiletry boxes holding the array of cosmetics and perfumes which the well-dressed woman applied before facing the day.

According to Lucian: 'a woman does not just wash away her sleepiness with cold water, and proceed to a serious day's work. No, innumerable concoctions in the way of salves are used to brighten an unpleasing complexion ... a multitude of boxes, enough to stock a chemist's shop, jars full of mischief, tooth powders, or stuff for blackening the eyelids'.[36] Ovid offered advice to young women on how to improve their appearance in order to attract men.[37] In his poem 'On Painting the Face', he started with the basics in the form of a face pack which included ten eggs with an equal measure of vetch to two pounds of skinned barley added to twelve ground narcissus bulbs, gum, 1/6 pound of Tuscan seed and 1.5 pounds of honey. To get rid of spots he recommended 'a remedy taken from the querulous nest of birds: halcyon cream they call it, mixed with Attic honey'.[38] For a toner he mentioned that he had 'seen one who pounded poppies moistened with cool water and rubbed them on the tender cheeks'.[39] Oyster shells mixed with water were recommended by Pliny to improve the complexion. Lomentus, or bean flower, was widely used to smooth out wrinkles and there were many imitations on the market. Juvenal complained, from the husband's point of view, about the use of highly scented night creams and bread face-packs.[40]

Once the skin was improved one could apply foundation. The most popular was called *oesyspum* – a preparation of the sweat and dirt extracted from sheep's wool and available throughout the Empire, although the product of Attica was acknowledged as being superior. A white foundation, known as *cerussa*, made from white lead, was popular and the product made in Rhodes by dissolving lead in vinegar was particularly prized.[41] The analysis of the contents of a small circular tin box, found recently in London, may suggest a similar foundation cream which would have provided a white base coat on which to apply further make-up (Fig 47). Rouge made from ochre or the lees of red wine was the next layer, according to Plautus and Tertullian, and Ovid commented that 'art gives complexion if real blood gives it not'.[42] If blemishes were still visible Ovid advised covering them up with small patches. The face could then be powdered with one of the many face powders available: Ovid recommended those which contained ground roast lupin seeds, white lead, foam of red nitre or Illyrian irises.[43]

From a number of references it is clear that it was the eyes that received the most attention. Tertullian referred to 'that black powder itself wherewith the eyelids and eyelashes are made prominent'[44] Pliny gave a recipe for mascara consisting of bear's fat and lampblack, but also mentioned ants' eggs and squashed flies.[45] Ovid suggested the use of 'powdery ash' and saffron as eye-shadow, and also mentioned that 'by art you fill up the bare confines of the brow'.[46] Juvenal recommended the use of soot to darken the eyebrows.[47]

The literature implies that the use of cosmetics was confined to aristocratic women or their less respectable sisters, and it is difficult to judge whether the ordinary women of the Roman Empire used cosmetics. Evidence of make-up in Egypt and the eastern provinces is well known, and there are hints that the use of cosmetics was widespread among the Celts. As early as 20 BC Propertius

47 Roman ointment pot: small tin container found by Pre-Construct Archaeology at Tabard Square, Southwark, London (Site LLS02)(Museum of London.© Pre-Construct Archaeology)

was commenting: 'even now, mad girl, dost [thou] ape the painted Briton and wanton with foreign dyes upon thy cheek? Beauty is ever best as nature made it; foul shows the Belgian rouge on Roman cheeks'.[48] In Britain a number of artefacts suggest that the use of cosmetics was common, although it is not always possible to say which instruments were used for medical purposes and which for toiletry. The contents of both ointment pots and make-up flasks would have been extracted by long-handled bronze or silver implements known as *ligulae*, hundreds of which have been found with long narrow spoon terminals, bulbous probes for mixing and applying ointments and tiny angled disc heads for extracting small amounts of powder.

Ralph Jackson has identified the boat-shaped pestle-and-mortar sets found throughout the south of Britain as cosmetic utensils used to grind the powders for mineral-based applications, and suggests that their size and shape make them particularly suitable for eye make-up such as mascara and eye-liner. Unfortunately, analysis of the substances left in some of the mortars has not yielded any clear proof. A fragment of a glass vessel shaped like a bird, found at Silchester, has been identified as a flask of the type used in the first century AD for exporting face powders from North Italy.

Scents were used extensively, particularly those made at Capua, and Nero's wife, the Empress Poppaea, is known to have introduced a very strong perfume which was named after her. Phials of perfume were also put into tombs and perfumed oils used to anoint corpses, using an ancient recipe of salt, cedar oil, honey, myrrh, and balsam. Analysis of basketwork found in a barrow at Bartlow Hills has revealed that it contained myrrh or frankincense, while a white substance found in a mid-second-century barrow at Weston Turville has proved to be frankincense.

It is believed that the perfumes used at the dressing table, in the baths and in funerary rites were imported in individual glass flasks known as *unguentaria*, also used for face powders and medical ointments. A squat vessel with a tulip-shaped neck and wide flat base from York has PATRIMONI on the base, which is considered to be the name of the manufacturer of the contents rather than the maker of the vessel. Late first- to second-century *unguentaria* tend to have long necks and conical or globular bodies, while some resemble waisted test tubes. Rarer forms include a ring-shaped bottle found in a grave at York with a bronze mounted casket and jet bracelets and the very long tubular container. with a jet lid and 'dip-stick' found with the fourth-century coffin at Spitalfields, London (Fig 48).

Glass *unguentaria* were mostly of 'uncoloured' glass which is light green in appearance, but tubular examples are known at Gloucester in yellow/green and blue/green, and globular forms are found in bright colours with white opaque spiral trails. Flasks were also made in pottery and metal: a very beautiful bronze example from Catterick is decorated with blue and red enamel and has an internal clip to keep the small knobbed top in position; sadly, this decorative piece ended its career rather ignominiously as a glue pot.

Chatelaines with ointment scoops, nail-cleaners and tweezers are found throughout the province (Fig 49). Tweezers were used by both men and women for removing unwanted hair and Ovid took it for granted that women would remove underarm hair as well as hair from the legs: 'how nearly did I warn you that no rude goat find his way beneath your arms and that your legs be not rough with bristling hairs'.[49] It is from his advice to men that we learn that hair was removed from the legs by the use of a pumice stone.[50] Pliny discussed depilatory creams made from various noxious substances, such as the blood of a wild she-goat mixed with sea-palm, and powdered viper or she-goat's gall.[51] Hares' blood was used to prevent plucked hairs from growing again. Luckily, Ovid, despite his encouragement of the use of make-up and depilatories, felt that their application should be a private act carried out behind locked doors.[52]

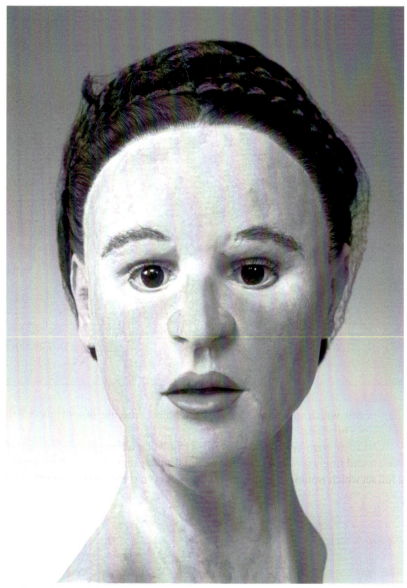

48 Reconstruction of lady found in a sarcophagus at Spitalfields, London (© Museum of London)

Lucian saw cleaning the teeth as a cosmetic practice rather than a matter of oral hygiene.[53] Ovid suggested that a man should make himself attractive to women by ensuring that his teeth 'be clear of rust' and took it for granted that women would clean their teeth: 'why should I enjoin that no laziness leave the teeth to darken'.[54] Powdered horn was the main ingredient of tooth powders, although oyster shell ash was also used, as were the ashes of dogs' teeth mixed

49 Chatelaine from London which includes all the tools required by a woman at her toilet; nail cleaners, tweezers and cosmetic scoops.
(© Museum of London)

with honey, which must have defeated the object. The use of toothpicks was acceptable in public.

False teeth were available, made of gold or ivory, although these have only been found singly or wired as a pair and it is unlikely that a dentist could supply a full set which would allow the wearer to eat or even speak. The false teeth were wired into place with gold wire, which was also used to anchor loose teeth to their neighbours.

Some cosmetic surgery was carried out, mostly removing slave brands from freed men and women. However, the raising of slack eyelids and patching of mutilated ears, lips and noses are recorded, although the lack of efficient anaesthetics must have limited such surgery to cases of dire need.

There was a great deal of interest throughout the Empire in new ways of dressing the hair, to the extent that Ovid commented that it would be easier to count the acorns on an oak tree than to list the number of different hairstyles in fashion in the first century.[55] That British women were just as fashion-conscious as their Mediterranean counterparts is clearly shown by finds of hair in gypsum burials and by sculpture. To keep up to date, women will have studied the portraits of empresses on coins and sculpture, travellers will have been questioned closely on their return from Rome and the wives of newly posted officers and civil servants relied upon to bring the latest ideas. Even so, it is likely that Britain would often be several years behind the times, and some hair-dos would continue to be popular despite the dictates of fashion (see Fig 48). Ovid advised women to stick to styles which suited their faces: 'an oval face prefers a parting upon the head left unadorned ... Round faces would fain have a small knot left on top of the head so that the ears show'.[56]

During the Republic it had been considered improper for women to resort to artificial aids to improve their looks, and most females wore their hair gathered into a simple loose knot at the back of the head. This style continued to be popular among the less fashion-conscious, even when very complex modes were in favour, and Tertullian considered it to be a suitable style for a Christian woman.[57] On a sculptured head of the late second or early third century (Bath 2) the woman has her hair parted in the centre, framing the high forehead, and drawn back behind the ears in a homely bun; Aelia Sentica at Low Borrow Bridge also has a centre parting with her hair tucked behind her rather prominent ears, whilst a tombstone from High Rochester shows the bust of a woman wearing her long straight hair drawn back into the nape of her neck. A young woman or goddess portrayed in stone from Aldborough wears her hair in a Greek version of the bun: very wavy with a centre parting and a raised braid over her forehead held in place by a piece of ribbon.

The head of hair discovered in a fourth-century burial at the Railway cemetery at York had been twisted into a loose bun which would have covered the whole of the back of the head (Fig 50). It was held in place by a couple of jet pins with cantharus-shaped heads. Mantinia Maerica preferred to wear her bun on the top of the head and cover it with a bonnet, but the mother and daughter on a tombstone from Halton Chesters leave their topknots uncovered (Halton Chesters I).

Women with social pretensions will have followed the lead of the empresses as closely as possible, so we cannot tell if a head from Bath (Bath 3) is a portrait of a member of the imperial family or an aristocratic citizen. The hair is parted in the middle and wound into a roll around the head, with the back hair plaited and looped into a clubbed ponytail of the type which Lady Evans called a 'catogan'. This particular catogan was carved separately and is now missing. Other strands of hair are wound over the head and a ringlet hangs down the side of the neck. The fashion is similar to that favoured by Agrippina I, the wife of Germanicus, and the two-piece hairstyle may confirm that this is an imperial portrait, as the statues of empresses often had some of the hair carved in different stones so that alterations could be made to keep pace with changing fashions.

Only one sculptural example of the complex hairdressing of the Flavian court is known from Britain, although a number of bone pins have been found decorated with elaborately coiffured busts, and a tiny gold bust from Richborough has curls across the forehead with the rest of the hair piled up under a net. The head of a woman from Walcot (Bath 4) is carved to twice

50 Auburn hair wound in a bun and secured by jet pins, found at the Railway cemetery, York (© York Museums Trust (Yorkshire Museum))

life-size and may portray an empress. The hair is divided into lots of thin plaits coiled into a heavy chignon at the back of the head. At the front a high diadem of bubbly curls, probably of false hair arranged over a frame, towers above the face. This was certainly not a style to be attempted without the aid of an accomplished hairdresser armed with curling tongs. Such a hair-do would have had to have been slept in overnight, as it would have taken a great deal of time to achieve, and if the style was copied in Britain it must only have been by those of the highest rank. A version may be seen on a wooden head from Llanio, where the hair has been divided into a series of plaits from the forehead and pinned into a flat bun at the back of the head. The effect is smoother and less fussy than the head from Walcot but would also have required the assistance of a hairdresser to be successful. Another example from York (York 3) shows a woman wearing her hair in a series of braids wrapped around the head with one wide plait starting from the forehead and running back over the crown, but unfortunately this may be a nineteenth-century import. The discovery of two six-strand plaits of brown hair at Poundbury may indicate a local fashion or, alternatively, may reflect the Roman custom of dividing a bride's hair into six parts fastened at the back of the crown.

The visit of Julia Domna to Britain in AD 208–11 led many British women to adopt the Syrian style of hairdressing, with the hair hanging in crimped waves on either side of the face and taken in a large roll up the back of the head (see Fig 13). The roll may have been interlaced with ribbons. Candida Barita wore her hair in this style at York, as did the figure behind Volusia Faustina on a tombstone from Lincoln, while Faustina herself wore the slightly later style which retained the crimped waves but rolled her back hair into a small tight knot at the nape of her neck.

In the mid-third century a variation on the Syrian tradition appeared, where the waves left the ears free but the back hair was carried in a single strip or a band of small plaits straight up the back of the head from the nape to the crown. This has been called the 'helmet' style, as it recalls a crested helmet. A good example of this fashion can be seen on the woman's head from Fishergate, York (York 2), and it was also affected by Aelia Aeliana and her companion.

Several of the styles known in Britain bear no resemblance to the styles of the empresses and may reflect an independent British tradition or local fashions. Decimina, from York, has her wavy hair parted in the centre and arranged in two long braids hanging loose down her back, and partly covering her ears. 'Ved ... ic ..', a tribeswoman of the Cornovii, has very thick hair which falls forward on either side of her face in two braids which reach to her lap. Sepronia Martina wears her long hair loose, but at the age of six she may not have been old enough to wear her hair up. Her mother, Julia Brica, has her hair combed back without a parting and tied at the nape of the neck. Shoulder-length hair is worn by Aurelia Aureliana from Carlisle (see Fig 38), as well as by the mother on a family tombstone from York (York 4), while another woman (Bewcastle 2) appears to wear her shoulder-length hair curled up at the ends. Short hair was preferred by the daughter of Blescius Diovicus and an anonymous woman (Halton Chesters 1). Ringlets appear to have been largely the prerogative of goddesses: Venus is often portrayed with her hair in a chignon with ringlets falling to both shoulders, although a bunch of auburn ringlets has been found in a York burial.

A head from Lansdown, Bath (Bath 1), is dressed in a most peculiar way, although it is possible that the hair is shown covered by a cap. The hair seems to have been secured in a flat bun at the back from which strands have been brushed forward into a roll framing the face. However, the arrangement bears some resemblance to an object of woven hair-moss discovered at Vindolanda, which has been identified tentatively as a wig or head-dress but may equally be a helmet cover as worn by Batavians. A similar object is known from Newstead.

False hair was often resorted to, either in the form of complete wigs or as extra tresses, particularly in the Flavian period when, as we have seen, the hairstyles were elaborate and required bolstering. Black hair from India was so popular that the government in Rome included *capilla Indici* among the commodities on which customs dues had to be paid. The blonde locks of the Germans were also popular, so some women may have sold their hair to supplement their income, while Ovid mentioned female prisoners-of-war having their hair cut off to supply the wig-makers[58] A chestnut wig has been discovered in the catacombs of Rome and a coil of false hair attached to a piece of leather is known from Les Martres-de-Veyre in France, but the hair found so far in British graves appears to have belonged naturally to the deceased. An exception may be some long brown hair which, according to the excavator, was found 'plaited and coiled around' in a cremation urn at Rainham Creek and could have been a hairpiece.

If one's hair was not the requisite colour it was always possible to dye it. Tertullian objected to women dyeing their hair with saffron,[59] whilst Ovid referred to women dyeing their 'whitening locks with German juices'.[60] Pliny and Martial described a dye invented in Gaul and used in Germany, called 'Mainz soap'.[61] This was a mixture of goat-fat and beechwood ash, which probably worked like a tinting shampoo. There are also references to 'Batavian foam' and 'Wiesbaden soap-tablets'. Propertius denounced those who dyed their hair with 'lying hue', but henna is known to have been extensively used.[62] Diodorus Siculus commented that the Celts washed their hair in lime water, which would have lightened the colour as well as stiffening the hair.[63] Tertullian, however, was against even washing the hair, as he warned that 'the force of the cosmetics burns ruin into the hair; and the constant application of even any undrugged moisture, lays up a store of harm for the head'.[64]

British women seem to have had an advantage over the women of Rome, as the coveted red hair was commonplace: Tacitus commented on the red hair of the Caledonians[65] and Cassius Dio recorded that Boudica had 'a great mass of bright red hair ... to her knees',[66] but brown and blonde hair has also been found in the Poundbury cemetery. There has been some discussion as to whether the predominance of red hair from graves is simply the result of melanin oxidation, but research on hair from Poundbury would seem to suggest that such 'oxidation' effects rely on the hair being red to start with. A head of hair and its associated plait from the same cemetery may give archaeological evidence for hair dye. The burial is likely to have been that of a man who wore his hair in a plait 18 inches (45 cm) long. Under the microscope the surface of the strands is pitted, as bleached hair would be. Unfortunately, when the hair was submitted for analysis the results were ambiguous – the only hint of artificial dye being an unexpected trace of nickel, a substance used in modern chestnut hair dyes. The pitted surface of the hair strands could also be the result of using curling tongs. Several of the styles mentioned above would have required the hair to be artificially curled, particularly the crimped waves of the Julia Domna style. The iron curling tongs were heated in braziers and even if the hairdresser didn't over-heat the tongs their use would have had an adverse effect on the hair; many fashionable women would have lost their hair at an early age because of overheated curling tongs.

Hairpins provide the best evidence that hair was worn piled up. Hilary Cool has described how pins became popular very rapidly in the first century AD, suggesting that hair was worn loose or braided before the invasion, although some Iron Age graves at Danes Graves, Driffield and Garton Slack have produced pins which could have been worn in the hair. They also reflect changes in style: the complicated towering fashions of the first and second centuries required long pins, while the simpler styles of the third and fourth centuries only needed short pins. The longer pins may have protruded some distance from the hair so that their decorated heads could add to the effect: some of the more elaborate have glass insets, beads fitted over the shanks, or pendants. Others have heads in the form of human busts, hands, vases, animals, and birds as well as religious symbols. One from London has the full figure of Venus standing on a Corinthian capital (Fig 51). In the later period pins were made in coloured materials: York, for example, has produced pins in gold, crystal, glass, silver, jet, and copper alloy as well as bone, and several sites have revealed bone pins stained red with madder or green with copper salts, which would have produced an attractive effect of dots of colour in the hair.

Bone and bronze are the most common materials for hairpins found today but it is likely that there were large numbers made in wood, either in the elaborate forms seen in bone or, at the bottom of the social scale, whittled from twigs. Metal pins tend to have straight shanks but those of bone, jet and shale, and presumably wood also, often expand in the middle to counteract the weakness of the shank. Bone, shale and jet pins have been found with reshaped ends – clearly if one snapped a hairpin it was worth re-sharpening.

Pins are found wherever women passed – road surfaces, domestic buildings and public buildings – as it is easy for such pins to slide out, particularly if they were used to fix buns low at the nape of the neck (Fig 52). Large numbers are found in bath-houses, either because women pinned their hair on the top of the head whilst bathing or lost them when rearranging their hair afterwards.

Few other hair decorations are known. Some jet and shale rings have been identified as ponytail restraints and illustrations from the Eastern Empire suggest that some coils of bronze were used to hold small tufts of hair on top of the head or at the sides. At Lankhills a pin was found on a child's brow where it may have secured an ornamental band. A pin found in a similar position in a grave at Butt Road, Colchester, recalls the hairstyle of the bust from Aldborough. Alice bands and ribbons of braid are presumed but traces are elusive, except for a decorated headband found in Grave 323 at Lankhills and the tabby headband found in Grave 530 at Poundbury. The band from Lankhills was of leather with six bronze-gilt scallop-shaped mounts sewn into position on either side of four yellow glass discs held in bronze frames. Comparable headbands have been found in Hungary, southern Bavaria and Gaul. A bone strip from Dunstable, thought to have been a hairband, is now considered to have been a necklace. At the upper end of the market a complex object from a child's grave from Southfleet has been identified tentatively as a hair ornament on the evidence of parallels from Palmyra whilst at East Hill, Dartford a Roman coffin was found to contain a female skeleton whose hair 'was a light brown colour, aparently clubbed at the crown of the head, and fastened with a brooch or bandeau of pearls'.

Early combs were single bone or antler plates with rounded backs and teeth cut along one edge. This type is not well represented in Britain, although there is a late Iron Age example from Ghegan Rock, Lothian. A preferred type was a

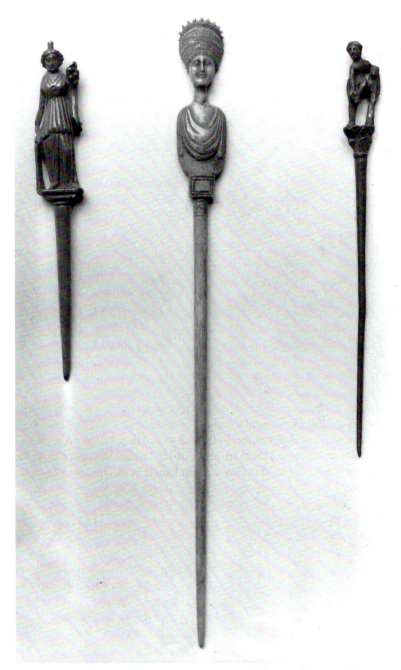

51 Silver and bone hairpins. The more expensive pins could be very elaborate and depictions of deities and empresses were popular: the bone pin on the left depicts Fortuna, while the silver pin on the right shows Venus. (© British Museum)

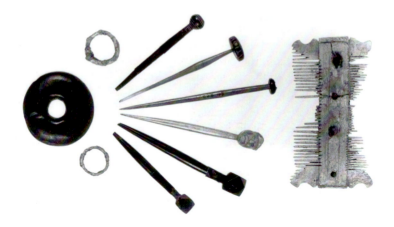

52 Roman hairdressing aids (© Museum of Antiquities of the University and Society of Antiquaries of Newcastle upon Tyne)

rectangular sheet of boxwood with teeth cut into two opposing edges, those of one side often being coarser than the other, like a nit comb. In the late first or second century, in an attempt to make a longer type of comb, plates of bone or antler were positioned side by side and fixed by a riveted bar along one edge. These were more popular in the eastern parts of the Empire, only appearing in any numbers in Britain at Richborough in the fourth century, where triangular-backed combs were preferred, many decorated with stamped dot-and-ring motifs and incised borders. In the late fourth century rectangular combs with a central 'handle', outswept ends and zoomorphic terminals appear in the south-east of Britain, with a few examples from York.

From the third century double-sided composite combs became common in Britain. These had rectangular strips holding the plates in the centre, the teeth being sawn after the plates were fixed. In the fourth century the decorative endplates became increasingly zoomorphic in appearance, as can be seen in the examples from Lankhills, twelve of which can be dated to after AD 365. The majority of combs were made of wood, bone or antler but a few survive in horn and bronze; iron combs seem to have been used only for dressing hides or weaving.

Once one's hair was dressed to one's satisfaction it was wise to secure it under a net, a fine example of which was found at York. Alternatively, animal fats were often used to keep the hair in place once the waves had been created.

In order to dress the hair neatly or apply make-up an essential piece of equipment is a mirror and these were available in various shapes and sizes. The most common were small rectangular or circular sheets of polished metal held in wooden frames or set into toilet-box lids. Circular mirrors with handles attached at one point of the circumference are known from Iron Age Britain, with magnificent examples from Desborough and Birdlip. These Celtic mirrors are noted for the elaborately incised or enamelled decoration on the backs and the handles. Roman examples can be seen on a tombstone from Chester (Chester 4) and falling from the hand of Venus on the Rudston mosaic. A complete hand mirror was found in 1973 at Whitchurch and proved to be of an alloy of copper and tin called speculum. It is circular with a series of holes around the edge and concentric rings on the reverse. The handle, which was originally soldered at the joint, is tapered with elegant moulded decoration. Traces of wood suggest that it was buried with its case.

Lidded mirrors are rare in Britain but a circular example is known from the St Pancras cemetery at Chichester. A more complicated lidded mirror was discovered at Coddenham. This is decorated with the head of Nero on the cover and a scene showing the emperor addressing the troops on the underside of the mirror. The largest surviving mirror from Roman Britain comes from Wroxeter: it is a circular mirror of silver with two rosette-decorated rod handles straddling the back with a central reef-knot (Fig 53). This is a particularly ornate example, dated to the late first or early second century, and simpler versions are known from Verulamium and Chester of silvered bronze. Glenys Lloyd-Morgan has

53 Silver mirror from Wroxeter, Shropshire – the largest found in Roman Britain – would have had to have been held by an attendant, as can be seen on the relief from Neumagen (© Shrewsbury Borough Museum Service)

commented that this must have belonged to a very wealthy woman who, like the aristocrat on a relief from Neumagen, had attendants to hold the mirror, which gives a better image if held at a distance.

Pliny referred to the use of glass mirrors, examples of which are known from Reculver and York as well as Ospringe (Kent), where one was found on the hip of a female skeleton and another showed traces of lead 'silvering' on the back. Square frames of decorated lead for glass mirrors are also known from Ospringe, Verulamium and Chester. Despite the paucity of surviving examples, glass mirrors must have been the most common type during the period and were cheaply mass-produced in the Balkans and Cologne. These glass mirrors, however, were very small and would have been most useful for applying make-up. Indeed, it is salutory to consider that most mirrors, whether of glass or polished metal, would have only given a flawed reflection and that, as none have been found larger than a hand mirror, women would have gone through life without ever having seen what they looked like from head to foot or from the rear.

Whether women dress for the men in their lives or to retain their standing among other women is a debate which has raged through the centuries. Ovid suggests that the former was the case in Rome, although he was directing his comments at courtesans rather than respectable matrons. It could be presumed from the evidence of sculpture and artefacts that many women in Britain tried to make the best of their appearance, although the very elaborate dresses and hairstyles and the excessive use of cosmetics and perfumes were probably confined to the middle and upper class women, particularly those with time on their hands. Among the slaves, freedwomen and country women the style of dress and use of cosmetics may have reflected their origins as much as their status or income.

Chapter 6

Religion

It would be impossible to discuss any inhabitants of Roman Britain without reference to their religious beliefs, as these dominated the lives of Romans and Britons alike on both a personal and a political level. This has been described by many writers on the period but the importance of their spiritual life to the female population, and the way in which religion emphasised the gulf between the sexes, has not received the attention it deserves.

Roman religion in the provinces was divided into the official state religions, classical cults, native cults and the exotic mystery religions of the east. The part which women played in these different cults varied between complete exclusion to full participation. To be sure which cults practised in Britain were open to women one has to rely on the sparse evidence afforded by inscriptions, so there are difficulties in judging the extent to which they participated. The cult of the Deified Emperors is a case in point.

It was recognised at an early stage that there was a need to weld together the provinces with their multitude of religious convictions in a way which bolstered the State. This was not achieved by establishing a single state religion and banning all other professions of devotion, but by adding another tier: the cult of the Deified Emperor.[1] As we will see later, this caused difficulties with some people whose religion, such as Christianity, recognised only one god, but was easily absorbed by the majority of the emperor's subjects, who had been brought up to believe in a multiplicity of gods. Even if an individual might have personal difficulties in according the Deified Emperor his full veneration as a god, it would not have offended most religious sensibilities and no doubt many went through the ceremonies in a spirit of civic duty rather than religious fervour.

One of the earliest public buildings to be built in Britain was the massive temple at Colchester, mentioned by Tacitus[2] as being dedicated to the Deified Claudius. The Britons saw this as a symbol of Roman dominance and it suffered accordingly at the hands of Boudica's tribesmen. As part of the drive to Romanise the population several leading citizens were appointed as priests of the Imperial Cult but at their own expense. Although they were in the post for only one year this proved to be a very costly honour, as Tacitus related: 'those who had been chosen as its priests found themselves obliged to pour out their whole fortune in its service'.[3] The *seviri* were wealthy men but this responsibility must have been a drain on their resources and inevitably have affected the domestic budget. Even if women had little active involvement in the ceremonies, the knock-on effect in financial terms will have touched them deeply, and the regulation that the *sevir* was expected to reside near the temple during his year of office must have brought its own problems. Despite the enhanced social standing it brought with it, the post must have been seen as a mixed blessing.

Colchester was not the only town to have a temple erected to the Deified Emperors, although it seems to have remained as the cult centre. Several inscriptions suggest that there was another substantial temple at London, where the governor resided. One of these is the tombstone of the nineteen-year-old Claudia Martina, whose husband Anencletus is referred to as 'slave of the province'. Anthony Birley, in 1979, interpreted this as meaning that he belonged to the *concilium provinciae*, the council to which each community sent representatives every year, and whose principal task was to conduct the annual ceremony of devotion to the Deified Emperors.

In the towns, ceremonies in honour of the Deified Emperors in temples and fora may have been open to women but it would be unlikely that female participation was allowed in any ceremonies held in the shrine of the headquarters buildings in forts, where the statue of the reigning emperor and the standards of the unit were kept. Outdoor ceremonies involving the whole unit and the local populace, at which the Commanding Officer officiated, may have been regular occurrences as part of the programme of Romanisation. No doubt the officers' wives and daughters were expected to turn out on these occasions to set a good example.

The worship of the personified virtues extended the worship of the Deified Emperors into more philosophical areas, and here we have evidence for the direct involvement of women. For example, at Maryport Diana Hermione dedicated an altar to the Emperor's Virtue and at Risingham Aelia Proculina erected an altar to the Emperor's Fortune. Both of these altars come from forts, and the worship of the Emperor's Virtue, Fortune, Discipline, and Victory may have appealed more to the wives and daughters of military men than to those of civilians.

The Roman invaders also brought with them the official state gods such as Jupiter, Juno and Minerva: the Capitoline Triad. These cults in Britain were largely supported by the army and dedications to the Triad by women are rarely found. An exception is an altar dedicated to Juno by Diana Hermione at Maryport. More dedications to Juno might have been expected, as she was the classical goddess who oversaw the lives of women and offered protection during major life events such as marriage and childbirth. A few statues have been tentatively identified as being of Juno but may be more accurately described as depicting empresses in the guise of Juno – a popular conceit. It may be that the women of Britain preferred to rely on their native deities in moments of stress and that Juno was only worshipped by women who had been born in Italy. Minerva, who was patroness of spinning and weaving among other crafts, had several altars erected in her name, although none in Britain by women, and a number of statuettes have been found in both temples and domestic shrines. Jupiter's only dedications by women equate him with the eastern god Dolichenus and bear little relation to his role as a member of the Capitoline Triad.

Other deities brought from Rome include Fortuna, Mars, and Diana. Sosia Juncina, wife of Quintus Antonius Isauricus, imperial legate at York, set up an altar to the goddess Fortuna, while at the other end of the social scale Antonia, the slave or daughter of Strato, dedicated to Fortune the Preserver at Kirkby Thore. No temples to Fortuna have survived in the province but altars and statuettes were often set up in bath-houses where extra protection was felt to be needed whilst one was in a state of undress. Fortuna was a particular favourite in Britain, where she personified Good Luck, appealing to the British love of gambling and their generally superstitious nature; occasionally she was linked with Bonus Eventus as in the dedication by Julia Belismicus and her husband Cornelius Castus at Caerleon. Mars was primarily a soldier's god, but temples for his worship have been tentatively identified at the civilian sites of Barkway, Kingscote, Kings Stanley, Lower Slaughter and Stony Stratford. He was also invoked in his role of Peace-bringer at Ribchester by a woman whose name is now lost,[4] and as Mars Corotiacus by Simplicia at Martlesham. No shrines have survived for the worship of Diana, the divine huntress, but as she was worshipped, traditionally, in a grove, this may not be surprising. A statue of her was found in a late temple at Maiden Castle and she also appears on a relief at Housesteads, but for evidence that she appealed to women we have to turn to an altar dedicated by Aelia Timo at Risingham. This altar was the result of the fulfilment of a vow and it may have been Diana's role as huntress which was invoked – Aelia Timo having taken to hunting in an attempt to while away the time at a remote outpost fort – or her more basic role as a fertility goddess.[5]

On a day-to-day level a woman's religious life was centred on the rituals carried out in the home. The household god was known as the *lar familiaris*, while the *penates* were the spirits of the store-cupboard. *Lararia* could come in many forms, either as niches set into the wall of the house or as miniature temples. The shrines in a shop and house at Verulamium, both destroyed by a fire in AD 55, were cupboards made of tile or stone, while a household shrine at Silchester consisted of a small room with a mosaic floor and a plinth to support the statuettes. *Lararia* were probably a feature of almost every home, although the majority may have been glorified wooden cupboards or shelves on which statuettes could be arranged, rather than architectural elements. One of a woman's daily tasks was to tend the domestic shrine and provide flowers to decorate it on special occasions. She also prepared the food for rituals, such as the purification of a new-born girl on the eighth day and the rites of puberty. A death in the family would also have meant complex rituals involving the whole family.

The cult of the ancestor was shared by Roman and Briton alike. The Romans kept alive the spirit of their ancestors by displaying busts of their deceased relatives in the *lararium*, or elsewhere in the house, and they were also carried at funeral ceremonies. There were traditional festivals which linked the living

141

and the dead, such as the Parentalia in February and the Rosalia in May, when the tombs were decorated with flowers and the whole family participated in a solemn picnic.

Orthodox Roman religion involved numerous rites and festivals for set days of the year when presents were given – Ovid mentions 1 April (the feast of Venus) and 1 March (the feast of the Matronalia) as days when presents should be given, as well as birthdays:[6] any one of these might account for the flagon from Ilchester given to 'little Vrilucolus' by Verina. In Britain only the army is likely to have followed the full calendar, with the civilian population confining themselves to the birthday of Rome[7] and other officially designated days, unless the Roman festival could be linked with the old Celtic feasts which divided the agricultural year: Imbolc (lambing), Beltine (spring), Lugnasand (late summer), and Samain (harvest). Henig has described the scene at a sanctuary on a festival day with sacrifices, theatrical performances, bear-baiting, acrobats, gladiatorial combat and an enormous consumption of food and drink.

Many of the classical religious rites would have been followed by army families and civil servants in the early years but as fewer and fewer Roman citizens of recent Italian descent were domiciled in Britain so these rites would have become less important and replaced or adapted by native, sometimes quite localised, rites.

At the end of the Republic and in the early days of the Empire, most citizens of Rome had a profound disbelief that anything existed after life on earth. By the Antonine period (AD 138 – 92), however, this mood seems to have changed and the rites of inhumation and more attention to the needs of the deceased indicate a more hopeful attitude. Henig has indicated that the Lullingstone temple-tomb, the Holborough sarcophagus and the fashion for surrounding the corpse with gypsum are indications of this trend. The Celts, on the other hand, had always considered that the soul was immortal and that the afterlife was superior to the bodily life. Iron Age graves throughout Europe were often lavishly equipped with food and drink and other necessities, and this native belief in another world also appears in the early Romano-British graves, although manifested in the provision of Roman artefacts.

After a death the women would have prepared the feasts which were held before and after the ceremony and on set days in the ensuing months. The anniversary of the death would also be marked by a feast, and some cremations at Caerleon were provided with a pipe through which wine could be poured, suggesting that the deceased was expected to participate fully in these meals. There were no markedly different funerary rituals for the sexes, although Lankhills cemetery gives the impression that at some periods and in some areas there were segregated burial plots, and in Britain, unlike the Rhineland, it was more common for the tombstones of women to show the deceased reclining at the funerary feast. There were large family tombs, but an anonymous body buried at York had a formal stone-and-tile mausoleum to herself, with a vaulted roof and a stone coffin, although few grave-goods (Fig 54). Some of

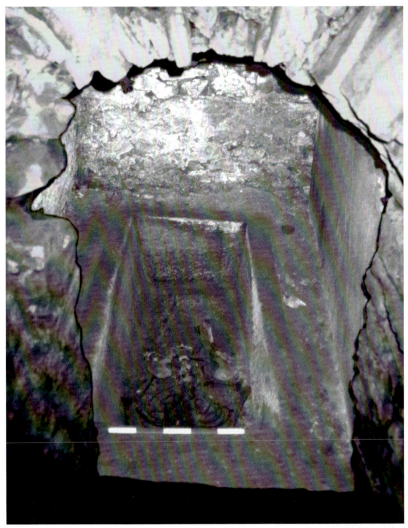

54 Romano-British woman still occupying her stone coffin in a mausoleum beneath York (© Allason-Jones)

her colleagues at York were accompanied by boxes of jewellery, phials of oil or perfume and other items of personal significance. Female graves elsewhere had spindles and spindle-whorls and a high proportion had oil lamps; others had kitchen pots and tableware. What accompanied a woman to the grave may have depended on the customs of her tribe or her personal preference although the ideas of those responsible for her burial or cremation may have influenced the final decision making.

Despite the home comforts provided in the tomb, and the carvings which simulated domestic architectural details, Martin Henig has expressed his doubts that many Romano-Britons expected to last out eternity camped in a hole in the ground even though many memorials, such as that to Aurelia Lupula, end with such phrases as 'may the earth lie lightly upon you'. The images of the next world, however, might make the confines of the tomb pleasant by comparison: Flaminius Pansa's gravestone at Risingham portrays the afterlife as a place where the ground is always frozen[8] and the general impression of Corellia Optata's memorial is of a world of dark and gloom. The worst fate which could be imagined was to wander forever haunting the living, and as a precaution many cemeteries were provided with perimeter fences or deep ditches. As the money found in graves may be to pay Charon to ferry the deceased across the River Styx, so the food may be seen as rations for the journey and the provision of shoes and boots in cremations and inhumations, reduced to a symbolic handful of hobnails at Cirencester, may reflect the thought that one needed a stout pair of walking shoes for the journey to the Underworld. Some people preferred to position this shadowy place above the earth or across the Ocean: the birds shown on Curatia Dinysia's tombstone have been interpreted as representing the flight of the soul, while symbols such as tridents, wind gods, shells and dolphins, as on Aelia Aeliana's tombstone, may also indicate the soul's voyage to the Islands of the Blessed.

The burial rites and beliefs of Roman Britain reveal an enormous variety of religious convictions. Fashions in rituals changed with time but there were also local traditions which meant that the rites followed and methods of burial at Dunstable would bear little similarity to those at Petty Knowes in Northumberland, or those at Lankhills, Winchester, to those at Guilden Morden in Cambridgeshire. In the face of death men and women may have felt that they had more chance in the afterlife if they followed the rituals of their own ancestors, and many foreigners will have been concerned to leave instructions so that even though they were far from home their bodies would receive the correct ceremonies.[9] This responsibility was usually left in the hands of the husbands or wives or heirs of the deceased, and many tombstones reflect these last requests: Placida's tombstone, at Wroxeter, for example, was set up 'under the charge of her husband', presumably following Placida's instructions. Others took no chances and, like Julia Velva's heir, had tombs made for themselves and their families during their lifetime. Some unmarried women, like Pervinca, may have joined burial clubs in order to ensure a decent burial. In mixed marriages the beliefs of the surviving partner could occasionally override those of the deceased; Regina's husband, Barates, put a phrase in his native Palmyrene language on his wife's tombstone, although she herself was British born and bred, and her tombstone in general bears more resemblance to those of Palmyrene women than of her fellow Catuvellaunians.

It is rare, as Joan Alcock has pointed out, to find a burial linked to a specific deity. Exceptions are pipeclay statuettes of Venus found in graves in the south-east. It has been suggested that these burials were of women who had died in childbirth, and a similar explanation has been given for the statuettes, also

55 Pipeclay mother goddess from Welwyn (© British Museum)

of pipeclay, of the Dea Nutrix (nursing mother goddess) found at Canterbury and Welwyn (Fig 55). The Canterbury Dea Nutrix, and a number of Venus figurines from Kent, had been deliberately broken before being added to the tomb, possibly in the belief that in doing so the spirit of the object would also die and so accompany the deceased. A figure of Cupid found in a woman's coffin at London is another deity associated with death, but female figurines found with cremations near Brighton, and from the cemetery outside London's north wall, may have been intended to represent the deceased.

The gods, on the whole, were seen as being more useful during life than after death, providing assistance in times of trouble and protecting their worshippers, and it was in this role that many native deities were invoked. The policy of the Roman state on conquering a province involved no missionary zeal to convert the population to their gods; as long as the inhabitants gave due reverence to the cult of the Deified Emperors and any other officially designated Roman deities, they were free to worship whom they pleased. Exceptions were those cults which involved human sacrifice or denied the existence of multiple gods, both because they could be seen as undermining the fabric of the Empire. Druidism was already an ancient religion in Gaul and Britain when it was discussed by Julius Caesar,[10] and its priests held a great deal of political and social power. The ancient authors depicted the Druids variously as philosophers, magicians, law-enforcers, theologians, bards, and poets, but invariably give the impression that the Druids were men. Who then were the 'black-robed women with dishevelled hair like Furies, brandishing torches' on the shores of Anglesey, whose gibbering so terrified the troops of Suetonius Paulinus?[11] Were these priestesses, or did they belong to the families of Druids? Or were they servants or devotees? It is not clear, but it is possible that they were priestesses: Strabo referred to a group of priestesses on an island at the mouth of the Loire who may have been Druids, and the prophecies to Severus Alexander, Aurelian and Diocletian were all made by female Druids, although by the third century the term 'Druid' may have just indicated someone with magical powers.[12] Pomponia Graecina, wife of the first governor of Britain, Aulus Plautius, was accused by her enemies of practising a foreign religion and there is a suggestion, albeit unlikely, that this was Druidism picked up in Britain.

Claudius was said by Suetonius[13] to have abolished Druidism on the grounds that its followers practised human sacrifice. There is no evidence that this was so and possibly the claim was merely an excuse to mask a shrewd political move which removed a potential focus of rebellion. The cult may not have been totally destroyed but driven underground, and there is evidence that human sacrifice as part of other cults continued in some rural areas, resulting in the crouched infant burials found under the foundations of the corners of Temple IV at Springhead in the second century and the young woman buried under a threshold at Piddington villa. There was also a long history of venerating the human head, which the Celts saw as the essence of the being and the repository of the soul. This belief survived into the Roman period in the representations of heads on metalwork and pottery, as well as on altars, and as simple stone carvings which are referred to as 'Celtic heads'. The discovery of one of these heads in the domestic shrine at Caerwent shows that the significance of the human head continued to be fundamental to some families' religious beliefs.

Under this heading may also come post-mortem decapitation, evidence for which has appeared on over thirty sites. The heads, when found, are normally placed between the knees. It has been suggested that beheading was the cause of death – capital punishment for some crime – but there is little conclusive proof for this and it is hard to imagine what horrendous crime the baby of six months at Dunstable or the three-year-old at Lankhills could have committed. Furthermore, Matthews has indicated that one in ten of the population in the Dunstable cemetery was decapitated; if all these were the result of capital punishment the crimewave in the area must have given cause for alarm. Matthews also mentioned that, although the methods of inhumation varied, all the bodies could be described as having had a decent burial.

Throughout the country more females than males were decapitated, according to present figures. However, at Dunstable the ratios were equal. At a recent excavation in Roman York, 30 out of 56 skeletons (all male) were decapitated (after death). This male bias probably reflects the military nature of the York cemetery although the decapitation rate is unusual for the province and might suggest that they were foreign soldiers. The skeletons date from about AD 200.

Decapitation has also been interpreted as a punishment for practising witchcraft and the severed head and neck of a woman deliberately placed behind the wicker lining of a well at Odell might support this theory. However, Henig has theorised that the practice was to stop ghosts walking,[14] a theory supported by the York evidence. Lethbridge commented that the rheumatoid arthritis suffered by one decapitated female at Guilden Morden had probably made her bad-tempered and therefore likely to return to haunt the living. It was a predominantly rural tradition and as such may reflect less sophisticated beliefs.

Other than the belief in the importance of the human head, the pre-Roman religious practices of Britain and the women's participation in them have left few traces. Except for a few timber shrines of the late Iron Age, there was no tradition of temple building or of imbuing gods with a recognisable human form. Centres for religious ceremonial were often groves in the forest or sacred enclosures, delimited by a boundary ditch and surrounding a focus for ritual such as a tree, a spring or a rock. This belief in the sacred nature of natural phenomena continued in a Roman form in the worship of the *genii loci* – the spirits of the place. Occasionally the location was specified, but was more often left vague. The altar at Lincoln dedicated by a woman in fulfilment of her vow to the *genius loci* shows that, although the majority of such dedications were made by military men, women were also devotees.[15]

Other Celtic gods were named, although their precise function is unknown and it is often difficult to be sure which deities were purely indigenous and which were imported by units or travellers from the other northern provinces. The appeal of these deities to women is also difficult to assess in the absence of clear written evidence. John Mann has suggested that it was due to the Roman invasion that local gods developed into individual personalities and that what seem to be different deities may be merely local names for more widespread divine powers. We know that Boudica sacrificed to the goddess Andraste[16] and Anne Ross has suggested that this goddess might be analogous with Andarte, worshipped by the Vocontii of Gaul. Romana at Great Chesters dedicated to the mysterious Veteres, whose name is variously spelt and may be a group of deities rather than an individual god. Mocuxsoma and Ivixa are also thought to have been female worshippers of Veteres. The small size of the altars and the crudeness of the inscriptions has led to the theory that this religion appealed to people of low social status, and was based on a pre-Roman cult, not necessarily of British origin, whose deity's name could not be expressed accurately in the Latin alphabet.

Nymphs may also have had a pre-Roman ancestry, personifying the hazier Celtic spirits of spring and wood. Specifically named nymphs, such as Coventina, have left no indications of female worshippers, although dedications have survived to anonymous nymphs: one at Risingham reads 'Forewarned by a dream the soldier bade her who is married to Fabius set up this altar to the Nymphs who are to be worshipped', while an altar at Carvoran was erected by Vettia Mansueta and Claudia Turianilla to 'the Goddesses the Nymphs'. A dedication by another mother and daughter, Brica and Januaria, at Greta Bridge seems to conceal the name of the local nymph in the letters NEINE. *Nymphaea* have been discovered in the grounds of villas, for example at Chedworth, where the shrine resembles a garden pavilion, or at Lullingstone, where one room in the house was dedicated as a *nymphaeum*.

Nymphs were often worshipped in groups of three, a trend shared by mother goddesses. Anne Ross has argued that the mother goddesses *(matres)* were introduced 'representationally' into Britain during the Roman period but that the depictions expressed a concept which was already entrenched in Celtic belief: that of a threefold goddess concerned with fertility (Fig 56) and childbirth. Such a triad can be seen in a relief from Cirencester where one mother is suckling a child while the others play with their offspring.

The majority of dedications which survive to the mother goddesses were made by men; a rare exception being the altar dedicated by Marulla at Ribchester. This may mean that men were more likely or in a better position to spend money on expensive dedications rather than that the women were not interested. This, of course, must hold true with all the other altars and religious dedications from the province, as female dedicators are considerably out-numbered by male. It is also possible that religion was largely a family affair, so women relied on the head of the family to make dedications on their behalf. One dedication to the Mother Goddesses Ollototae ('of other peoples'), however, was erected by Julius Secundus and Aelia Augustina, and there is no reason to suppose that they were

56 Triad of mother goddesses with unruly children (Corinium Museum, Cirencester:© Cotswold District Council, rights reserved)

related in any way. Simplicia's dedication to Mars Corotiacus took the form of a bronze statue, while at Carrawburgh Tranquila Severa took the responsibility of dedicating an altar to Cybele on her family's behalf. Women clearly could, if they had the funds, dedicate on their own and other people's behalves.

The surviving evidence for women worshipping in Roman Britain is unlikely to give a full picture. Noticeable by its absence is the devotion of women to female deities, although Ross has commented that 'the function of the goddess must, to a certain extent, reflect the function of the woman, and her most potent and striking characteristics'. There is also a surprising lack of a recognisable British goddess of love; even Venus appears as a fertility goddess (Fig 57) rather than the last resort of the lovelorn. John Clayton suggested that the rings and brooches found in Coventina's Well were thrown there 'by love-sick damsels ... in the hope of obtaining the countenance of the goddess in their views', but it is more likely that such offerings were seen as being appropriate gifts for a goddess, rather than revealing the sex of the worshipper.

Recent finds of curse tablets at Bath and other sites have revealed a rich spiritual life, in which women were fully involved, running alongside the formal rituals. The tablets are sheets of lead on which was scratched a demand for action from the gods. These could be used to ensure luck for someone or to correct one's own misfortune and have been called by Roger Tomlin 'the loser's last resort'. Of those so far interpreted, about 70 are concerned with theft: a 'memorandum' from Uley asks Mercury and/or Mars Silvanus to retrieve a stolen piece of linen for Saturnina, for example (Fig 58). The god, sometimes named, but occasionally left unspecified, is expected to perform like a celestial hybrid of Sherlock Holmes and Gilbert and Sullivan's Lord High Executioner, not only discovering the perpetrator of the crime but also exacting a fitting punishment. In order not to influence the deity by unjust suspicions, many use the formula 'whether man or woman, whether boy or girl, whether slave

57 The goddess Venus as depicted by a native mosaicist at Rudston is surrounded by huntsmen, exotic animals and birds. She appears to have been startled into dropping her mirror by a Triton holding a torch. (© Hull City Museums and Art Galleries)

or free', but some name names, such as Anniola and her accomplices, who are accused of taking six silver coins. The deity could also be offered suggestions as to a suitable punishment, and these give a splendid picture of frustrated fury: Basilia asked that her silver ring be returned and that the thief and any accessories, 'be cursed in [his] blood and eyes [and] every limb, or even have all [his] intestines eaten away'.

Some tablets do not explain the cause of the curse but still express themselves with choleric spleen: 'I curse Tretia Maria and her life and mind and memory and liver and lungs mixed up together, and her words, thoughts and memory: thus may she be unable to speak what things are concealed'. Unfortunately the rest of the curse is missing so we do not know how long the invective continued, nor what Tretia Maria had done to deserve it. This particular *defixio* shows the shadowy line between religion and magic, as no deity is named and the names Tretia and Maria may be reversed – a powerful curse. Some are simpler, such as 'Tacita, hereby accursed, is labelled old like putrid gore', which has a flavour of pure vindictiveness.

Not all the tablets are curses. Examples from Bath are more in the nature of swearing a sacred oath; for example, 'Uricalus, Docilosa his wife, Docilis his son, and Docilina, Decentinus his brother, Alogiosa; the names of those who have sworn at the spring of the goddess Sulis on the 12th of April. Whosoever there has perjured himself you are to make him pay for it to the goddess Sulis in his own blood'. Others ask favours, such as a gentleman at Old Harlow who

58 The curse tablet commissioned by Saturnina at Uley (© British Museum)

petitions 'To the god Mercury, I entrust to you my affair with Etterna, and her own self, and may Timotneus feel no jealousy of me at the risk of his own life blood'. The author of this touching revelation of a love triangle, however, loses some sympathy as on the other side he takes the opportunity to ask Mercury to look after a business transaction!

These tablets reveal not only fascinating personal details of a level of society which rarely leaves any record, but also the business-like relationship between mankind and the gods. If the deities play their part they will be rewarded. A striking example of this is set out in a tablet from Caistor-St Edmund, where the theft of 15 *denarii*, a wreath, bracelets, clothes, a mirror and two pewter vessels is recorded and Neptune told firmly: 'if you want the pair of leggings they shall become yours at the price of his [the thief's] blood'.[17] What Neptune was expected to do with the leggings is left to our imagination but they no doubt joined the rings, cloaks, bathing costumes and other impedimenta which he had also recovered.

Superstition played a major part in everyday life. Tacitus[18] recorded that prior to Boudica's rebellion the statue of Victory fell at Camulodunum and 'women, converted into maniacs by excitement, cried that destruction was at hand'. Seeing visions and interpreting signs was common and we have already seen that Fabius' wife at Risingham and Antonia at Kirkby Thore paid due attention to visions and dreams. Sorcery as an act was illegal because magic could be used to destabilise the settled pattern of society, but the confused thinking behind the curse tablets shows that the situation was not black-and-white and even if the State banned witchcraft a large proportion of the population believed in it and carried amulets as a protection against ill-luck. The phallus, in particular, was a powerful symbol against evil and as such appears on buildings, on pottery and on jewellery: small gold rings found at London and Faversham decorated with phalli may have been worn by the children of the wealthy to ensure their protection. Bells were also used to ward off evil.

The evils against which these amulets were directed were usually nameless and unspecified, but to the living a fear of disease was an ever-present worry. Physicians and surgeons, mostly of Greek origin, are known to have practised in Britain although the only ones known by name were attached to the army.[19] One can only presume that women living in the *vici* had access to these military medical men for their own ailments and those of their children. The civilian situation is less clear, as no inscriptions have survived naming civilian doctors, nor have any buildings been identified as civilian hospitals. In other parts of the Empire physicians were employed by the town councils to provide treatment for any citizen who might require it and there seems no reason to doubt that this system was followed in Britain.

Roman doctors were highly trained and mostly remarkably competent, given their limited scientific knowledge. The treatment of wounds, the repair of broken limbs and many complex operations were carried out with confidence, even if a lack of anaesthetics other than opium, henbane and mandrake, made them ghastly experiences for the patients. Many doctors, such as Soranus, Galen and Celsus, wrote treatises on medical practice which would have been read widely, so patients in Britain could have expected their treatment to be as up-to-date as if they were being treated in Rome or Athens. However, doctors were not expected to act alone: the gods were required to play their part and many people put more faith in divine treatment than in practical remedies; going to see the doctor might be seen as a last resort rather than a first call. This was recognised by the doctors themselves, who did not scorn divine intervention: Abrocomas at Binchester[20] is known to us only because he dedicated an inscription to Aesculapius and Salus, both deities with an acknowledged role in healing. The sick would either make offerings to a god of healing – there were plenty to choose from, both Roman and non-Roman – in the hope of receiving a cure in return, or could visit a shrine famous as a centre of healing, such as the temple of Sulis Minerva at Bath. There are indications that the native goddess Sulis was worshipped at Bath before the Roman invasion, but the magnificent temple erected over the spring was firmly in the classical manner and must have been an overwhelming sight to the sick and lame who visited it. The water at Bath has medicinal properties and is still used for this purpose, but in the Roman period visitors were prepared to make sacrifices to the goddess as part of their cure as well as immersing themselves in the water or imbibing it. Sulis Minerva was expected to cure a multitude of complaints and may have done so in cases of gout, arthritis and rheumatism. In other cases her skill was supplemented by various physicians of differing levels of competence. The stamp for an eye-salve found in the baths suggests that Titus Iunianus, for example, may have had a permanent surgery on the site.[21]

The number of women visiting the shrine is hinted at by the names mentioned on the curse tablets, but some models of parts of the anatomy, known as *ex votos*, such as ivory or bronze breasts (Fig 59), also suggest that Sulis Minerva assisted in female ailments. Fewer *ex votos* have been found in Britain than in Italy or Gaul, but at Wroxeter thirty-five eyes carved from wall-plaster and two from sheet gold indicate a shrine which specialised in eye troubles.

The visitors to Bath or Wroxeter relied on a mixture of practical relief and faith to heal them, but another method in which Greek and Celtic traditions came together could be found at the temple of Nodens at Lydney. This was a temple with an adjacent bath suite and a guest house for visitors, as well as a long narrow building which has been identified as an *abaton* in which the patient slept overnight in the hope of being visited by the god and healed, or at least given a prescription in the form of a dream message which could be interpreted by the priests. Among the offerings to Nodens were statuettes of dogs, an *ex voto* of a miniature bronze arm and a bone plaque of a naked woman clutching her stomach. This temple complex has been dated to the fourth century and might indicate that the emergence of Christianity had not diminished the appeal of the healing gods.

It was in the eastern religions, of which Christianity was one, that women seem to have shown most interest. The only priestess known by name is Diodora at Corbridge, who dedicated an altar in Greek to Herakles of Tyre. Other priestesses must have had full-time employment or officiated on a voluntary

59 Ivory *ex voto* from Bath. The two breasts carved on the front indicate that the petitioner suffered from a breast complaint such as mastitis. (© Institute of Archaeology, Oxford)

60 Bronze statuette from South Shields of a priestess with her head veiled for sacrifice (© Museum of Antiquities of the University and Society of Antiquaries of Newcastle upon Tyne)

basis, as a number of statuettes of women with veils drawn over their heads in preparation for sacrifice have been found (Fig 60).

Some eastern cults had a strong appeal for women. The worship of Isis, for example, had its origins in Egypt and was introduced into Rome as a mystery cult in the second century BC. Its secret foreign nature led to its suppression by Augustus but it was supported by Gaius Caligula, who erected an Iseum in the Campus Martius. Isis was a mother goddess, described by Apuleius as 'the natural mother of all things, mistress and governess of all the elements' who could dispose of 'the planets of the sky, the wholesome winds of the seas, and the lamentable silences of hell'.[22] The cult's appeal lay not in its doctrines, which differed little from those of other mother goddesses, but in the fact that worshippers of both sexes took part in the ceremonies, supervised by professional priests, instead of watching others performing the rituals.

Although the cult demanded abstinence from the pleasures of the flesh at certain times, it was seen in the first century in Rome to be an unsavoury religion which appealed to courtesans, and Ovid offers the excuse of a visit to the Iseum as a suitable cover for an assignation with a lover.[23] However, by the time it reached Britain the cult had become respectable: an altar from London records the restoration of the Temple to Isis by a third-century governor of Britannia Superior, Marcus Martiannius Pulcher.[24] This may be the same temple referred to on a buffware jug of first-century date found at Tooley Street, London, which has *Londinii ad Fanum Isidis* (London at the Temple of Isis) scratched on the shoulder (Fig 61).

Devotees of the cult may have been scattered throughout the province and may not have been able to participate regularly in the rites. There is evidence of followers of Isis at Wroxeter, Silchester, Exeter and Dorchester, and there may have been temples in these towns. An oval amulet of haematite found at Dicket Mead shows Isis with a lion and the god Bes within a frame formed by the Ouroboros, the Serpent devouring its tail. Below the goddess there is a stylised representation of a womb, and around the edge there is an invocation in Greek to Typhon, the elemental force. On the reverse there is a scarab and a second Greek legend which invokes Ororiouth, the spirit which gives protection against women's diseases, and Iao, the Jewish Jahweh. Haematite amulets were carried in pockets or strapped to the thigh to relieve labour pains and this example may have belonged to a woman of eastern descent, although there is no evidence to indicate that she was a slave as has been suggested.[25]

A particularly interesting religious dedication by a woman is that to the Silvanae and to the Quadruviae (the goddesses who presided over crossroads) by Vibia Pacata at Westerwood. This association of deities is characteristic of Upper Pannonia (modern Hungary), but the epithet *Caelestis* which is attached to the deities is of African origin. Eric Birley has suggested that Vibia Pacata had been influenced by the African cult of the Punic Tank, either as a result of her husband, the centurion Flavius Verecundus, having had a posting in Africa, or because she herself was of African origin.

The dedication to 'The Goddess Mother of the Gods' by Tranquila Severa at Carrawburgh, points to another eastern cult, that of Cybele; a theogeny from Carvoran claims that she is the 'Mother of the Gods, Peace, Virtue, Ceres, the Syrian Goddess, weighing life and laws in her balance'.[26] The worship of Cybele was a complex cult which also involved worship of Atys, her lover who castrated himself in her service, in memory of which priests of Cybele castrated themselves during initiation rites. A temple to Cybele and Atys is thought to have existed in London on the grounds of sculptural evidence and others may have been built outside the forts on Hadrian's Wall.

Some eastern religions, like Mithraism, were specifically barred to women, although they would be well aware of the importance of the cult to their menfolk – Julia Similina carefully included Mithraic figures on her husband's tombstone as the widow of a Freemason today might include Masonic symbols. Other cults were open to both sexes: a case in point is the worship of Jupiter Dolichenus. Dolichenus was an ancient Hittite sky-god who was assimilated with the Roman sky-god, Jupiter. This habit of pairing off Roman gods with

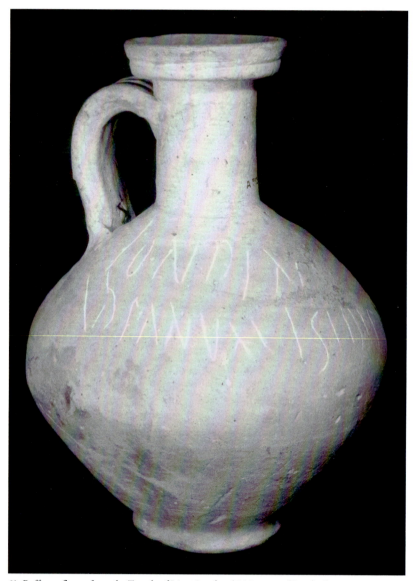

61 Buffware flagon from the Temple of Isis at London (© Museum of London)

those of other lands, known as syncretism, was common and seems to have been an attempt to render the exotic more familiar or to draw foreign elements into the standard Roman framework. Jupiter Dolichenus largely appealed to army officers, who linked his worship with the health and safety of the emperor. The cult never achieved official status but became closely connected with the Severan emperors, and the third century saw an increase in dedications, with temples built at Cirencester, Customs Shrubs and most of the Wall forts. Why the cult should have appealed to women is not clear; possibly the element of emperor veneration was responsible, as neither Magunna at Birrens nor the daughter of Sabinus at Great Chesters appear to have had an eastern origin.

The eastern cult which appealed most to women was Christianity, but despite later claims that it was brought to Britain by Helen, the mother of Constantine the Great, St Paul or Joseph of Arimathea, it is more likely that its origins lay in the visits of traders and merchants. British Christians start to be mentioned in the works of Tertullian and Origen in the second century but the church does not seem to have become openly established until the fourth century. There is a likelihood that individual Christians lived in the province as early as the late first century but anti-Christian sentiment, which lasted until the late third century, will have kept the religion underground. This lack of sympathy may have been a reaction to what Charles Thomas has called 'the stubborn exclusivity of the Christians', which cannot have endeared them to their neighbours, some of whom may have seen the cult as a threat to the delicate balance between man and the gods, to disturb which might result in major natural disasters. It was only after AD 313 that Christians could feel confident enough to build churches, and even martyria, to those like Albinus, Aaron and Julius who had suffered under the persecutions of Decius and Valerian (AD 250–9). By the mid-fourth century textual evidence referring to Christian bishops at London, York, Cirencester and Lincoln, confirms how established the Christian religion had become.

There is not the space here to give a detailed history of Christianity in Roman Britain: interested readers can do no better than read Thomas's masterly and very readable account. However, it is worth noting the effect it had on the women of the province to whom several aspects of the new religion appealed. First, and most important, it offered a more optimistic view of the afterlife than any other religion. This hope of a better world must have attracted people whose lives were often hard and restricted, particularly as this better life was available to everyone, rich and poor, slave and free, male and female. Membership of many of the eastern cults and the classical Roman religions had been denied to the poor because worshippers were expected to donate large sums of money to support a priesthood or stage festivals. Christianity relied on its richer members for practical support: silver vessels for use in ceremonies were donated by the wealthy such as Innocentia and Viventia at Water Newton, but the religion did not close its doors to the poor (Fig 62).

The development of Christianity and its establishment as the state religion had a more basic effect on women than just fulfilling a spiritual need. The belief that it was necessary to preserve the body so that it could be resurrected on the Day of Judgement led to cremation being replaced by inhumation, often with the bodies preserved in gypsum. Even Christian women, however, despite the strictures of Tertullian, insisted on being accompanied to the grave by their jewellery and personal items in caskets: a grave at York, for example, contained *unguentaria* and jewellery as well as an openwork bone plaque which contains

62 Silver vessel from Water Newton inscribed with the Christian *chi-rho* symbol and the names Innocentia and Viventia (© British Museum)

the Christian message 'Hail sister, may you live in God'.[27] Christian symbols and imagery also began to appear on mosaics and wall-paintings as well as on domestic items, such as spoons and bowls, and jewellery, such as the gold finger-ring from Corbridge which carries the motto 'Aemilia Zesis' (Aemilia May You Live) (see Fig 46).

The silver votive plaque from Chesterton in Cambridgeshire which was embossed with a ChiRho symbol as well as having an inscription which reads 'Iancilla fulfilled the vow that she promised', suggests that the worship of the Christian god had much in common with that of the pagan gods.

Christianity had an effect on the appearance and manners of women. Tertullian gave specific instructions as to how a Christian woman should conduct herself: he deprecated the use of make-up, allowed only the plainest of hairstyles, and directed that only the simplest garments of uncoloured cloth should be worn.[28] The increase of infant burials in the fourth century may also be the result of the spread of Christianity as the early Christian writers disapproved of contraception, abortion and infanticide, which may have led to a sharp increase in the birth rate. Lactantius preached that a Christian couple who were too poor to have a family should remain celibate, and that abortion and infanticide were against Christian principles.[29] However, as Valentinian I had to decree infanticide illegal in the Western Empire as late as 370, it would appear that the practice continued.

The number of eastern cults known to have thrived in Britain highlights the difficulties of following one's religion in a foreign country. Many of the cults were brought into the province by the army, and shrines and temples proliferated around forts, so women attached to the army had a reasonable chance of finding a shrine to their favourite deity close at hand or at least other adherents with whom to share their devotions. However, with the number of mixed marriages and the trade in foreign slaves there may have been many women who were cut off from the comfort of familiar ritual, particularly if they were devotees of a cult which involved elaborate ceremonial. The aristocratic lady from Rome, Julia Lucilla, for example, may well have missed worshipping at the Temple of Vesta or the excitement of the Lupercalia, when young men dressed in the skins of sacrificed goats ran through the streets of Rome striking at bystanders with thongs. Even Britons moving around the country might find themselves among strangers who had different festivals and ceremonies, as their deities, by their very nature, were limited to a small locality.

It is, therefore, likely that it would be her religious beliefs which would emphasise to a woman how far she was from home if she married outside her tribe or followed her male relatives to a different area or province. It would be important for these women to meet like-minded people with whom to attend religious services or carry out simple rituals. Even within the family a wife might follow a different religion to her husband, and as family ritual was led by the *pater familias* any children of a marriage would be brought up with the religious beliefs of their father taking precedence over those of their mother. Mothers would have introduced their daughters to those cults which allowed them access or which were confined to female worshippers, but they would have been isolated from their sons when it came to religions which were totally or partially closed to women. Unfortunately, it was these latter groups which had the greatest influence on the social and political life of the province.

Chapter 7

Entertainment and recreation

A woman's day would not necessarily be a round of toil from dawn to dusk. Various entertainments were available to her, both inside and outside the home: time would be spent playing with her children, the household might include numerous pets, the family might enjoy listening to music or playing board games, and there would be other occupations in which she could participate for pleasure and relaxation.

In the cradle babies played with rattles and bells until they were old enough for more sophisticated toys. Dolls, in particular, were popular; a jointed doll of wood found at Hitchin resembles others found elsewhere in the Empire in bone, wood or clay (Fig 63). It was customary in Rome for brides to dedicate their dolls to Venus or the *lares* and *penates* before their marriage as a sign that their childhood was over. Examples found in Egyptian tombs of the period demonstrate that even the rag doll has a very respectable lineage. Other cuddly toys may have been common but have left no trace unless some of the 'pets' seen on tombstones come into this category.

Wall-paintings from Pompeii and Herculaneum show cupids playing games such as leap-frog, blindman's buff and hide-and-seek, which of course leave no evidence for archaeologists to find. A bone spinning top from South Shields and balls, seen clutched in the hands of the young Ertola at Corbridge and Flavia Augustina's offspring, indicate that simple games were enjoyed. Balls may also not have been purely for children: a mosaic at Piazza Armerina, in Sicily, shows two bikini-clad females playing handball with a ball which has clearly depicted seams like a cricket ball, and was presumably of leather stitched in gussets.

Board games have left evidence in the form of the boards themselves and gaming pieces. Many of these have been found in military contexts, as might be expected, but there is enough evidence to suggest that women were also keen players; Ovid was of the opinion that all women should include games of chance among their skills of seduction.[1]

Four games involving the movement of counters on a board are known. *Duodecim scripta* was played on the same principles as backgammon, with two players moving fifteen counters each in opposite directions around a board of twenty-four squares. The moves were controlled by throwing three dice and the object was to move one's own counters to safe squares while knocking off the opposition's isolated pieces. The first player to move her counters around the board won. A pottery board decorated with rows of incised ivy leaves found at Holt is thought to have been a sophisticated *duodecim scripta* board.

63 Wooden puppet from Hitchin, its hinged arms now missing. The hair is dressed in the elaborate style of the Flavian empresses. (© British Museum)

A second game, which may simply have been a version of *duodecim scripta*, was played on a board with six six-letter words arranged into columns of three. Unfortunately, although fragments of boards survive, we have no clear idea of how the game was played. *Terni lapilli* was the Roman version of noughts and crosses played on a square board with nine squares, each with incised diagonals. Boards for this game are known from a number of sites.

The best known of the Roman board games is undoubtedly *ludus latrunculorum* (Fig 64), also known as 'soldiers' as it was a battle game requiring great skill. The pieces were used like the rook in chess and the player's aim was to capture the counters of her opponent by surrounding an opposing piece with two of her own. This game was extremely popular and boards made of stone, pottery, wood and even marble (at Richborough) have been found, with exotic

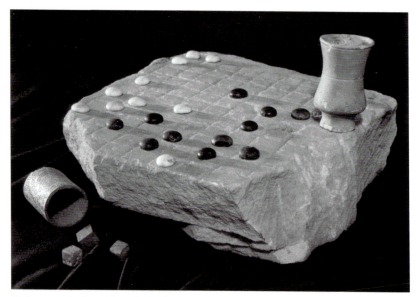

64 Stone gaming board from Corbridge (© English Heritage)

boards in precious metals referred to in literature. *Ludus latrunculorum* was exempt from the ban on gambling because the moves depended on the players' skill and foresight, and it may well have been regarded as a spectator sport as well as a private battle.

Dice were required to play *duodecim scripta* and the word game, and no doubt throwing dice was regarded as a game in itself; it may be that the cube found at Southwark, which has incised letters on its faces reading P/VA/EST/ ORTI/URBIS/ITALIA, was used in such a game.[2] This item was made from basalt but most dice were made in bone and pottery; some of the bone dice found at South Shields and Corbridge were loaded, suggesting that cheating was commonplace. The game for the long bone dice found in Iron Age contexts, mostly north of Hadrian's Wall, is puzzling as their shape would seem to preclude normal methods of dice throwing. However, their use seems to have continued well into the Roman period.

Simple guessing games were played at home. The Emperor Augustus enjoyed playing *par impar* or 'odds and evens' with his family, allotting them 250 *denarii* a piece to make it more fun. The game appears to have needed all the help it could get as one merely betted on the odd or even number of pebbles hidden in the player's hands. In *inicatio* two players each raised the fingers of the right hand, varying the number raised and calling out the total number of fingers raised by both, until one or other guessed correctly. This game still survives in Italy today as *morra*.

Nine men's morris is commonly regarded as a medieval game but stone boards for nine- and three-men's morris have been found at Corbridge and other sites in Britain in Roman contexts. In three-men's morris the squared

162

board has nine points and each player has four counters which are placed alternately on points. The first player to place three counters in a straight line wins. In six-men's morris each player has six pieces and in nine-men's morris they have nine, with the rules and the board becoming correspondingly more complicated.

Literary references suggest that Roman women at all levels of society kept pets for companionship and protection, and coped with the demands for exercise and feeding, as well as the extra housework involved. Animal bones reveal the presence of a large number of cats and dogs in domestic contexts. These may have been kept as guard dogs and vermin catchers but some will have been regarded purely as pets. The evidence of animals found in burials or depicted on gravestones is ambiguous as they could have had a funerary significance, but a tiny dog, like a chihuahua, found in a coffin at Stanwick villa must have been the pet of the deceased. In an early fifth-century family burial at Canterbury, where the parents had been buried seated, one child was on the mother's lap while the family dog had pride of place on the father's lap. Dog pawprints of various sizes are common on tiles and a small dog must have incurred wrath at Lullingstone when he trotted over the wet cement of a low barn wall. A dog jumping up for titbits on a woman's tombstone from Bowness appears to have been a favoured animal. Cats regularly occur on tombstones in Gaul although not so far in Britain, where evidence for their place in the home relies on bones found on such sites as Lullingstone and Vindolanda, and the pawprints of full-grown cats as well as kittens on tiles. A small boy from Lincoln appears on his tombstone with a hare on his knee and another hare is carved on the tombstone of Anicius Ingenuus from Housesteads – both could have had religious significance but it is not difficult to see them as pets. No doubt children also kept beetles, mice and orphan ducklings as they do today and it is tempting to see a dormouse found in the hypocaust of one of the South Shields granaries as the Roman equivalent of the modern family hamster disappearing behind the central heating pipes.

Birds were particularly popular as pets for women. Pliny referred to those which could be taught to talk, such as starlings and magpies,[3] and Indian parrots were imported into Rome. Nightingales and other birds were kept for their song. The child on the Murrell Hill, Carlisle, grave relief is shown playing with a bird on the mother's knee, and Julia Velva's companion and Sepronia Martina both hold birds. The woman on a Bowness tombstone holds a dove in one hand.

Wild animals were captured alive for displays and combat in the arena. Not every town was provided with an amphitheatre – so far only nine in Britain have produced clear evidence of an amphitheatre, although there are possible examples at York and Leicester. It is unlikely that British spectators were often treated to the sight of gladiators in combat with lions, tigers, panthers or rhinoceroses, nor does the *venatio*, or wild beast hunt, appear on British mosaics, which may suggest that it was not to British taste or that there were practical or economic difficulties in producing exotic beasts for popular edification. Bear-baiting and bullfights were a different matter, as there were ready supplies of both animals, bears being a regular export from Scotland. A scene on a beaker from Colchester may show a scene of bear-baiting although no dogs are shown. Hand-to-hand fighting between both male and female gladiators also took place in the amphitheatre and the evidence for regular bouts being held in Britain includes a fragment of graffiti from Leicester which refers to 'Lucius a gladiator' (boyfriend of Verecunda) as well as a gladiatorial helmet from Hawkedon. Various representations on pottery, glass, mosaics and wall-paintings show gladiators in training or in combat, so whether or not women were allowed to witness such displays, they would have accepted the amphitheatre as a part of everyday urban life. Their possible exclusion from the audience may be suspected from various rules and regulations in force in other parts of the Empire: in Rome women had to sit at the back at gladiatorial shows by decree of Augustus,[4] and were barred from watching athletic contests. This was an attempt to prevent disorderly behaviour and may not have been in force in Britain. The amphitheatres were also used to mete out various punishments, including the death penalty, and there is no reason to believe that women were not as keen to witness these treats as their menfolk.

Celtic women are known to have been enthusiastic race-goers, and in the Roman Empire race tracks called circuses were often built in association with amphitheatres. None have so far been identified in Britain, although a pair of parallel walls below Knightrider Street in London has been tentatively suggested as a circus. Again, circuses appear often enough in artistic impressions for it to be concluded that formalised horse racing was known in Roman Britain. Many of the products of the Nene Valley and Colchester pottery factories show chariot and horse races, which may reflect a long British tradition of interest in racing even before the Roman conquest.

Women would also have attended theatrical performances. Theatres are known at Canterbury, Verulamium, Colchester, and Gosbecks Farm, although the latter may have been intended primarily for religious performances. Tacitus also mentions the theatre at Colchester at the time of the Boudican revolt,[5] and there is an inscription referring to a theatre at Petuaria (Brough-on-Humber) although the actual structure has yet to be found.[6] The only completely exposed theatre in Britain is at Verulamium, first built in the mid-first century (Fig 65). It was built in conjunction with a temple and originally served the needs of priestly ceremonial. The earliest building had a central orchestra surrounded on all sides, bar the north-east, by an earthen bank supporting wooden seating. In the north-east section there was a small stage building which was built with a raised wooden floor and a small dressing-room behind. Three aisles led under the stands to the orchestra and wooden staircases against the outer walls allowed the public access to their seats. It was more common in Roman theatre architecture for the orchestra to be semicircular in shape and at Verulamium many members of the audience would have had a poor view of the stage,

65 Theatre at Verulamium. The stage is on the left with the column marking the scenery. (© Allason-Jones)

although a performance taking place in the orchestra would have been visible. This may support the theory that the theatre had a dual purpose, with religious or state ceremonies being enacted in the orchestra and theatrical performances on the stage.

Most of the plays performed in British theatres are likely to have been the same old favourites which had first been played in Rome during the Republic, and there is little evidence for new plays being produced in quantity. Tragic and comic masks were used by actors to identify their characters; an ivory tragic mask from Caerleon and pottery masks from Baldock and Catterick used as decorative appliqué may suggest that bands of travelling players brought popular productions to rural or military areas. The owners of a house at Leicester may have been theatre buffs, as they chose to decorate a room with a painting of tragic masks. A rare figurine from Colchester shows an actor in the guise of Priapus and hints at the Rabelaisian character of the comedies.

The status of an actor was not high and persons of quality who appeared on the stage did so at the risk of losing their standing in society. Actresses were even less highly thought of, and Augustus decreed that no-one of senatorial rank could marry an actress. In Italy the behaviour of actresses had become a byword as early as the time of Cicero and full-frontal nudity was a commonplace on the Roman stage. In Britain there is a fragment of pottery graffiti which links Verecunda, an actress, with Lucius, a gladiator. Unfortunately pots are transportable and we cannot assume that Verecunda or Lucius ever appeared nightly or 'for a short season only' at Leicester. However, it is likely that actresses regularly formed part of the company at Canterbury, Verulamium and Colchester, as well as being members of the smaller travelling groups.

We have little evidence for the proportion of women making up the audience at these performances. If the theatre at Canterbury could hold seven thousand we must assume that it was open to men, women and children, otherwise there would rarely have been a full house. Nor do we know if the sexes were segregated; Ovid's advice to predatory men to 'do your hunting in the round theatre' suggests that they were not.[7] One wonders, however, whether the British theatre bore much resemblance to the Italian in the quality and regularity of the performances, which may often have resembled pantomime rather than high drama, with both tragedies and comedies accompanied by singing and dancing – the audience joining in with favourite verses. In some plays the music got the upper hand and the performance approached modern opera in character, while on other occasions there would be just solo or harmony singing. Soranus referred to the medical fates, such as failure to menstruate, which could befall professional female singers, particularly those who took part in competitions,[8] and there is little reason to suppose that female singers received any more respect than actresses.

Remarkably little is known about music in the Roman period even though it played an important part in religious and civic ceremony as well as public and private entertainment. Ovid, among others, considered it essential for an educated woman to be able to sing and play both the lyre and Phoenician harp,[9] but very few pieces of manuscript have survived to indicate the level of skill required. In Britain we have to rely on rare finds of instrument fragments and representations in art for any impression of the musical life of the inhabitants. Some of the latter are rather fanciful and show deities or nymphs at play: a mosaic at Sherborne, for example, shows Apollo playing the lyre in competition with Marsyas on the double pipes. Orpheus is depicted on several mosaics playing an instrument which could be either a lyre or a *cithara*. The Mildenhall plates show several instruments being played by frolicking bacchanalian revellers: cymbals, tambourines, double pipes and panpipes, all used in the worship of Bacchus (Fig 66).

Religious ritual in general would have involved the use of the larger brass section, such as the *tuba*, the *litmus*, the *cornu* or the *carnyx*, all of which also had a military role. The *sistrum*, a rattle with loose discs strung along metal bars within a small frame, was mostly associated with the worship of Isis, a sect which particularly appealed to women, and is occasionally found decorating the heads of hairpins. Women would therefore have been familiar with the appearance and sound of many instruments even if they were not competent musicians themselves.

Fragments of musical instruments have been found which might indicate that music was also played in the home. A set of bone mounts from the yoke of a lyre was found in a fifth-century context at Abingdon and a similar piece of antler from Dinorben suggests that the lyre had been played in Britain from the late Iron Age. A fragment of ivory from Cirencester has been identified as part of a *cithara*, an instrument like a lyre but with more strings and a broader

66 The Mildenhall silver platter showing a maenad playing the double pipes whilst dancing. (© British Museum)

sound box. Both instruments had their strings attached to bone tuning pegs and were either plucked with both hands or with a plectrum.

A small figurine of a young woman from Silchester holds a *tibia*, a reed pipe which was played either singly or in pairs (Fig 67). An eight pipe *syrinx* found at Shakenoak is inscribed with the name Bellicia, presumably the owner, although her skill is unrecorded. It is possible the graded bone pipes found at Corbridge came from a similar instrument. Small pipes have been found in ivory and bone on several sites in London but, unfortunately, none comes from an unequivocally Roman context. One has a single note and might be more accurately described as a whistle. The pipe found in a well at Ashton, however, was provided with a reed as was the baked clay pipe found at Lydiard Tregaze in Wiltshire.

Some instruments, such as the lute and the harp, both considered by classical writers to be female instruments, have left no record in Britain, so their use has to be assumed from Continental evidence and literary references. More exotic instruments such as the bagpipes – tentatively identified as being played by an

Atys figure from Gloucester – might not bear much relationship to everyday life, but there is some evidence that the *hydraulis* might have been quite commonly played by women as a tombstone from Aquincum in Hungary records the death of Aelia Sabina, a professional singer and musician who surpassed her husband, a *hydraulis* player with the IInd Legion Adiutrix, when she played at the local amphitheatre. The *hydraulis* was a form of organ invented by Ctesibios of Alexandria at the end of the third century BC, in which air was pumped by hand into a chamber containing a bronze bell surrounded by water. Notes were played by opening and closing vents by means of a keyboard, which forced air through pipes by altering the balance of pressure between the water and the air coming from the bellows. The appearance of this instrument is known from clay models as well as remains found at Pompeii and Aquincum in Hungary; its use in Britain is attested by its appearance, standing on a pedestal, as decoration on Castor ware vessels made in the Nene Valley.

Some householders would hire musicians and singers to entertain their guests at dinner whilst others relied on their womenfolk performing traditional melodies. No doubt there were some airs which were never written down but passed through the generations from prehistoric origins, and women from other provinces will have brought with them the melodies of their native areas. Traditional dances are also likely to have been performed, particularly on festival days, although nothing is known of their form. The motif of three female figures dancing in a ring has a very long ancestry and may reflect one of these old dances. In Rome dancing was regarded as respectable only if it took place in the home, professional dancing being regarded as immoral unless it formed part of a religious ritual.

Singing, dancing and playing musical instruments would have been taught initially by mothers, with music teachers hired if affordable or if the children showed aptitude. Mothers were also responsible for teaching their children the elementary skills of reading and writing before both boys and girls were sent to school or had home tutors. In Rome formal education began at the age of seven and this practice may have been followed in Britain.

It is possible that formal education was confined to the middle and upper classes who could afford to pay for schooling or the upkeep of an educated slave. Some children went on to secondary education which was in the hands of Greek *grammatici* who taught in rooms in fora or in private houses. Agricola made it a priority during his governorship of Britain to ensure that the sons of leading Britons received a thorough grounding in the Latin language, rhetoric and literature, and was of the opinion that the Britons were naturally more able than the hardworking Gauls at learning Latin once they set their minds to it.[10] Whether this opportunity was extended to daughters is not mentioned. The only teacher known by name in the province is Demetrius of Tarsus, who took part in the reconnaissance of the Western Islands in AD 82 and is known to have resided in York for a time.[11] He may not have been actively involved in teaching whilst in Britain, but the results of his many anonymous colleagues' efforts is visible in the number of inscriptions, graffiti and lettered pottery stamps which appeared from the first century AD onwards.

The majority of the native rural population will have continued to speak Celtic dialects as their first language, with enough dog-Latin to get by in trading and in any brushes they might have with officialdom. Survivals in the Welsh language, for example, suggest that in some areas Latin was, at best, only a second language and it is possible that some women in the rural backwaters never bothered, or needed, to know more than a few basic words. Contact with merchants and the army helped to spread the Latin language, while those who had had some education or close contacts with officials would have been fluent. Kenneth Jackson considered that the Latin spoken in Britain remained purer and of a more archaic form than that spoken in other provinces simply because it was a second language, learnt with all its grammatical subtleties at school rather than in a looser form at mother's knee. The well-educated minority, and those of eastern origin, would also have been familiar with Greek. By the end of the first century AD the increasingly cosmopolitan flavour of the urban population will have resulted in many languages being heard in Britain with the consequence that a knowledge of Latin would have been essential for efficient communication between people who could have originated as far afield as Scotland, Africa or Turkey. Native Britons are unlikely to have abandoned their Celtic dialects entirely but over the years the increasing number of mixed marriages will have added to the number of families speaking Latin.

The many finds of graffiti indicate that most people could not only speak Latin but also write it down. The cultured pre-Roman Briton, often educated in Gaul, may have been able to write, but the Celtic language had no script – any written Celtic words, as on Belgic coins, were in Latin characters. The concept of ordinary people being able to write was new, therefore, and shows how successful Agricola's policy of education had been. Writing was employed to keep tallies, make lists, ask favours of the gods – the number of inscriptions to native deities indicates that the population presumed that the gods, too, had taken part in this education programme – as well as to send letters and make bizarre comments, such as 'Austalis has been wandering off on his own every day for a fortnight' which is scratched on a tile from London.[12] The new-found skill was also used to write obscenities on wall-plaster at Leicester, showing familiarity with slightly more than mere text-book Latin. Graffiti, however tends to be confined to urban sites and rarely appears in the country, which may reflect social factors or the limits of education.

A number of letters have survived, mostly from military men, but three examples from Vindolanda show that women also sent and received letters. These letters are all that survive of what seems to have been a regular correspondence between Claudia Severa, wife of Aelius Brocchus, and Sulpicia Lepidina, wife of Flavius Cerialis, prefect of the ninth Cohort of Batavians. One letter invites Sulpicia Lepidina to Claudia Severa's birthday party and is written by a scribe but with a postscript added by Claudia Severa herself: 'I shall expect you, sister. Farewell, sister, my dearest soul, as I hope to prosper, and hail'. This has been described by Bowman and Thomas as the earliest known example of a woman's handwriting in Latin, as even the literate regularly used scribes.

The Vindolanda writing tablets, in general, indicate that letter-writing for purely personal reasons was common and that families kept in touch over great distances by this method. Sons in the army regularly wrote home asking for food parcels or extra socks. So far no love letters have come to light although, no doubt, they were also common, and the love of a woman called Armea apparently moved one lovesick youth at Binchester to express himself in hexameters on the tiles he was making, foreswearing all other women. Ovid referred to confidantes carrying letters concealed in their bosoms, stocking tops or shoes, and even goes so far as to recommend the use of new milk and 'stalks of moistened flax' for secret writing.[13] Most letters, luckily, were inscribed in wax or written in ink on wooden tablets or papyrus. A number of styli have been found but only a few bronze pens and iron nibs; quills or brushes may also have been used. Inkwells of pottery, metal and glass are also regular, if not common finds, using ink of carbon black mixed with gum and water.

Writing tablets which have survived intact consist of rectangular leaves hinged together in pairs or in sets opening out like a concertina. The letters were tied shut with string and sealed with wax or lead, stamped with a personal seal, so that they could travel without anyone but the recipient being able to read the contents. The name of the recipient was written on the outside and occasionally that of the sender was added. One letter from Vindolanda is unusual in that the text is written on both sides of a single piece of wood, like a postcard. Sending the letter depended on finding someone reliable who was travelling in the right direction, possibly an easier task for the female relatives of the military than civilians.

Letters were not the only reading matter available. Books were written on papyrus and stored in cylindrical boxes (the lid of one has been found at Housesteads) and some wealthy families may have had small libraries. Through these books Britons would have been introduced to the classical writers. In 1978 Barrett published a catalogue of allusions to the *Aeneid* of Vergil found in the province. These include a wall-painting from Otford showing Turnus riding out to battle, and mosaics from Lullingstone and Keynsham, which both relate the tale of Europa's abduction by Jupiter in the guise of a bull. Barrett considered that, whereas many of the depictions of the *Aeneid* might be explained away as the result of pattern books or the use of well-known phrases or sayings, the Lullingstone mosaic indicates a personal knowledge of the story on the part of the owner of the villa as it is accompanied by a couplet commenting on the scene. He also concluded that the composition of this couplet indicates that the author had had a thorough grounding in the works of Ovid. The works of Vergil appear to have been a popular source of writing exercises – an example from Vindolanda which copies a line from the *Aeneid* was marked as being 'slack' – and as such his writings would have been more familiar than those of other authors. Certainly as a theme in interior design its influence would have extended beyond the literate, as would a quote from *Aeneid* II on coins of Carausius.

After Vergil the works of Ovid were the most popular in the Empire as a whole and there was a revival of interest in his writings in the fourth century. It is less easy to pinpoint his influence on life in Britain than Vergil's, but a scene showing the birth of Dionysus on a mosaic at East Coker, the Labours of Hercules at Bramdean and the life of Cyparissus at Leicester may all have originated in a knowledge of Ovid. There is no reason to believe that reading these classical authors was a male privilege and women must also have read for pleasure and instruction.

The depths to which education had penetrated into society might be seen in references on tombstones such as one from Lincoln where a parent's grief at the loss of a 9-year old daughter is compared with the grief which accompanied the Rape of Proserpine.[14] Eumenius, writing about Constantine's victory in Britain, took it for granted that his audience would have read both Caesar and Tacitus and one wonders what the Britons of the third and fourth centuries thought of these descriptions of their forebears and the invasion of Britain.

For those who could not read, and probably many who could, stories would be related verbally, some giving the British version of history and others continuing a long story-telling tradition of heroes and heroines, gods and battles. No doubt mothers told their children simplified versions of the old tales. Little is known of the sagas of prehistoric Britain except what can be distilled from surviving Welsh and Irish stories but the importance of these stories in keeping alive a tribal identity should not be disregarded even if, in Roman Britain, the tradition of telling the old stories may have survived into the fourth century only in the more remote rural areas. In towns tales told by travellers from distant lands may have taken the place of the native sagas and enlarged the gulf between the sophisticated town dwellers and the simpler rural inhabitants.

One form of entertainment which would be familiar in both town and country, appealing to aristocrat and slave alike, was gossip. Women from settlements and villas would have looked forward to trips to market to catch up on the latest gossip and those in towns foregathered in the forum or the shops to discuss their neighbours, events and scandals. The best place for a good gossip was the baths, and it was here that women of different racial origins, ages and status would have been most likely to meet and exchange opinions, as well as beauty tips and recipes.

Bathing to the Romans was not just a matter of hygiene; it was a relaxation, a social activity in which one met one's friends, ate and drank, took exercise and transacted business. The authorities saw bathing as such a civilising activity that the provision of public bath-houses was made a priority and substantial civic baths were built as soon as towns were established. Villas, too, had bath suites or separate bath-houses erected as soon as the inhabitants could afford them and the lavish decoration expended on these indicates that it was a matter of etiquette to offer one's guests a bath.

A bath-house consisted of a series of rooms graded in temperature (Fig 68). The bather, once divested of clothing and wrapped in a linen towel, moved from room to room getting progressively hotter until reaching a steamy room like a Turkish bath, where dirt was sweated out and scraped away with a metal blade called a *strigil*. Scented bath oils were used but not soap, and after immersion in a hot bath the pores were closed by a quick plunge into cold water. Women might bathe naked or wear a two-piece bathing costume, like a bikini, although the more sedate matrons preferred a shift or a capacious towel.

Hadrian and other emperors issued edicts forbidding mixed bathing, possibly in vain. Modesty was otherwise catered for in the larger establishments, such as Huggin Hill in London, by separate suites for men and women, children usually bathing with their mothers. In the smaller baths arrangements were made for specific opening hours for the sexes. In Rome the sixth to eighth/ ninth hours were reserved for women, with the rest of the day for men. At Vipasca, a mining district in Portugal, the terms of the lease stipulated that the baths were to be open for use by women from daybreak to the seventh hour at a charge of one *as* each.[15] Balsdon has indicated that the charge for women was often more than for men, which seems a little unfair as female bathing establishments were rarely as well appointed and were usually kept at a lower temperature. This matter of temperature, however, may be explained by the popular theory that bathing in very hot water was not good for women or for the more prosaic reason that steam makes the hair go frizzy. Subsidies from public benefactors meant that only a nominal charge needed to be made at the main public baths, and children, soldiers and slaves were usually admitted free.

The legionary fortress baths at Caerleon were clearly open to women and children, as can be seen from the finds discovered in excavation. Some of these people may have been the dependants of the garrison but it is likely that the

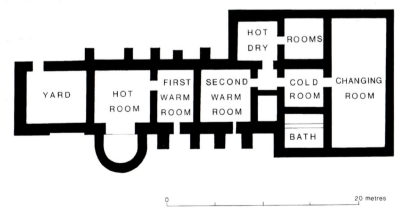

68 The baths at Halton Chesters show the sequence of heated rooms in a Roman bath-house (© D A Welsby)

local residents were also allowed, even encouraged, to use the facilities. A lead bath ticket found at Caerleon indicates that some control was kept over the comings and goings of the civilian customers. All the forts along Hadrian's Wall were provided with baths for the use of the military and it has been suggested that some were enlarged in the third century to accommodate the increased numbers of wives and children. Certainly provision must have been made at an early stage for the wives and families of the commanding officers to have a bath; women such as the senator's daughter Julia Lucilla at High Rochester are unlikely to have given up the pleasures of bathing without a fight even if, as Pliny mentioned, 'sitting baths' were used for day-to-day washing.[16]

Private bath-houses in villas would have been for the use of the whole household, not just the landowner and his immediate family: possibly mixed bathing was more usual *en famille* than in public baths. At some sites there is a bath suite in the main building and a separate bath-house but whether this catered for a division of sexes or a division of class is not clear. It may be that the bath-houses were intended for the farm-workers and their families with access also allowed to local villagers.

The social aspect of bathing is particularly notable in villas as it formed part of the entertainment offered to an honoured guest, but some baths appear never to have been fired, remaining as status symbols rather than useful fixtures. Firing private baths may have involved considerable expense but experiments have shown that, like hypocausts, once the furnaces were lit it was more economical to keep them going. It follows, therefore, that villa inhabitants may have been in the habit of bathing every day rather than having the baths heated once a week, or alternatively the baths were fired only rarely, on special occasions.

Private baths are known in town houses but are comparatively rare. Such was the multiplicity of public baths that private suites may have been regarded as unnecessary luxuries, or possibly the population preferred the sociability of mass bathing. Baths would have been very crowded: Wacher has estimated that in a town like Leicester with a population of between three and four thousand even a weekly bath per person would result in nearly five hundred people a day using the baths, that is fifty or sixty an hour. With such numbers of clients it is hardly surprising that various traders converged on the baths. Seneca referred to the sale of ready-made snacks[17] and at Caerleon the remains indicate the consumption of food which could be eaten in small portions with the fingers, such as chicken legs, chops and shellfish. The other services available included massage, hairplucking, dentistry, medical advice, and the repair of clothes, while bath oils and the other accessories of bathing would also have been on sale. At Caerleon there is even evidence of a goldsmith working on the premises, possibly selling or repairing jewellery.

The large number of clients also led to crime and 'bath-house thieves' were a recognised problem as bathers had to leave their belongings unguarded if they were not accompanied by a slave or could not afford to pay an attendant. The curse tablets at Bath refer to several thefts of clothing or jewellery. One could also lose one's shirt through gambling: gaming counters, dice and boards have been found in profusion in bath-houses and there is evidence at Caerleon and Exeter that cock-fighting bouts were laid on by the management. These extra facilities may have been confined to male bathers, the women indulging in more sedate activities. The picture painted by the number of handicraft tools found at Caerleon is of the women sitting sewing or making braid while they gossiped and sweated, although many will have taken the opportunity to shave their legs and cream their faces. Martial describes the particularly unlovely sight of a female called Thais who, 'in order craftily to substitute for such a reek another odour, whenever she strips and enters the bath she is green with depilatory, or is hidden behind a plaster of chalk and vinegar, or is covered with three or four layers of sticky bean flower'.[18]

The entertainments discussed so far have been rather sedentary and there is little evidence of women participating in more energetic pursuits for pleasure. A dedication to Diana, goddess of hunting, by Aelia Timo at Risingham may be a reference to at least one woman using hunting as a way of keeping herself amused. Although there are no sculptural representations of women hunting or fishing for sport, some may have done both as part of their food-gathering role. Skating may have been a winter pastime as well as a means of transport: skates made from the *metapodia* or *radii* of horses have a long history stretching back into the Bronze Age, with several examples known from Iron Age contexts. Sledges made from *radii* and *metapodia* of cattle, unfortunately, come from undated contexts but examples have been found from the late Hallstatt period on the Continent and it is possible that they were used in Britain.

In Italy much attention was given to gardens and gardening, and many leisure hours were spent out of doors. Unfortunately, excavation in Britain has tended to concentrate on buildings and has largely ignored the ground in between, so archaeological evidence for horticultural enthusiasm is limited. The most extensively excavated garden, and the most impressive, is at the first-century palace at Fishbourne. To build the residence a rectangular platform of land had to be levelled, which involved filling in part of the harbour and diverting two streams. This impressive engineering feat meant that extensive gardens could be laid out on level ground but it left large areas of stripped, ill-drained clay which had to be prepared very carefully before planting, particularly in the formal garden in the central court. As a result the bedding trenches when excavated showed black against the orangey clay, revealing a formal pattern down both sides of the central path as well as edging the lawns or gravelled areas. These trenches probably held low box hedges.

The bedding trenches form regularly spaced niches, either to avoid uninteresting straight lines or to frame statuary or ornamental shrubs in the manner illustrated in Italian wall-paintings. In the north-west corner of the garden a large pit filled with topsoil was found (Fig 69), probably the bedding trench for a tree screening the awkward junction of the two building wings as well as providing visual interest. The eastern side of the garden was more elegantly

175

69 The bedding trenches in Fishbourne palace garden showed up clearly against the natural clay and gravel in excavation(© Fishbourne Roman Palace/Sussex Archaeological Society)

laid out than the northern or western, possibly because it formed the backdrop to the principal view from the terrace in front of the west wing. Close to the east path a row of post-holes packed with stones alternating with loam-filled pits was found, which may hint at a trellis supporting climbing plants designed to screen the entrance hall until the final approach – a dramatic visual device much appreciated by the Romans. It is this formal planning which gives the gardens at Fishbourne their typically Roman atmosphere and implies that they must have been designed by an immigrant landscape architect, well-trained in contemporary gardening techniques.

The south garden may have been designed as a 'natural' landscape to merge with the countryside on the opposite side of the salt-water inlet. This is the only garden in Britain to suggest that some of the larger villas might have had great parks in the eighteenth century English manner. In Italy landowners such as P. Cornelius Scipio Aemilianus Africanus Minor and Decimus Brutus Augur had had pleasure grounds as early as the late second century BC, modelled on the eastern *paradeisoi* and Hellenistic public gardens.

The arrangement of the wings at Fishbourne villa creates five small internal courtyards or peristyles. In Italy these were seen as extensions to the house; areas for dining or lounging in fine weather. Diodorus referred to such gardens as 'a useful device for avoiding confusion when crowds are present',[19] and they were filled with flower beds, statuary and fountains which the owner could show off to guests. Unfortunately, little is known of the five peristyle gardens at Fishbourne; on the evidence of gardens in Pompeii and Herculaneum, however, it is likely that they were laid out rather formally in smaller versions of the great courtyard garden.

At Frocester villa the gardens were not laid out until the fourth century and consisted of two formal flower beds near the house, a hedge and two long beds on either side of the approach road. Again the bedding trenches had been dug into the stone and gravel of the courtyard and filled with topsoil which contained sherds of pottery, bits of animal bone and small items of jewellery, suggesting to the excavators that the gardeners had used composted kitchen refuse and that the women of the villa had taken an interest in the garden. It is not clear whether the area of the courtyard was laid out to lawn or was gravelled, although there were grass verges between the flower beds and the drive.

Mention has been made of box hedging, but for an indication of the other plants grown in Romano-British gardens we have to rely on pollen analysis. Silchester has revealed mallow, rose, violet, ox-eye daisy and white campion as well as various types of buttercup, speedwell and other plants which may have been regarded, then as now, as weeds. At York there is evidence of heather and red campion, as well as such horrors as stinking mayweed, deadly nightshade, hairy buttercup, stinging nettle, and the lesser nettle. Alcester has produced columbine and London corncockle and corn marigold, which must have been imported from the eastern Mediterranean. Even without exotic imported species a garden could have had a very impressive display, particularly in the spring, with native plants such as irises, honeysuckle, snowdrops, violets, daffodils, primroses, and bluebells; later in the year windflowers, bellflowers, cowslips, forget-me-nots, foxgloves, globeflowers, marguerites, pasque flowers, pinks, and scabious would be in flower.

There are also several species of rose native to Britain, but none were listed by Pliny as being worthy of note. He preferred the roses of Praeneste and Campania, although he allowed that the Milesian rose had a good fiery red colour even if it was not a prolific bloomer.[20] Pliny and Varro[21] both gave advice for taking cuttings and recommended the correct soil for the best results, so it is possible that some immigrants to Britain may have brought cuttings of their favourite roses for their gardens.

Whilst many plants will have been grown for display in the garden and particularly for their pleasant smell, a number will have been intended for cutting. A pottery vessel from London has been identified tentatively as a flower vase and simple flower arrangements can be seen on wall-paintings from Rome, suggesting that flowers were used for domestic decoration. Aurelia Aureliana is shown holding a bouquet on her tombstone(see Fig 38), which may be an allusion to the custom of decorating the tombs of the recently deceased with flowers at the festival of the Rosalia. Cut flowers were also in demand for other festivals, banquets and weddings, either loose or wound into garlands. These would have been grown commercially as well as domestically, although no plant nurseries of the Pompeian type with rows of broken *amphorae* used as seed trays have so far been found in Britain.

At Fishbourne there was a kitchen garden in the north-west corner, immediately adjacent to the ovens. Every villa would have had a large kitchen garden to supply the kitchen with its needs and, according to Pliny, 'it was immediately concluded ... that a woman was a poor housewife when the kitchen garden – for this was considered to be the woman's department – was badly cultivated.'[22] At Latimer a formally arranged garden with an orchard and vegetable garden beyond shows the blend of formal aesthetics and practicality typical of Roman taste.

In towns the atrium houses will have incorporated peristyle gardens of the Italian type with vegetable gardens and orchards in vacant building plots. Houses IIIS, IIS, and VIIS at Caerwent, for example, had peristyle gardens, IIIS having a statue base opposite the main entrance to the east wing. In the larger towns, where there was less space, the Italian habit of growing kitchen herbs and flowers in window boxes may have been introduced, and roof gardens may also have been popular.

The planting of flower gardens indicates that the householders had reached a certain social level where there was no economic need for all their land to be utilised for growing food. It also suggests time to design the arrangement, supervise the gardeners and wander about, appreciating the sights, smells and sounds. How was this leisure time available? In the more extensive establishments enough slaves will have been kept to ensure that the day-to-day tasks were undertaken and a few lucky women will have had little to occupy their hours except the pursuit of pleasure. In other homes the womenfolk will have been run off their feet trying to cope with the kitchen garden, the cooking, the children, and helping their husbands in their work. Yet even they would have had occasions when they could relax. There was no concept of a regular weekend off or annual holidays, but certain days were set aside for religious festivals and once the formal ceremonies of the day were over the rest may have been free. These days seem to have occurred on average about every ten days. To many women, particularly slaves, these days may have made little difference to the amount of work which needed to be done, but some festivals will have attracted travelling traders and entertainers like a medieval fair, and these would have provided diversion.

Some of the wealthier families may have adopted the Roman habit of moving to a second home in the country or at the seaside in the warmer months but the majority of women will only have travelled any distance when following their husbands or masters in career moves. Another reason for travel might have been to visit a famous temple or shrine of healing, such as Bath or Lydney, for a cure. Evidence is beginning to emerge, however, that women travelled for social reasons, such as a visit to the theatre or amphitheatre or a party. The writing tablet found at Vindolanda, which Claudia Severa had sent to invite her friend Sulpicia Lepidina to her birthday celebrations, appears to presume that her guest would travel some distance to be at the party. Around AD 100 – 05 the possible places within easy travelling distance of Vindolanda were limited and all were at least half a day's march away, so we might assume that Sulpicia Lepidina was not expected to walk. Some women will have travelled on horseback; a skeleton of a woman from Bradley Hill seems to suggest that she was a rider, but most of the sculptural depictions of women on horseback are of the goddess Epona sitting either astride or sideways and cannot be taken as evidence that riding was a regular means of female transport. The best saddle horses would inevitably be reserved for cavalrymen, hunters or dispatch riders, and if women did ride it was more likely to have been on a mule or donkey.

Another method of travel was the carriage, of which several types are known to have been used in the Empire. The wheels were made of wood with iron tyres and as none of the carriages were sprung, travelling in them must have been an uncomfortable business, even on the excellent surfaces of the Roman road system. The subsequent jolting might explain why Soranus recommended horse-riding and light carriage exercise as useful aids to convalescence and helpful during pregnancy.[23] Litters, carried by men or mules, were a common sight in Rome but it is not known if they were ever popular in Britain.

A relief from Shirva in Scotland has been interpreted as showing a woman reclining in a canopied carriage drawn by a mule, but could equally show a high-backed couch with the animal and wheel present in a symbolic role. Gaul, Hungary and Italy have produced some delightful reliefs showing couples or families driving along in carriages but none so far have been discovered in Britain (Fig 70).

The ordinary person who did not have access to a carriage or a mule would have had to walk or hitch a lift, or series of lifts, from traders' waggons.

Anyone wishing to indulge in foreign travel would have found it a relatively simple business, as there were no customs barriers for private travellers to cross. From Britain to Turkey, northern Germany to North Africa one could use the same language, the same currency and be expected to abide by the same general

70 Relief from the church of Maria Saal, Austria, showing a covered wagon. Fitted with beds like a modern caravan, these were used by families and merchants travelling about the Empire. (© Foteca Unione, Rome)

laws. An elaborate network of roads with inns and posting stations linked the towns and cities, and merchant vessels would usually take passengers if the price was right. How many women availed themselves of these facilities is unknown but many will have only done so when accompanying their husbands or joining them on a foreign posting, as did Claudia Rufina, a British woman living in Rome in the first century AD whose charm and manners were applauded in an epigram by Martial. There is a theory that Egeria, a nun in the fourth century who travelled to the Holy Land, was by birth a Briton and, although her birthplace is doubtful, her urge to travel may not have been unique. Certainly British women are known all over the Empire: for example, Lollia Bodicca at Lambaesis in Algeria, and foreign women from Sardinia, Greece, Raetia, Gallia Narbonensis, Aquitania and Italy are attested in Britain. This gives a picture of continual movement but this is likely to have been confined to a minority of the population with the majority of women never travelling further than their nearest market town.

The way they could spend their leisure hours emphasises the difference between the urban women and the women of the country districts, as well as between civilians and army wives. In the large towns women will have been able to attend theatrical and musical performances, as well as contests in the amphitheatre or circus. They would also have been able to spend time at the large public bath-houses with all the added side attractions, and no doubt street life, markets and fairs would have had considerable entertainment value. It is unlikely that an urban woman in Roman Britain ran the risk of being bored, whatever her class. In the smaller towns, villages and villas there was less opportunity for formal entertainment and women will have had to entertain themselves and their families at home with music, story-telling and dancing, with occasional trips to larger centres. There may, of course, have been compensations in country life, such as gardening and walking, hunting and hare-coursing.

It was the women of the military who ran the most risk of boredom. These women were often very far from their homelands and the companionship of family and childhood friends, as well as the entertainments linked to the religious or tribal festivals they were accustomed to. Women attached to military units which were garrisoned at one fort for a long time or which moved as a unit would have made lifelong friends and developed a settled social life; those whose menfolk were transferred as individuals, such as centurions, would have had to make new friends constantly and find new sources of entertainment to counteract their loneliness. Although *vici* housed jugglers and other entertainers, these may have appealed more to male tastes than to those of the wives and daughters of prefects or centurions. In the frontier zones there would not even have been the compensations of a garden or activities outside the fort, unless accompanied by guards. Entertainment for many of these women would have been limited to board games, music, reading, playing with their children, and conversation with their household servants or other wives, as well as corresponding with other women in similar situations.

Chapter 8

Finale

The end of the Roman occupation of Britain is traditionally dated to AD 410, when the Emperor Honorius wrote to the city fathers telling them that in future they would have to provide for their own protection.[1] Britain had already been subject to raids from several directions for some years and few women living on the coast can have slept soundly in their beds. Most towns had been provided with fortifications as early as the late second century, but initially these had been intended to protect people and property from brigands and outlaws, and did not prove their real usefulness until the fourth and fifth century raids by Saxons, Jutes, Franks and Picts. Some coin hoards deposited in the late 260s and 270s may reflect the fears brought about by the Saxon raids – fears which led families to hide their valuables and treasured possessions. The destruction suffered by some towns (Colchester, Chelmsford), villages (Park Brow) and villas (Preston) show that these precautions were justified. In the fourth century even small settlements, such as Margidunum, were provided with walls, and an inscription from Dorchester-on-Thames referring to a *beneficiarius* of the Governor may suggest that some housed police posts.[2] Towns which already had defences improved them at this time and there is some evidence for the strengthening of town garrisons.

The general sense of insecurity at this time must have caused distress to many women and might be compared to the tensions felt in Britain during the Napoleonic era or during the Second World War, when again there were constant fears of invasion. Women living in the towns may have derived some comfort from the increased defences but otherwise would have been fearful for their husbands, who faced the possibility of having to defend their homes and families. Britain was also racked by internal dissensions caused by localised peasant revolts, and was occasionally caught in the cross-fire of the power struggles between ambitious generals and would-be emperors, as for example when Constantius wrested London back from the troops of Carausius and Allectus.

In the country women will have had less protection from invaders as most villas lacked defensive walls. The villa at North Wraxall, on the evidence of bodies and architectural fragments flung down a well, seems to have been destroyed by enemy action in the early fifth century, and country folk will have lived in daily fear of having their homes attacked and burned (a fate suffered by the villa at Great Casterton), their food crops and stock captured, and themselves or their families raped, killed or carried off into slavery. In these circumstances most women will have preferred to have kept their families under their eye all the time.

Between AD 378 and 388 the number of new coins being minted was drastically reduced and the use of coins for daily transactions appears to have been increasingly rare. This may have been due to the difficulties in transporting the cash but was more likely the result of the periodic inflation which affected the Empire as a whole. The modern reader needs no description of the effect of economic inflation on daily life. The rise in prices and the difficulties in obtaining basic essentials must have been exacerbated by the destruction of stock and crops by raiders and a barter system may have developed. It could have been the lack of cash with which to effect repairs which led to the abandonment of the majority of villas or the evacuation of the owners, who sought safety in the towns, the old hillforts or even Gaul. Some villas such as Bignor fell into decay, while the ruins of Great Casterton were taken over by squatters, possibly dispossessed refugees from other villas or settlements.

The insecurity of the times and the rate of inflation also affected the merchant classes and craftsmen, particularly the potters. The steady decrease in pottery in the archaeological record during the fourth and fifth centuries suggests that factory owners had had to pay off their work-force and housewives to replace their broken pots with wooden or leather vessels. Unemployment will have taken its toll in many families and having to 'make do and mend' will have become a way of life even for women of some pretension.

In the military north the situation was even more complex. We have already seen (Chapter 2) that there is some difficulty in identifying the accommodation of the women and children of the military in the third and fourth centuries. The activities of various emperors in Gaul and Germany had depleted the garrisons of Britain considerably and the *Notitia Dignitatum* records several British units serving in the Continental provinces as well as in Egypt and the East. The womenfolk of centurions and the other ranks will once again have had to pack their belongings and move to a new land. They were replaced to some extent by German troops and their families, such as the group led by Hnaudifridus at Housesteads, leading to a change in the make-up of the population along the frontier. This population faced innumerable dangers brought about by the uniting of the Pictish tribes in Scotland with the Scotti from Ireland and the Attacotti. People in Wales had already suffered several invasions from Irish tribes and matters were brought to a head in AD 367, with the barbarian conspiracy recorded by Ammianus Marcellinus.[3] Some military men may have thought it wise to evacuate their families to the southern fortified towns or back to their homelands.

In fact, there may have been few soldiers left to hold the northern frontier by the time the troops' pay failed to arrive in AD 410. There was no formal withdrawal of the army from Britain and the fate of the soldiers and their dependants after 410 is open to speculation. Some will have returned to their homelands or made their way to the Continent to join up with other units. Some may have become mercenaries with the local tribes or joined the defending forces of the towns. These courses of action may have appealed more to bachelors than to married men with responsibilities. It is possible that the majority, many of whom were of British descent or had married into local families, were absorbed into the local community, either as farmers or craftsmen.

The early years of the fifth century may have been characterised by a continual movement of population: country people moving to the safety of the towns or the refortified hillforts of their ancestors; refugees escaping from massacres, such as that experienced at Caistor-by-Norwich where excavations uncovered the skeletons of thirty-five men, women and children huddled under the ruins of one house; escaping slaves taking advantage of the confused times; unemployed craftsmen looking for work; foreign mercenaries being hired by townspeople to aid their defence; soldiers making their way home or to a new posting. Throughout the country there would be people on the move, with the women trying to retain some semblance of family routine as they abandoned their homes and belongings through fear or necessity, and struggled to feed and clothe their children and ensure their safety. Evidence from the recent excavations at Birdoswald on Hadrian's Wall indicates that some people gathered together under the protection of a local lord, either renewing their ancient tribal loyalties or forming new ones.

So ended a unique period in British history – a period which had seen Britain at its most cosmopolitan, part of an empire which covered most of the then known world. It is difficult to imagine the impact of Roman rule on the native women of Britain as evidence for their way of life in the periods immediately before and after the occupation is limited. Iron Age Britain gives the impression of being a somewhat introspective country with few people having any interest in the rest of the world; the social unit was the extended family which formed part of a tribe, but there was little sense of the tribes making up a larger entity. Some groups along the east coast, particularly in the south-east, had had trading and cultural links with the Continent but these links had not opened up the rest of the country to merchants or travellers to any great extent.

Women at the time held a respected position as wives and mothers; some, such as Cartimandua, had political status. The Bath curse tablets suggest that British women in the Iron Age may have had a stronger position at law than their contemporaries in Rome, or even their descendants until the twentieth century, and the evidence from excavations might suggest that this position was based on their involvement in the production and supply of food. Despite these possibilities, however, their horizons were strictly limited. Britain was then invaded by an army which represented a major power, and within a generation everything had changed. At first most of the invaders may have been of Italian, Gallic, Spanish or German descent but within a few years the full cross-section of the Roman populace would have been found in the new province. Some of the side-effects of the Boudican revolt suggest that it took at least a generation for intermarriage between invaders and the native women to be accepted, but once accepted, liaisons between Britons and Africans, Pannonians, Gauls, Italians, Germans, Greeks and Syrians became commonplace.

The result was an extraordinary mixture of races and languages. Within a generation a woman whose mother would rarely have met anyone outside her own tribe would have become acquainted with women from all over the world. Even if their facility with the Latin language was limited, the great sisterhood of women will have ensured that they would have been able to communicate on the subjects of most interest to them. Conversations in the privacy of the baths during the hours open to women must have been fascinating as they exchanged their common experiences and opinions. With only a towel around them the differences in race or between free, freed or slave may have been of little importance.

We have sparse evidence as to whether there was any racial prejudice in Britain at this time. It is likely that those of Italian descent would have regarded themselves as superior but the attitude of the other races to each other is not well recorded. A reference to 'Brittunculi' – possibly a disparaging term – on one of the Vindolanda writing tablets[4] may suggest that Britons were not highly thought of by some army personnel. A poem published by the Bordeaux poet Ausonius in AD 382, about the British poet Silvius Bonus, makes a play on his name:

> What? Silvius Good?
> No Briton could
> Be – better he had
> Been Silvius Bad

Again, the implication is that the Britons did not enjoy a good reputation in other provinces, but there is no reason to believe that the incoming women shared these views or that the natives looked down on the newcomers.

Despite the possible camaraderie, the feature which has emerged most strongly from this study is the sense of loneliness which many women will have experienced in Roman Britain. The extended family system provides support for every member of the group, each of whom is aware of their place in the order of things. Young wives can draw upon the experience of their mothers and grandmothers and their children grow up with their cousins: the system may be introspective but it has its strengths. The undermining of the tribal system, the introduction of towns and the recruitment of British young men into the Roman army broke up the extended family units and the native women who moved to the towns would have found themselves in strange surroundings with foreign neighbours, cut off from the assistance of their families. The isolation of many mothers of small children on today's housing estates might be seen as a close parallel. The phenomenon will have been particularly noticeable in the first century AD but may have continued throughout the centuries of Roman rule as the population shifted.

Women from other parts of the Empire who emigrated to Britain will have found much that was familiar, but would not necessarily have been able to find women from their own province or background to turn to for advice or to exchange reminiscences with. They may have found their dress, hairstyles or diet different from those with whom they were in daily contact, and in particular they may have been isolated by their religious beliefs and practices. It is only too easy to overestimate the ease with which a provincial used the Latin language or the extent to which it was used. To the majority of women it would have been a second language, with all the frustrations inherent in having to use a second language all day and every day. Many women will not even have shared a first language with their husbands or children. They may have been able to make themselves intelligible when shopping or in general conversation but in more complex situations misunderstandings may have been a regular hazard.

The impact of the invasion on the physical appearance of the country is undeniable. The building of roads, forts, towns, frontiers and villas were obvious changes. The long-term cultural impact is less easy to evaluate and the speed with which the trappings of Roman domination broke down in the early years of the fifth century may suggest that Romanisation to most people was at best only skin deep. Even after four centuries the bulk of the population rapidly returned to the ways of their ancestors: even the new religion of Christianity disappeared so effectively that it had to be reintroduced by missionaries several generations later. In the process the average woman may have lost a great deal. With the breakdown of the Roman legal system the women did not regain the position they appear to have enjoyed in the native British code, but became even more dependent on the men in their family. Power was now estimated in terms of land owned, and a woman's place in the new scheme of things was to provide land by means of her dowry. The collapse of the coinage system meant that there was less to spend on fripperies and the closing of the trade routes deprived people of many materials, semi-precious stones, spices and foreign ideas that had previously been imported into the country. Britain retreated into itself once more and the horizons open to women were drastically reduced. Many generations had to pass before women in Britain could once again have an extensive knowledge of the world and a balanced view of their place in it.

Women mentioned in the text

Any letters in the names which are uncertain due to the incomplete state of the stone or to abbreviations used by the inscriber are in brackets.

ABUDIA MEGISTE: seller of grain and pulses at the Middle Stairs, Rome. *CIL* VI. 9683 (tombstone)

AELIA AELIANA: died in York. *RIB* 682; *CSIR* I.3, no 40 (tombstone)

AEL(IA) AMMILLUSIMA: widow of Marcus Trojanius Augustinus. Lived at Stanwix. *RIB* 2029 (tombstone).

AELIA AUGUSTINA: co-dedicator of an altar to the Mother Goddesses Ollototae with Julius Secundus, at Heronbridge. *RIB* 574

AEL(IA) COMINDUS: wife of Nobilianus, a military decurion. Died at Carrawburgh aged thirty-two. *RIB* 1561; *CSIR* I.6, no 194 (tombstone)

AEL(IA) MATRONA: 'incomparable' wife of Julius Maximus, *singularis consularis* of the Cavalry Regiment of Sarmatians; mother of Marcus Julius Maximus; daughter of Campania Dubitata. Died at Ribchester aged twenty-eight. *RIB* 594 (tombstone)

AEL(IA) PROCULINA: dedicator of an altar to the Emperor's Fortune at Risingham. *RIB* 1211

AELIA SABINA: wife of T Aelius Iustus, *hydraularius salariarius* of IInd Legion Adiutrix at Aquincum in Hungary, who was herself a skilled singer and musician. *CIL* III.10501

AELIA SENTICA: wife of Aurelius Verulus who died at Low Borrow Bridge, Cumbria aged 35. *Britannia* XXIII (1992) 312, no 8

AEL(IA) SEVERA: widow of Caecilius Rufus. Died at York aged twenty-seven; her coffin was paid for by her husband's freedman, Caecilius Musicus. *RIB* 683; *CSIR* I.3, no 64 (coffin)

AEL(IA) TIMO: dedicator of an altar to Diana at Risingham. *RIB* 1209

AEMILIA: owner of a gold *interasile* finger ring, which was lost at Corbridge; possibly a Christian. *RIB* 2422.1

AHTEHA: daughter of Nobilis. Died at Corbridge aged five. *RIB* 1180; *CSIR* I.1, no 66 (tombstone)

AICETUOS: wife of Limisius; mother of Lattio. Died at Old Penrith aged forty-five. *RIB* 936 (tombstone)

ALBIA FAUSTINA: widow of Flavius Agricola, soldier of VIth Legion Victrix. Lived in London. *RIB* 11 (tombstone)

ALOGIOSA: presumed wife of Decentinus; sister-in-law of Uricalus and Docilosa; aunt of Docilis and Docilina. Swore an oath against perjury at Bath. *Tab Sul* 94 (lead tablet)

AMABALIS: daughter of Firmus, daughter-in-law of Ramnio, wife of a retiring soldier specifically named on a military diploma found at Middlewich, Cheshire. Her husband retired in the summer of AD 105. *RIB* 2401.3

AMANDA: widow of Julius Julianus, soldier of IInd Legion Augusta. Lived at Caerleon. *RIB* 360 (tombstone)

ANNIOLA: accused of stealing six silver coins at Bath. *Tab. Sul.* 8 (curse tablet)

ANTONIA: daughter or slave of Strato who dedicated an altar to Fortune, the Preserver at Kirkby Thore, Cumbria 'following a vision'. *RIB* 760

ARMEA: girlfriend of tile-maker at Binchester. *Britannia* IX (1978), 477, no 27; *RIB* 2491.146; 2491.147 (tile graffiti)

ATINIA TYRANNIS: seed seller at the Porta Triumphalis in Praeneste, Italy. *CIL* XIV, 2850 (altar)

AUR(ELIA) AIA: daughter of Titus from Salonae in Dalmatia; wife of Aurelius Marcus in the century of Obsequens. Died at Carvoran aged thirty-three. *RIB* 1828 (tombstone)

AUR(ELIA) AURELIA(NA): wife of Ulpius Apolinaris. Died at Carlisle aged forty-one. *RIB* 959; *CSIR* I.6, no 493 (tombstone)

AURELIA CAULA: sister of Aurelia S...illa. Died at Great Chesters aged fifteen. *RIB* 1745 (tombstone)

AURELIA CENSORINA: widow of Aurelius Super, centurion of VIth Legion Victrix. Lived at York. *RIB* 670 (tombstone)

AUREL(IA) CONCESSA: died on a villa estate at Branston, Lincolnshire. *Britannia* VI (1975), 212 (tombstone)

AURELIA E(G)LEC(T)IANE: wife of Fabius Honoratus, tribune of 1st Cohort of Vangiones; mother of Fabia Honorata. Lived at Chesters. *RIB* 1482 (tombstone)

AUR(ELIA) LUPUL(A): mother of Dionysius Fortunatus. Died at Risingham. *RIB* 1250 (tombstone)

AURELIA NAIS: wholesale fish-seller at the warehouses of Galba in Rome. *CIL* VI. 9801 (inscription)

AURELIA PHILMATIO: child bride. Died in Rome aged forty. *ILS* 7472 (tombstone)

AURELIA ROM(ANA): sister of Aurelia Sabina. Lived at Greta Bridge. *RIB* 749 (tombstone)

AURELIA SABIN(A): sister of Aurelia Romana. Lived at Greta Bridge. *RIB* 749 (tombstone)

AUR(E)LIA S...ILLA: sister of Aurelia Caula. Lived at Great Chesters. *RIB* 1745 (tombstone)

AURELIA VICTOR(I)NA: daughter of Aurelius Victor. Died at Halton Chesters. *RIB* 1435 (tombstone)

AURELIA ...ILLA: widow of Gracilis, centurion of XXIInd Legion, from Upper Germany. Lived at Piercebridge. *RIB* 1026 (tombstone)

AVITA: daughter of Carinus, citizen of Rome, and his wife Romana; sister of Rufinus and Carina. Lived at Dorchester (Dorset). *RIB* 188 (tombstone)

BASILIA: victim of theft who petitioned Mars at Bath for the return of her silver ring. *Tab Sul* 97 (curse tablet)

BELLICIA: owner of a pottery *syrinx* at Shakenoak. *Britannia* IV (1973), 332, no 30 (graffiti)

BOUDICA: wife of Prasutagus, king of the Iceni; mother of two daughters. Tacitus *Annals* XIV; Tacitus *Agricola* 16; Cassius Dio LXII 2.7

BRICA: daughter of Januaria with whom she dedicated an altar to the Nymph Neine at Greta Bridge. *RIB* 744

CAESORIA CORO(C)CA: wife of Ren[tiu]s and mother of Munatius, Lestinus and Leontius; died aged forty-eight at Caerleon. *RIB* 371 (tombstone)

CALPURNIA TRIFOSA: freedwoman and widow of Gaius Calpurnius Receptus, priest of Sulis. Lived at Bath. *RIB* 155 (tombstone)

CAMPANIA DUB(I)TATA: mother of Aelia Matrona; grandmother of Marcus Julius Maximus; 'most steadfast mother-in-law' of Julius Maximus, *singularis consularis* of the Cavalry Regiment of Sarmatians. Died at Ribchester aged fifty. *RIB* 594 (tombstone)

CANDIDA BARITA: mother of Mantinia Maerica; mother-in-law of Marcus Aurinius Simnus. Died at York. *RIB* 689; *CSIR* I.3, no 43 (tombstone).

CANDIEDINIA FORTUNA(TA): died at Adel aged fifteen. *RIB* 632 (tombstone)

CARINA: daughter of Carinus, a citizen of Rome, and his wife Romana; sister of Avita and Rufinus. Lived at Dorchester (Dorset). *RIB* 188 (tombstone)

CARSSOUNA: wife of Sacer, a citizen of the Senones (Gaul); daughter-in-law of Bruscus; presumed mother of Quintus. Died at Lincoln. *RIB* 262 (tombstone)

CARTIMANDUA: Queen of the Brigantes; wife of Venutius; mistress of Vellocatus. Tacitus *Histories* III.45; Tacitus *Annals* XII.36.40

CATIA MARIA: possibly the owner of a *mortarium* at Brockley Hill but more likely to be non-existent. *JRS* LIX (1969) 237, no 14; *RIB* 2409.2 (graffiti)

CLAUDIA CATIOTUOS: mother or second wife of Aurelius Senecio, a member of the *ordo* of Lincoln. Died at Lincoln aged sixty. *RIB* 250 (there translated as Claudius Catiotus); Birley 1979, 117 (tombstone)

CLAUDIA CRYSIS: died at Lincoln aged ninety. *RIB* 263 (tombstone)

CLAUDIA MARCIA CAPITOLINA: widow of Petronius Fortunatus, centurion of VIth Victrix among other legions; mother of Petronius Fortunatus. She was fifteen years younger than her husband and was thirty when her son was born. Lived at York, in Arabia, the Upper Euphrates and on the Danube. Died at Cillium in Tunisia. *ILS* 2658 (monumental inscription)

C(LAUDIA) MARTINA: wife of Anencletus, slave of the province. Died at London aged nineteen. *RIB* 21 (statue base)

CLAUDIA RUFINA: wife of a friend of the poet Martial. Lived in Rome but of British origins. Noted for her charm. Martial *Epigrams* II.53

CLAUDIA SEVERA: wife of Aelius Brocchus, cohort commander at one of the forts in the north of England around AD 100. Mother of one son. Friend and correspondent of Sulpicia Lepidina. Bowman and Thomas 1994, Letters 244, 291-4 (writing tablets)

CLAUDIA TURI(A)NILLA: daughter of Vettia Mansueta with whom she dedicated an altar to the Nymphs at Carvoran. *RIB* 1789

CLEUOMEDES: owner of a lead phylactery protecting her against gynaecological problems, found at West Deeping, Lincolnshire. *Britannia* XXVII (1996) 443-5, no 10

COCCE(IA) IRENE: wife of Gaius Valerius Justus, *actarius* (record clerk) of XXth Legion Valeria Victrix. Died at Chester aged thirty. *RIB* 507 (tombstone)

CORELLIA OPTATA: daughter of Quintus Corellius Fortis. Died at York aged thirteen. *RIB* 684; *CSIR* I.3, no 52 (tombstone)

COSC(ONIA) MAMMIOLA: wife of Aurelius Serenus. Died at Sutton-under-Whitestone Cliff. *JRS* XLVII (1957) 228 (coffin)

CURATIA DINYSIA: died at Chester aged forty. *RIB* 562 (tombstone)

DECIMINA: daughter of Decimius. Died at York. *RIB* 692; *CSIR* I.3, no 45 (tombstone)

DEMETRIA: Egyptian woman, mother of Justus and Gemmelus; plaintiff in a court case to prove that she had been married to Gemellus. *P Mich* VII.442

(D)IANA HERMIONE: daughter of Quintus. Dedicated an altar to Juno (*RIB* 813), and an altar to the Emperor's Virtue (*RIB* 845) at Maryport (altars)

DIODORA: priestess of the cult of Heracles of Tyre at Corbridge. *RIB* 1129; *CSIR* I.1, no 49 (altar)

DOCILINA: daughter of Uricalus and Docilosa, sister of Docilis and niece of Decentinus and Alogiosa; swore an oath against perjury at Bath. *Tab Sul* 94 (lead tablet)

DOCILOSA: wife of Uricalus; mother of Docilis and Docilina; sister-in-law of Decentinus and

Alogiosa. Swore an oath against perjury at Bath. *Tab Sul.* 94 (lead tablet)

DOMITIA SATURNINA: died at Chester aged forty-one. Possibly the wife of a stone mason. *RIB* 564 (tombstone)

EGERIA: occasionally known as Etheria or Silvia. Nun who wrote travelogue of her journeys through Egypt, Syria, Turkey and the Holy Land in 4th century AD. Thought to have originated in one of the western provinces on the Atlantic coast, possibly Britain. *Egeria's Travels*, trans. J. Wilkinson 1971.

EMI(LIA) THEODORA: mother and heir of Valerius Theodorianus. Lived at York. *RIB* 677 (tombstone)

ERTOLA: nickname of Vellibia; presumed daughter of Sudrenus. Died at Corbridge aged four. *RIB* 1181; *CSIR* I.1, no 71 (tombstone)

ET(T)ERNA: the female member of a love triangle with Timotneus and an anonymous man, at Old Harlow. *Britannia* IV (1973), 325, no 3 (lead tablet)

FABIA HONORATA: daughter of Fabius Honoratus, tribune of the 1st Cohort of Vangiones, and his wife Aurelia Eglectiane. Died at Chesters. *RIB* 1482 (tombstone)

FLAMMA: wife, daughter or girlfriend of Senovarus at Colchester; owner of a knife with a bone handle. *RIB* 2441.8

FLAVIA AUGUSTINA: wife of Gaius Aeresius Saenus, veteran of VIth Legion Victrix; mother of Saenius Augustinus and a daughter. *RIB* 685; *CSIR* I.3, no 39 (tombstone)

FLAVIA BAETICA: widow of Afutianus, centurion of 2nd Cohort of Tungrians; daughter-in-law of Bassus. Lived at Birrens. *RIB* 2115 (tombstone)

FLA(VIA) INGENUA: widow of Flavius Helius, a Greek. Lived at Lincoln. *RIB* 251 (tombstone)

FLAVIA PEREGRINA: widow of Crotus, veteran of the 4th Cohort of Gauls; daughter-in-law of Vindex. Lived at Templebrough. *RIB* 620 (tombstone)

FL(AVIA) VICTORINA: wife of Titus Tammonius Victor. Lived at Silchester. *RIB* 87 (tombstone)

FORTUNATA: a member of the Diablintian tribe; a slave girl sold to Vegetus, a Roman official in London, by Albicianus for 600 *denarii* c AD 75-125. *Britannia* XXXIV (2003) 41-51

GERMANILLA: daughter of a governor of Britain, Caerellius Priscus, and his wife Modestina, sister of Caerellius Marcianus. *CIL* XIII.6806 (inscription)

GERMANILLA: possible kidnapper of Vilbia at Bath. *RIB* 114; *Britannia* XXX (1999) 384b

GRATA: wife of Solinus, daugher of Dagobitus. Died at Lincoln aged forty. *RIB* 22 (tombstone)

GRECA: sister of Crotilo Germanus and Vindicianus. Died at Old Penrith aged four. *RIB* 934 (tombstone)

IANCILLA: Christian dedicator of a silver votive plaque at Chesterton, Cambridgeshire. *RIB* 2431.1

INNOCENTIA: co-dedicator of a piece of Christian silverware at Chesterton with Viventia. *Britannia* VII (1976), 385, no 32; *RIB* 2414.1

IVIXA: dedicator of an altar to the Veteres at Carvoran. *RIB* 1804

JANUARIA: daughter of Brica with whom she dedicated an altar to the Nymph Neine at Greta Bridge. *RIB* 744

JANUARIA MARTINA: widow of Vivius Marcianus of the IInd Legion Augusta. Lived at London. *RIB* 17 (tombstone)

(JAVOLENA) MONIME: dedicated an altar at Netherby. *RIB* 967; Birley 1979, 112

JOVINA: possible kidnapper of Vilbia at Bath. *RIB* 154; *Britannia* XXX (1999) 384b

JULIA: wife of Lurio, a German; mother of Canio; sister-in-law of Ursa. Died at Chesters. *RIB* 1483 (tombstone)

JULIA BELISMICUS: wife of Cornelius Castus; dedicated an altar with her husband to Fortune and Bonus Eventus. *RIB* 318; *CSIR* I.5, no 1

JULIA BRICA: presumed wife of Sepronius Martinus and mother of Sepronia Martina. Died at York aged thirty-one. *RIB* 686; *CSIR* I.3, no 41 (tombstone)

JUL(IA) FORTUNATA: Sardinian wife of Marcus Verecundius Diogenes, *sevir* of York and a tribesman of the Bituriges Cubi (from Bourges). *RIB* 687; *CSIR* I.3, no 60 (stone coffin); see also *RIB* 678 (stone coffin)

JUL(IA) INGENUILLA: died at Horsley, near Nailsworth, aged twenty. *RIB* 133 (tombstone)

JULIA LUCILLA: widow of Rufinus, prefect of the 1st Cohort of Vardulli, 1st Cohort Augusta of Lusitanians and 1st Cohort of Breuci, sub-curator of the Flaminian Way and Doles in Rome as well as sub-curator of Public Works. An altar to Silvanus Pantheus was set up on their behalf by their freedman Eutychus and his dependents. A senator's daughter. Lived at High Rochester. *RIB* 1271 (altar); *RIB* 1288 (tombstone)

JULIA PACATA I(NDIANA): widow of Gaius Julius Alpinus Classicianus, procurator of Britain; daughter of Julius Indus, a Treveran nobleman; daughter-in-law of Gaius. Lived in London. *RIB* 12 (tomb inscription)

JUL(IA) SECUNDINA: widow of Julius Valens, veteran of the IInd Legion Augusta; mother of Gaius Julius Martinus. Died at Caerleon aged seventy-five. *RIB* 363; 373 (tombstones)

JUL(IA) SIMILINA: widow and heiress of Titinius Felix, *beneficiarius* of the legate of XXth Legion Valeria Victrix. Lived at Chester. *RIB* 505 (tombstone base)

JULIA VELVA: relation or freedwoman of her heir Aurelius Mercurialis. Died at York aged fifty. *RIB* 688; *CSIR* 1.3, no. 42 (tombstone)

JULIANA: wealthy owner of a gold, pierced work bracelet found at Hoxne, on which she is referred to as *domina* (lady). *Britannia* XXV (1994), 307, no 62

LATTIO: daughter of Limisius and Aicetuos. Died at Old Penrith aged twelve. *RIB* 936 (tombstone)

LIFANA: niece of Lucius Senofilus. Died at Carvoran. *RIB* 1830 (tombstone)

LOLLIA BODICCA: widow of Titus Flavius Virilis, who died at Lambaesis in Algeria. He was a centurion of five legions including IInd Augusta, and may have been a Briton or a Numidian. She was British. *ILS* 2653 (tombstone)

LOVERNISCA: victim of theft who petitioned Sulis Minerva at Bath for the return of her cape. *Tab Sul* 61 (curse tablet)

MAGUNNA: dedicator of an altar to Jupiter Dolichenus at Birrens. *RIB* 2099

MANTINI(A) MAERICA: wife of Marcus Aurinius Simnus; daughter of Candida Barita. Died at York. *RIB* 689, *CSIR* I.3, no 43 (tombstone)

MARITIMA: Relation or freedwoman of Julius Marinus, a centurion. Lived at Maryport. *RIB* 858 (tombstone)

MARTIOLA: daughter and heiress of Flavius Martius, *senator* of the Carvetii. Lived at Old Penrith. *RIB* 933 (tombstone)

MARULLA: wife or daughter of Insequens, possibly a Norican, who dedicated an altar to The Mothers at Ribchester. *Britannia* XXV (1994), 298, no 3

MATUGENA: owner of a pottery flagon at Neatham. *Britannia* VI (1975), 286, no 10 (graffiti)

MELANIA: Italian heiress who owned large estates in Britain. *Vita Melania* (10) Latin; (11) Greek.

MENIMANE: widow of Blussus, a ship's captain; daughter of Annius Brigionis. Lived at Mainz Weisenau, Germany. Espérandieu 1922, no 5815

MERC(ATILLA): freedwoman and foster-daughter of Magnius. Died aged eighteen months at Bath. *RIB* 162 (tombstone)

MINERVINA: presumed wife of Cunomolius and daughter-in-law of Minicus. A witness to a petition or curse at Bath. *Tab.Sul.* 9 (lead tablet)

MODESTIANA: wife of Caerellius Priscus, a governor of Britain; mother of Germanilla and Caerellius Marcianus. *CIL* XIII.6806 (inscription)

MOCUXSOMA: dedicator of a silver ansate plaque to the god Veteris at Thistleton, Leicestershire. *JRS* LII (1962), 192, no 6; *RIB* 2431.3

OCONEA: victim of a theft who petitioned Sulis Minerva at Bath for the return of her pan. *Tab. Sul.* 60 (curse tablet)

ONERATA: widow of Valerius Verecundus, veteran of IInd Legion Augusta. Lived at Caerleon. *Britannia* VIII (1977), 429, no 15 (tombstone)

PATERNA: friend of Sulpicia Lepidina. Bowman and Thomas 1994, Letter 294 (writing tablet)

PERVICA: died at Great Chesters. *RIB* 1747; *CSIR* I.6, no 216 (tombstone)

PERVINCA: daughter of Quartio; benefactress of Delfinus from Upper Germany. Possibly a member of a burial club. Died at Housesteads. *RIB* 1620 (tombstone)

PLACIDA: died at Wroxeter aged fifty-five in the thirtieth year of her marriage. Possibly related to Deuccus. *RIB* 295 (tombstone)

POMPONIA GRAECINA: wife of Aulus Plautius who led the invasion force to Britain in AD 43. Tacitus *Annals* XIII.32

PUSINNA: widow of Dagvalda, soldier in the 1st Cohort of Pannonians. Lived in the central sector of Hadrian's Wall. *RIB* 1667 (tombstone)

REGINA: British freedwoman and wife of Barates of Palmyra, a flag maker or standard bearer. She was a Catuvellaunian by tribe but died at South Shields aged thirty. *RIB* 1065; *CSIR* I.1, no. 247 (tombstone); see also *RIB* 1171 (tombstone)

ROMANA: dedicator of an altar to the Veteres at Great Chesters. *RIB* 1729

(R)OMANA: widow of Carinus, a citizen of Rome; mother of Rufinus, Carina and Avita. Lived at Dorchester (Dorset). *RIB* 188 (tombstone)

RUSONIA AVENT(I)NA: benefactress of Lucius Ulpius Sestius and tribeswoman of the Mediomatrici (centred on Metz in France). Died at Bath aged fifty-eight. *RIB* 163 (tombstone)

SALVIENA METILIANA: widow of C Julius Maritimus of Cologne, centurion of the three legions of the British army of occupation in turn before his death whilst attached to IIIrd Legion Augusta at Lambaesis in Algeria. *CIL* VIII. 2907 (tombstone)

SATURNINA: victim of theft who petitioned Mercury and/or Mars Silvanus at Uley for the return of her linen cloth. *Britannia* X (1979), 343, no 3 (curse tablet)

SECUNDA: owner of a grey-ware pot at Billericay. *Britannia* IV (1973), 330, no 19 (graffiti)

SENOVARA: 'wife' of Cunitius, the slave of Cunomolis and Minervina. Witness of a petition or curse at Bath. *Tab. Sul.* 9 (lead tablet)

SEPRONIA MARTINA: daughter of Sepronius Martinus and Julia Brica. Died at York aged six. *RIB* 686, *CSIR* I.3, no 41 (tombstone)

SIMPLICIA: dedicator of a statuette to Mars Corotiacus at Martlesham; customer of the metal worker Glaucus. *RIB* 213 (bronze statuette base)

SIMPLICIA FLORENTIN(A): daughter of Felicius Simplex of VIth Legion Victrix. Died at York aged ten months. *RIB* 690 (stone coffin)

SOSIA JUNCINA: wife of Quintus Antonius Isauricus, imperial legate. Dedicator of an altar to Fortuna at York. *RIB* 644.

SULICENA: died at Lasborough, near Wotton-under-Edge, aged fourteen. *RIB* 134 (tombstone)

SULPICIA LEPIDINA: wife of Flavius Cerialis, perfect of 9th Cohort of Batavians at Vindolanda. Correspondent of Claudia Severa and Paterna. Bowman and Thomas 1994, Letters 247, 257, 274, 288(?), 291-4 (writing tablets)

TACITA: cursed by an anonymous enemy at Clothall. *RIB* 221 (curse tablet)

TADIA EXUPERATA: daughter of Tadia Vallaunius; sister of Tadius Exuperatus. Lived at Caerleon. *RIB* 369 (tombstone)

TADIA VALLAUN(I)US: mother of Tadia Exuperata and Tadius Exuperatus. Died aged 65, possibly at Caerleon. *RIB* 369 (tomsbtone)

TANCORIX: died at Old Carlisle aged sixty. *RIB* 908 (tombstone)

TIBERIA: heiress of (Ti)berius. Lived at Chester. *RIB* 554 (tombstone)

TITIA PINTA: wife of Valerius Vindicianus; mother of Valerius Adjutor and Varialus. Died near Eastness aged thirty-eight. *RIB* 720

TITULLINIA PUSSITTA: a Raetian who died at Netherby aged thirty-five. *RIB* 984 (tombstone)

TRANQUILA SEVERA: dedicator on behalf of herself and her family of an altar to the 'Goddess Mother of the Gods' (Cybele) at Carrawburgh. *RIB* 1539 (altar)

TRETIA MARIA (or Maria Tretia): cursed by an anonymous enemy at London. *RIB* 7 (curse tablet).

TULLIA TACITA: named on a bronze die or stamp from Carrington, Lothian Region. *RIB* 2409.36

URSA: sister of Lurio, a German; sister-in-law of Julia; aunt of Canio. Died at Chesters. *RIB* 1483; *CSIR* I.6, no 192 (tombstone)

VACIA: sister of Aelius Mercurialis, a staff clerk (*cornicularius)* Died at Great Chesters. *RIB* 1742; *CSIR* I.6, no 213 (tombstone)

VACIA: died at Carlisle aged three. *RIB* 961; *CSIR* I.6, no 495 (tombstone)

VAL(ERIA) FRONTINA: widow of Marcri...us, an *Eques Romanus*. Lived at Colchester. *RIB* 202 (tombstone)

VED..IC..: tribeswoman of the Cornovii. Died at Ilkley aged thirty. *RIB* 639; *CSIR* I.3, no 98 (tombstone)

VELLIBIA: proper name of Ertola who died at Corbridge aged four. *RIB* 1181; *CSIR* I.1.no 71 (tombstone)

VELORIGA: head of a Bath family. *Tab Sul* 53 (lead tablet)

VELVINNA: possible kidnapper of Vilbia at Bath. *RIB* 154; *Britannia* XXX (1999) 384b (lead tablet)

VERECUNDA: actress and girlfriend of Lucius, a gladiator at Leicester. *CIL* VII, 1335, 4 (graffiti)

VERECU(N)D(A) RUFILIA: wife of Excingus; tribeswoman of the Dobunni. Died at Templebrough aged thirty-five. *RIB* 621 (tombstone)

VERINA: gave a buffware flagon to 'little Vrilucolus' at Ilchester. *Britannia* VIII (1977), 444, no 101 (graffiti)

VETTI(A) MANSUETA: mother of Claudia Turianilla with whom she dedicated an altar to the Nymphs at Carvoran. *RIB* 1789

VIBIA PACATA: wife of Flavius Verecundus, centurion of VIth Legion Victrix. He was a Pannonian, while she may have been an African. Dedicated an altar to the Silvanae and the Quadruviae at Westerwood on the Antonine Wall. *JRS* LIV (1964), 178; *CSIR* I.4, no 86

VILBIA: slave or concubine whose kidnapping(?) by Velvinna, Exsupereus, Severinus, Augustalis, Comitianus, Castusminianus, Germanilla or Jovina is recorded on a curse tablet from Bath. *RIB* 154; see also *Britannia* XXX(1999) 384b

VITELLIA PROCULA: mother and heiress of a thirteen-year-old child who died at York. *RIB* 696 (tombstone)

VITIA: illiterate owner of a grey-ware jar at Darenth villa ('Vitia X: her mark'). *Britannia* II (1971), 298, no 54 (graffiti)

VIVENTIA: co-dedicator with Innocentia of a piece of Christian silverware at Chesterton. *Britannia* VII (1976), 385, no. 32; *RIB* 2414.1

VIVENTIA: wife or daughter of Victoricus. Owner of a pewter plate at Verulamium. *JRS* XLVII (1957), 232, no 23; *RIB* 2417.35

VOLUSIA FAUSTINA: wife of Aurelius Senecio, a decurion. She was a citizen of Lincoln where she died aged twenty-six. *RIB* 250 (tombstone)

UN-NAMED WOMEN

CONCUBINE(?) OF TAGAMATIS, the flag-bearer: postulated from a letter from Vindolanda. Bowman and Thomas 1994, Letter 181; Birley, R 1990, 30

DAUGHTER OF BLESCIUS DIOVICUS: died at Risingham aged one year and twenty-one days. *RIB* 1254; *CSIR* I.1, no 267 (tombstone)

DAUGHTER OF CRESCENS, an *imaginifer*; died at Kirby Thorne. *RIB* 769 (tombstone)

DAUGHTER OF SABINUS: presumed relation of Regulus, who set up an altar to Jupiter Dolichenus at Great Chesters. *RIB* 1726; *CSIR* I.6, no 119.

MOTHER OF SECUNDUS: member of a three generation family at Usk. *RIB* 396 (tombstone)

SLAVE OF M COCCEIUS FIRMUS: servant who, on being found guilty of a crime, was condemned to serve as a cook at the salt-mines in south-west Scotland. She was ransomed after being kidnapped and re-claimed by M Cocceius Firmus, a centurion at Auchendavy. Justinian *Digest* 49.15.6

WIFE OF CASSIUS SECUNDUS, a veteran who died at Chester when he was eighty. *RIB* 526 (tombstone)

WIFE OF FABIUS: set up an altar to the Nymphs at Risingham after an anonymous soldier was 'forewarned in a dream'. *RIB* 1228

WIFE OF MARCUS AURELIUS NEPOS, centurion of the XXth Legion Valeria Victrix. Lived at Chester. *RIB* 491 (tombstone)

OTHER ANONYMOUS WOMEN

ALDBOROUGH: *CSIR* I.3, no 15 (sculpture)

BATH 1 (Landsdown): *CSIR* I.2, no 144 (sculpture)

BATH 2 (Winterslow): *CSIR* I.2, no 94 (sculpture)

BATH 3 (R. AVON): *CSIR* I.2, no 2 (sculpture)

BATH 4 (WALCOT): *CSIR* I.2, no 1 (sculpture)

BEWCASTLE: *CSIR* I.6, no 180 (relief)

BIRRENS: *CSIR* I.4, no 20 (sculpture)

BOWNESS-ON-SOLWAY: *CSIR* I.6, no 233 (tombstone)

CAERWENT *CSIR* I.5, no 14 (sculpture)

CARLISLE: *CSIR* I.6, no 497 (tombstone)

CASTLESTEADS: *CSIR* I.6, no 228 (tombstone)

CHESTER I: Wright and Richmond 1955, no 66, pl XIX (tombstone)

CHESTER 2: Wright and Richmond 1955, no 117, pl XXX (tombstone)

CHESTER 3: Wright and Richmond 1955, no 119, pl XXXI (tombstone)

CHESTER 4: Wright and Richmond 1955, no 120, pl XXXI (tombstone)

CHESTER 5: Wright and Richmond 1955, no 118 pl XXXI (tombstone)

CHESTER 6: Wright and Richmond 1955, no 112, pl XXIX (tombstone)

CORBRIDGE: *CSIR* I.1, no 15 (relief of Maenad)

HALTON CHESTERS 1: *Britannia* V (1974), 462, no 61 (tombstone)

HALTON CHESTERS 2: *CSIR* I.1, no 261 (tombstone)

HIGH ROCHESTER: *CSIR* I.1 no 271; *RIB* 1293 (tombstone)

ILKLEY: *CSIR* I.3, no 99 (tombstone)

LLANIO: *CSIR* I.5, no 56 (wooden sculpture)

MIDLOTHIAN: *CSIR* I.4, no 61 (relief of three mother goddesses)

YORK 1: *CSIR* I.3, no 59 (tombstone)

YORK 2 (FISHERGATE): *CSIR* I.3, no 71 (sculpture)

YORK 3: *CSIR* I.3, no 132 (sculpture)

YORK 4 (MICKLEGATE): *CSIR* I.3, no 54 (tombstone)

Abbreviations and Notes

The majority of the classical authors referred to below have been translated into English in the Loeb Classical Library volumes.

CIL Corpus Inscriptionum Latinarum 16 vols (Berlin, 1863 -)

CSIR Corpus Signorum Imperii Romani (London)

ILS Inscriptiones Latinae Selectae 3 vols (Berlin, 1892-1916)

JRS Journal of Roman Studies (London)

RIB The Roman Inscriptions of Britain (Collingwood and Wright 1965)

Tab Sul Tomlin in Cunliffe 1988

Introduction

1. Tacitus *Annals* II.24
2. Strabo *Geography* .V.2
3. Caesar *De Bello Gallico* II.4
4. Ehrenberg 1989
5. Millett 1990, 181-6
6. Roberts and Cox 2003, 142
7. The popular spelling 'Boudicea' was the result of the miscopying of Tacitus' text. Kenneth Jackson has recently shown that the correct spelling is 'Boudica'
8. Cassius Dio *Roman History* LXII.2.4
9. Strabo *Geography* XVII
10. Cicero *Pro Murena* 27
11. Tacitus *Histories* III.45
12. Tacitus *Annals* XII.36
13. Tacitus *Histories* III.45
14. Tacitus *Histories* III.45
15. Tacitus *Annals* XII.40
16. Tacitus *Annals* XIV.30; Tacitus *Agricola* XVI; Cassius Dio LXII.2.7
17. Tacitus *Annals* XIV.30
18. Ruffus, Article 40 in C.E. Brand *Roman Military Law* (1978)
19. Cassius Dio *Roman History* LXII.2.2
20. Cassius Dio *Roman History* LXII.2.2
21. Cassius Dio *Roman History* LXII.3-6; Tacitus *Annals* XIV
22. *Henry V* Act III, Scene I
23. Tacitus *Agricola* 31
24. *Antiquaries Journal* XXXIII (1953), 206-8; *British Museum Quarterly* XXXI

(1967), 101-3; however, for an alternative translation see RIB 2443.7.
25. *Britannia* XXXIV (2003), 41-52.
26. RIB 560; see also Birley 1979, 146 for alternative reading of the children's names.
27. Justinian *Digest* 37.15.11
28. Allason-Jones 1996

1. Birth, Marriage And Death

1. Soranus *Gynecology* II.10 (see Temkin 1956)
2. Soranus *Gynecology* II.12
3. Molleson 1989, 17-38
4. Soranus *Gynecology* I.20
5. Soranus *Gynecology* I.23
6. Soranus *Gynecology* I.20, 24
7. Soranus *Gynecology* I.29
8. Soranus *Gynecology* I.26
9. Tacitus *Annals* III.28
10. Hopkins 1965; *ILS* 7472
11. Tacitus *Germania* 20
12. Caesar *De Bello Gallico* VI.21
13. Diodorus Siculus V.32.3; Strabo IV.5.4; Caesar *De Bello Gallico* V.14
14. Cassius Dio *Roman History* LXXVII.16.5
15. Soranus *Gynecology* 1.34
16. Aulus Gellius *Noctes Atticae* 3.10.8; 3.16. Curiously, a superstition that an eighth month baby 'wouldn't thrive' was still current in the North of England in the 20th century.
17. Soranus *Gynecology* 1.48
18. Soranus *Gynecology* 1.55
19. Claudia Trophima: *CIL* VI.9720; Poblicia Aphe: *CIL* VI.9723
20. RIB 560 (see also Introduction note 26)
21. Pliny *Naturalis Historia* VII.37
22. Tacitus *Germania* 20
23. Soranus *Gynecology* II.19
24. Soranus *Gynecology* II.19
25. Soranus *Gynecology* II.49-54; 46; 45
26. RIB 188, 371, 15, 934
27. Hopkins 1967, 126
28. Aristotle *Historia Animalium* 583a
29. Hippocrates *Natura Mulierum* 98; *Muliebria* 1.76
30. Pliny *Naturalis Historia* XXIV.II.18
31. Pliny *Naturalis Historia* XXIX, 27.85
32. Dioscorides *De Materia Medica* 3.34; 1.77.2; 3.130; 5.106

33. Caelius Aurelianus *Gynaecia* (ed. Drabkin, 29, 1.83)
34. Lucretius *De Rerum Natura* IV.1265ff.
35. Soranus *Gynecology* I.60
36. Soranus *Gynecology* I.61
37. Soranus *Gynecoloy* I.60
38. St John Chrysostom *Epistle to the Romans* 24.4
39. Dioscorides *De Materia Medica* 2.159.3
40. Pliny *Naturalis Historia* XXV.37.75; XXVII.55.80
41. Soranus *Gynecology* II.10
42. Plautus *Gasina* prol. 41, 79; *Cistellaria* I.3, 17,31
43. Tacitus *Germania* 19; Cassius Dio LXXVII.12
44. Mays 1995
45. Soranus *Gynecology* II.12
46. Cocks 1921
47. Columella *De Re Rustica* 1.8.19
48. Soranus *Gynecology* II.10
49. *RIB* 681
50. *RIB* 1292
51. *RIB* 937
52. Oribasius *Ecloga Medicamentorum* 132.1
53. Galen *On Prognosis* 6
54. Plato *Timaeus* 91C; *Britannia* XXVII (1996), 443-6, no 10
55. *Britannia* XX (1991), 292-311
56. *RIB* 2446.1-32
57. Roberts and Cox 2003, 142
58. Roberts and Cox 2003, 118-9
59. Roberts and Cox 2003, 140
60. Roberts and Cox 2003, 131-2
61. Molleson 1989, 27-38

2 Women in the Army

1. Tacitus *Annals* III.34
2. *Scriptores Historiae Augustae Hadrian* II.3
3. Tacitus *Annals* III.33
4. Tacitus *Agricola* 29
5. Juvenal *Satires* VI.398ff
6. *CIL* XIII.6806
7. *ILS* 1092
8. Allason-Jones 1999
9. Cassius Dio *Roman History* LX.24.3
10. Herodian *Histories* 3.8.4-5
11. Birley, R 1990, 30
12. Justinian *Digest* XLIX.17.13
13. Roxan 1989, 462-7
14. Roxan 1981, 265-86
15. Cassius Dio *Roman History* LVI.20.2-5
16. Caesar *De Bello Africo* 75
17. *RIB* 1700
18. *RIB* 369: Tadius Exuperatus is presumed to have borne in the *canabae* of Caerleon but this is not explicitly stated. For reference

to people born *ex castris* elsewhere in the Empire see J C Mann (ed M M Roxan) *Legionary Recruitment and Veteran Settlement during the Principate* (London 1983)
19. Van Driel Murray 1995
20. *RIB* 2401.1
21. *CIL* XVI, 49
22. *RIB* 1064
23. Justinian *Digest* 49.15.6
24. *RIB* 2059
25. *RIB* 2182
26. Birley, Charlton and Hedley 1933

3 Women of Town and Country

1. Nennius *Historia Brittonum* 31; see also Gildas *The Ruin of Britain* 25, and Bede *Ecclesiastical History* 1.16
2. Tacitus *Annals* XIV.32
3. Cassius Dio *Roman History* LXII.2.7
4. Caesar *De Bello Gallico* IV.20
5. *RIB* 69; 70; 71
6. *Britannia* VIII (1977), 430-1
7. *Britannia* IV (1973), 332
8. *Britannia* III (1972), 359
9. *JRS* LI (1961), 195
10. *CIL* VII.1238, *Britannia* II (1971), 297
11. *CIL* VI.9846; 9848; 37820
12. *CIL* VI.10006; 33928; X.1965
13. *CIL* II.53
14. *CIL* VI.9488
15. *CIL* VI.9855
16. Allason-Jones 1996; see also Crummy 1996
17. Birley, Charton, and Hedley 1933
18. Bradley 1985
19. Horace *Epistles* I.I4.21
20. Horace *Satires* 1.2.36; Ovid *Fasti* 4.134; Ovid *Ars Amatoria* 1.31ff.
21. *Scriptores Historiae Augustae Hadrian* 18.8
22. Suetonius *Caligula* 40

4 At Home

1. Justinian *Digest* 47.2.12
2. *CSIR* 1.1 no. 248
3. Wright and Richmond 1955, pl. XXXVII.156
4. *CSIR* 1.2, no.41
5. Unfortunately, the marble tombstone from London, which shows a female resting her feet on a small elaborate footstool, is now considered to be a recent import. R E M Wheeler, *London in Roman Times* (London 1930), pl XVIII
6. Diocletian's *Edict* XIX.28-35; Lucretius *De Rerum Natura* IV.1029; IV.1123

7. Strabo *Geography* X.1.6; Pliny *Naturalis Historia* XIX.19
8. Apicius *The Art of Cooking* published as *The Roman Cookery Book* by B Flowers and E Rosenbaum, London 1958
9. Caesar *De Bello Gallico* V.12
10. Caesar *De Bello Gallico* V.12
11. Tomlin 2003, 176; see also *Britannia* XXXI (2000) 438, no 19 for a Spanish amphora which contained 'the product of Proculus and Urbicus'.
12. *Martial Epigrams* XIII.103
13. Pliny *Naturalis Historia* XXI.93
14. Byron 1981, quoted in Tomlin 2003, 176
15. Petronius *Satyricon* LXVI
16. Pliny *Naturalis Historia* XVIII.12.68; 26.102-4
17. Pliny *Naturalis Historia* XI.240-2
18. Athenaeus *Deipnosophistae* 152
19. Ovid *Ars Amatoria* III.765
20. Plutarch *Moralia* 244A
21. Diodorus Siculus *Library of History* XXIII.21
22. Pliny *Naturalis Historia* XXVIII.4.19

5. Fashion

1. Suetonius *Augustus* 73
2. Columella *De Re Rustica* XII, pref.9
3. Wild 1968, 212-6
4. Soranus *Gynecology* II.9.14
5. *Tab Sul* no.61
6. Gabra-Sanders 2001
7. *Scriptore Historiae Augustae Alexander Severus* 27
8. Ovid *Ars Amatoria* 3.261.4; Cicero *Clodius* 15.21-4; *Scriptores Historiae Augustae Clodius Albinus* 5.9
9. Martial *Epigrams* 3.87
10. Van Driel-Murray 1999; 2002
11. *Tab Sul* no 55
12. Palladius *De Re Rustica* I.42(43)4; Ionas *Vita Columbari* 1.15
13. *Tab Sul* 5; see also *Britannia* XXXV (2004), 337, no 3 for a lead tablet from Radcliffe-on-Sea which also refers to a pair of gloves.
14. Woad, dog's mercury, bilberry, whortleberry; seeds of woad have been recorded in a late Iron Age deposit at Dragonby.
15. Elder bark, meadowsweet and woad; a black yarn found at Arrington, Cambridgeshire appears to have been dyed with woad.
16. Rhizomes of bracken, the flowering shoots of heather, pine-cones, pear leaves and gorse; weld has also been recorded at York, London, and Carlisle.
17. Flowerheads of reeds
18. Onion skins
19. A fragment of textile found in a late Roman burial near Dorchester had been dyed with either *murex* or *thais* whelk and was, presumably, an import. The Atlantic whelk (*nucella lapillis* L.), found on the North Devon coast would have produced a similar colour.
20. Orchil lichen
21. Madder
22. Tacitus *Annals* XIV.30
23. Ovid *Ars Amatoria* III.170-83
24. Ovid *Ars Amatoria* III.190
25. Tacitus *Germania* 17; see also Wild 2002, 8
26. Tertullian *On Female Dress* VIII
27. Cassius Dio *Roman History* LXII.2.4
28. Cool 2000
29. Aulus Gellius *Noctes Atticae* 10.10
30. Tertullian *On Female Dress* X
31. *CIL* VI.1527
32. Pliny *Naturalis Historia* XXXVII.30
33. Artemidorus *Onirocritica* 2.5
34. Tacitus *Agricola* 12
35. Pliny *Naturalis Historia* XXXVI. 14102
36. Lucian *Amores* 39
37. Ovid *Ars Amatoria* 111.10ff
38. Ovid *On Painting the Face* 75-80
39. Ovid *On Painting the Face* 100
40. Juvenal *Satires* 6.461-74
41. Plautus *Mostellaria* 258; Pliny *Naturalis Historia* XXXIV.175
42. Plautus *Truculentus* 294; *Mostellaria* 258; Tertullian *On Female Dress* V; Ovid *Ars Amatoria* III.200
43. Ovid *On Painting the Face* 66-71
44. Tertullian *On Female Dress* II
45. Pliny *Naturalis Historia* XXVIII.46.166
46. Ovid *Ars Amatoria* II.202
47. Juvenal *Satires* 2.93
48. Propertius *Elegis* II.18B, 1-4
49. Ovid *Ars Amatoria* III.197
50. Ovid *Ars Amatoria* I.505-6
51. Pliny *Naturalis Historia* XXVIII.249 and 255
52. Ovid *Ars Amatoria* III.215
53. Lucian *Amores* 39
54. Ovid *Ars Amatoria* III.193
55. Ovid *Ars Amatoria* III.149
56. Ovid *Ars Amatoria* III.140
57. Tertullian *On Female Dress* VII
58. Ovid *Amores* I.14-45
59. Tertullian *On Female Dress* VI
60. Ovid *Ars Amatoria* III.165
61. Pliny *Naturalis Historia* XXVIII.191; Martial *Epigrams* 8.33.20;14.26
62. Propertius *Elegis* 11.18B

63. Diodorus Siculus *Library of History* V.28
64. Tertullian *On Female Dress VI*
65. Tacitus *Agricola II*
66. Cassius Dio *Roman History* LXII.2.4

6 Religion

1. Henig 1984, 68-71
2. Tacitus *Annals* XIV.31
3. Tacitus *Annals* XIV.31
4. RIB 584
5. Diana is known to have been entreated to increase the population of Rome on occasions: Horace *Carmen Saeculare* 17.20
6. Ovid *Ars Amatoria* I.400-40
7. *RIB* 1270
8. *RIB* 1253; see also Henig 1984
9. See Cool 2004: the cemetery at Brougham shows that some Pannonians were continuing their ethnic burial traditions
10. Caesar *De Bello Gallico* VI.13
11. Tacitus *Annals* XIV.30
12. Strabo *Geography* IV.4.6; *Scriptores Historiae Augustae Severus Alexander* IX; *Aurelianus* XLIV; *Numerianus* XIV. See Chadwick 1966
13. Suetonius *Claudius* XXV.5
14. Henig 1984, 203
15. *RIB* 246
16. Cassius Dio *Roman History* LXII.7
17. *Britannia* XIII, 1982, 408-9
18. *Tacitus* Annals XIV.30
19. Anicius Ingenuus at Housesteads; *RIB* 1618; Abrocomas at Binchester:*RIB* 1618; Hermogenes at Chester: *RIB* 461
20. *RIB* 1028
21. *Victoria Country History: Somerset* (1906), 283, no. 46
22. Apuleius *The Golden Ass* XI.4
23. Ovid *Ars Amatoria* III.636
24. C Hill, M Millett and T Blagg *The Roman Riverside Wall and Monumental Arch in London* 1980, 196-8

25. *RIB* 2423.1
26. *RIB* 1791
27. Tertullian *On Female Dress* VIII
28. Lactantius *Institutiones Divinae* 6, 20, 18ff

7 Entertainment and Recreation

1. Ovid *Ars Amatoria* III.355-63
2. *Britannia* XXXII, 2001, 397
3. Pliny *Naturalis Historia* X.59
4. Suetonius *Augustus* 44
5. Tacitus *Annals* XIV.32
6. *RIB* 707
7. Ovid *Ars Amatoria* 1.90
8. Soranus *Gynecology* I.22
9. Ovid *Ars Amatoria* II.320-5
10. Tacitus *Agricola* 21
11. *RIB* 662; 663; Plutarch *On the Cessation of Oracles* 410A
12. *Ephemeris Epigraphica* VII.1141; *RIB* 2491.147
13. Ovid *Ars Amatoria* III.620-30
14. *RIB* 265
15. *ILS* 6891; *CIL* II.5181
16. Pliny *Naturalis Historia* XXXIII, 54.152
17. Seneca *Epistulae Morales* 56
18. Martial *Epigrams* VI.93
19. Diodorus Siculus *Library of History* V.40
20. Pliny *Naturalis Historia* XXI.10.10-22
21. Varro *De Re Rustica* 1.39 ff
22. Pliny *Naturalis Historia* XIX, .19.57
23. Soranus *Gynecology* 47

8 Finale

1. Zosimus *Historia Nova* VI. 5-2
2. *RIB* 235
3. Ammianus Marcellinus *History* XXVII, 8, 1-3, 5-8
4. Bowman and Thomas 1994, no164

Bibliography

To cover the topics discussed adequately would require a bibliography of enormous size. The list is, therefore, confined to those modern authors cited in the text and a selection of some general works which will lead interested readers to more specialise works.

ALCOCK, J 1980. 'Classical religious belief and burial practice in Roman Britain', *Archaeological Journal* CXXXVII, 50-85

ALCOCK, J P 2001. *Food in Roman Britain* (Stroud)

ALLASON-JONES, L 1996. 'The Actress and the Bishop: evidence for working women in Roman Britain', in *Women in Industry and Technology* ed Devonshire, A, and Wood, B (London)

ALLASON-JONES, L 1999. 'Women and the Roman Army in Britain', in *The Roman Army as a Community,* ed Goldsworthy, A, and Haynes, I. Journal of Roman Archaeology Supplementary Series 34, 41-51

ALLASON-JONES, L 2004. 'The Family in Roman Britain', in *A Companion to Roman Britain* ed Todd, M, (Oxford)

APPLEBAUM, S 1975. ' Some observations on the economy of the Roman villa at Bignor, Sussex', *Britannia* VI, 118-32

BALSDON, J P V D 1962. *Roman Women* (London)

BARRETT, A A 1978. 'Knowledge of the literary classics in Roman Britain', *Britannia* IX, 307-13

BIRLEY, A 1979. *The People of Roman Britain* (London)

BIRLEY, A 1981. *Life in Roman Britain* (London)

BIRLEY, E, CHARLTON, J AND HEDLEY, P 1933. 'Excavations at Housesteads in 1932', *Archaeologia Aeliana* 4th series, X , 82-96

BIRLEY, R 1990. *The Roman documents from Vindolanda* (Newcastle upon Tyne)

BLAGG, T F C AND KING, A C 1984. *Military and Civilian in Roman Britain: Cultural Relationships in a Frontier Province* (Oxford)

BOON, G C 1974. *Silchester: the Roman Town of Calleva* (London)

BOON, G C 1983a. 'Potters, oculists and eye troubles, *Britannia* XVIII, 125-42

BOON, G C 1983b. 'Some Romano-British domestic shrines and their inhabitants', in *Rome and her Northern Provinces* ed Hartley, B and Wacher, J (Gloucester)

BOWMAN, A K AND THOMAS, J D 1978. 'New texts from Vindolanda', *Britannia* XVIII, 125-42

BOWMAN, A K AND THOMAS, J D 1994. *The Vindolanda Writing Tablets (Tabulae Vindolandenses* II) (London)

BRADLEY, K 1985. 'Child labour in the Roman world', *Historical Reflections* VII, 311-30

BRAUND, D 1984. 'Observations on Cartimandua', *Britannia* XV, 1-6

BREEZE, D 1982. 'Demand and supply on the northern frontier', in *Rural Settlement in the Roman North,* ed Clack, P and Haselgrove, C (Durham)

BROTHWELL, D 1972. 'Palaeodemography and earlier British populations', *World Archaeology* 4.1, 75-87

BURNHAM, B C AND WACHER, J 1990. *The 'Small Towns' of Roman Britain* (London)

BYRON, R 1981. *The Road to Oxiana* (London)

CAMPBELL, B 1978. 'The marriage of soldiers under the Empire' *Journal of Roman Studies* LXI, 153-66

CARCOPINO, J 1956. *Daily Life in Ancient Rome,* trans. E O Lorimer (London)

CASSON, L 1974. *Travel in the Ancient World* (London)

CHADWICK, N K 1966. *The Druids* (Cardiff)

CLARKE, G 1979. *The Roman Cemetery at Lankhills* (Winchester)

CLAYTON, J, in Allason-Jones, L 1985 *Coventina's Well* (Chollerford)

COCKS, A H 1921. 'Romano-British homestead in the Hambledon valley, Bucks.' *Archaeologia* LXXI, 141-98

COOL, H E M 1991. 'Roman metal hairpins from Southern Britain', *Archaeological Journal* CXLVII, 148-82

COOL, H E M 2000. 'The significance of snake jewellery hoards', *Britannia* XXX, 29-40

COOL, H E M 2004. *The Roman cemetery at Brougham, Cumbria. Excavations 1966-7* (London)

CRUMMY, N 1996. 'Granny's old bones: Women boneworkers in Roman Britain', in *Women in Roman Industry and Technology* ed Devonshire, A, and Wood, B (London)

CUNLIFFE, B 1981. 'Roman gardens in Britain. A review of the evidence', in *Ancient Gardens* ed MacDougall, E B, and Jashenski, W F (Washington)

CUNLIFFE, B 1988. *The Temple of Sulis Minerva at Bath.* II *The Finds from the Sacred Spring* (Oxford)

DAVEY, N and LING, R 1982. *Wallpainting in Roman Britain* (London)

DIMBLEBY, G W 1978. *Plants and Archaeology* (London)

DIXON, S 1988. *The Roman Mother* (London)

DUDLEY, D R AND WEBSTER, G 1962. *The Rebellion of Boudica* (London)

EHRENBERG, M 1989 *Women in Prehistory* (London)

ESPÉRANDIEU, C 1907-38. *Recueil General des Bas-Reliefs, Statues et Bustes de la Gaule Romaine* 10 vols (Paris)

EVANS, M M 1906. 'Hairdressing of Roman ladies as illustrated on coins', *The Numismatic Chronicle* 4th series, VI, 37-65

FARWELL, D E AND MOLLESON, T I 1993. *Poundbury. Volume 2. The Cemeteries* (Dorchester)

FLOWER, B AND ROSENBAUM, E 1958. *Apicius: The Roman Cookery Book* (London)

FRERE, S S 1987. *Britannia* (London)

GABRA-SANDERS, T 2001. 'The Orkney Hood re-dated and re-considered', in *The Roman Textile Industry and its Influence* ed Walton Rogers, P, Jørgensen, L B, and Rast-Eicher, A, 98-104 (Oxford)

GARBSCH, J G 1965. 'Die Norisch-Pannonische Frauentract im I and 2 Jahrhundert', *Munchener Beitrage zur Vor-u Fruhgeschichte XI*

GARDENER, J F 1986. *Woman in Roman Law and Society* (London)

GREEN, M 1986. *The Gods of the Celts* (Gloucester)

GUIDO, M 1979. 'Beads and necklaces', in G Clarke *Pre-Roman and Roman Winchester* II *The Roman Cemetery at Lankhills* (Oxford)

HANLEY, R 1987. *Villages in Roman Britain* (Aylesbury)

HARRIS E and HARRIS J R 1965. *The Oriental Cults in Roman Britain* (Leiden)

HENIG M 1984. *Religion in Roman Britain* (London)

HOPKINS, K 1965. 'Age of Roman girls at marriage', *Population Studies* XVIII, 309-27

HOPKINS, K 1967. 'Contraception in the Roman Empire', *Comparative Studies in Society and History* VIII (1965-6), 124-51

JACKSON, K 1953. *Language and history in early Britain* (Edinburgh)

JACKSON, R 1985. 'Cosmetic sets from the late Iron Age and Roman Britain', *Britannia* XVI, 165-92

JACKSON, R 1988 *Doctors and Diseases in the Roman Empire* (London)

JOHNSON, P 1982 *Romano-British Mosaics* (Aylesbury)

JOHNSON, S 1980 *Later Roman Britain* (London)

JONES, G D B 1984. 'Becoming different without knowing it. The role and development of vici', in Blagg and King 1984

KILBRIDE-JONES, H 1938. 'Glass armlets in Britain', *PSAS* LXXII, 366-95

KING, A 1984. 'Animal bones and the dietary identity of military and civilian groups in Roman Britain', in Blagg and King 1984

LETHBRIDGE, T C 1936. ' Further excavations in the early Iron Age and Romano-British cemetery at Guilden Morden', *Cambridge Antiquarian Communications* XXXVI (1934-5), 109-20

LEWIS, M J T 1966. *Temples in Roman Britain* (Cambridge)

LING, R 1985. *Romano-British Wallpainting* (Aylesbury)

LIVERSIDGE, J 1955. *Furniture in Roman Britain* (London)

LIVERSIDGE, J 1957. 'Kitchens in Roman Britain', *Archaeological Newsletter* VI, 82-5

LIVERSIDGE, J 1973. *Britain in the Roman Empire* (London)

LLOYD-MORGAN, G 1977 'Mirrors in Roman Britain', in *Roman Life and Art in Britain*, ed. Munby, J and Henig, M (Oxford)

MACDONALD, G 1919. 'A sculpture relief of Roman period at Colinton', *Proceedings of the Society of Antiquaries of Scotland* LII (1917-18), 38-48

MACGREGOR, A 1985. *Bone, Antler, Ivory and Horn* (London)

MANN, J 1971. 'Spoken Latin in Britain as evidenced in the inscriptions', *Britannia* II, 218-24

MATTHEWS, C L 1981. 'A Romano-British inhumation cemetery at Dunstable', *Bedfordshire Archaeological Journal* XV, passim

MAYS, S 1995. 'Killing the unwanted child', *British Archaeology* 2 (March) 8-9

MAXFIELD, V A1995. 'Soldier and civilian: life beyond the ramparts', *The Eight Annual Caerleon Lecture* (Cardiff)

MILLETT, M 1990. *The Romanization of Britain* (Cambridge)

MILNE, G 1985. *The Port of Roman London* (London)

MOLLESON, T I 1989. 'Social implications of the mortality patterns of juveniles from Poundbury Camp Romano-British cemetery', *Anthropogsche Anzeiger* XLVII, 27-38

NEAL, D S 1981. *Roman Mosaics in Britain* (London)

OGDEN, J 1980. Note in *The Society of Jewellery Historians Newsletter* IX

PEACOCK, D P S 1982. *Pottery in the Roman World: an Ethnoarchaeological Approach* (Harlow)

PIGGOTT, S 1968. *The Druids* (London)

POTTER, T W 1983. *Roman Britain* (London)

PRITCHARD, F A 1986. 'Ornamental stonework from Roman London', *Britannia* XVII, 169-89

RANSOM, C L 1905. *Studies in Ancient Furniture, Couches and Beds of the Greeks, Etruscans and Romans* (Chicago)

RHODES, M 1980. 'Leather footwear', in *Excavations at Billingsgate Buildings, Lower Thames Street, London 1974* ed Jones, D M (London)

RICHMOND, I A 1954. 'Queen Cartimandua' *Journal of Roman Studies* XLIV 43-52

RIVET, A L F 1964. *Town and Country in Roman Britain* (London)

ROBERTS, C AND COX, M 2003. *Health and Disease in Britain from Prehistory to the Present Day* (Stroud)

ROSS, A 1974. *Pagan Celtic Britain* (London)

ROXAN, M M 1981. 'The distribution of Roman military diplomas', *Epigraphic Studies* XII, 265-86

ROXAN, M M 1989. 'Women on the frontiers', in *Roman Frontier Studies 1989: Proceedings*

of the XV International Congress on Roman Frontier Studies, ed Maxfield, V A and Dobson, M J, 462-7 (Exeter)

SALWAY, P 1981. *Roman Britain* (Oxford)

SMITH, J T 1963. 'Romano-British aisled houses', *Archaeological Journal* CXX, 1-30

SOMMER, C S 1984. *The Military Vici in Roman Britain* (Oxford)

STEPHENS, G R 1985. 'Civic aqueducts in Britain', *Britannia* XVI, 197-208

STEVENSON, R B K 1957. 'Native bangles and Roman glass', *Proceedings of the Society of Antiquaries of Scotland* LXXXVIII (1954-6), 208-21

STRONG, D AND BROWN, D 1976. *Roman Crafts* (London)

SWAN, V 1988. *Pottery in Roman Britain* (Aylesbury)

TEMKIN, O 1956. *Soranus' Gynecology* (Baltimore)

THOMAS, C 1981. *Christianity in Roman Britain to AD 500* (London)

TOMLIN, R S O 1988. ' The Curse Tables', in Cunliffe 1988

TOMLIN, R S O 2003. 'Documenting the Roman Army at Carlisle', in *Documenting the Roman Army* ed Wilkes, J J, 175-87 (London)

TOYNBEE, J M C 1952. 'A Roman(?) head at Dumfries', *Journal of Roman Studies* XLII, 63-5

VAN DRIEL-MURRAY, C 1987. 'Roman footwear: a mirror of fashion and society', *Recent Research in Archaeological Footwear,* Technical Paper 8, Association of Archaeological Illustrators and Surveyors

VAN DRIEL-MURRAY, C 1995. 'Gender in question', in *Theoretical Roman Archaeology: Second Conference Proceedings ,* 3-21, ed Rush, P, (Aldershot)

VAN DRIEL-MURRAY, C 1999 'Roman leather bikinis', *Archaeological Leather Group Newsletter* Issue 9, March 1999, 6-9

VAN DRIEL-MURRAY, C, 2002. 'Leather bikini or briefs' in Lakin, D *The Roman Tower at Shadwell, London: a reappraisal,* 57-60 (London)

VERMASEREN, M J 1977. *Cybele and Atys: The Myth and the Cult* (London)

WACHER, J 1974 . *Towns of Roman Britain* (London)

WACHER, J 1979. *The Coming of Rome* (London)

WALTHEW, C V 1975. 'The town house and the villa house', *Britannia* VI, 198-205

WEBSTER, G 1978. *Boudica: The British Revolt against Rome AD 60* (London)

WEBSTER, G 1986. *The British Celts and their Gods under Rome* (London)

WILD, J P 1968. 'Clothing in the North-west provinces of the Roman Empire', *Bonner Jahrbucher* CLXVIII, 166-240

WILD, J P 1970a. *Textile Manufacture in the Northern Roman Provinces* (Cambridge)

WILD, J P 1970b. 'Button-and-loop fasteners in the Roman Provinces', *Britannia* I, 137-55

WILD, J P 2002. 'The textile industries of Roman Britain', *Britannia* XXXIII, 1-42

WRIGHT, R P AND RICHMOND, I A 1955 *The Roman Inscribed and Sculptured Stones in the Grosvenor Museum, Chester* (Chester)

Endpiece Bronze head from Otterbourne depicting a young woman. The features are typical of Celtic sculpture during the Roman period. (© Warburg Institute)

201

Index

The figures in italic refer to illustrations